A Select Body

The Gay Dance Party Subculture and the HIV/AIDS Pandemic

Lynette A. Lewis
University of New South Wales, Sydney

Michael W. Ross
University of Texas, Houston

CASSELL

To all those who have experienced the destructive effects of low self-esteem and high external threat

Cassell
Wellington House, 125 Strand, London WC2R 0BB
215 Park Avenue South, New York, NY 10003

British Library Cataloguing-in-Publication Data
A catalogue record for this book is available from the British Library.

ISBN: 0–304–33510–X (hardback) 0–304–33511–8 (paperback)

Typeset by York House Typographic Ltd
Printed in Great Britain by Biddles Limited, Guildford & Kings Lynn

Lynette A. Lewis was educated in psychology at the University of Wollongong and completed her doctorate in community medicine at the University of New South Wales, Australia. She is currently a psychologist in private practice and conducts a research and development consultancy with her husband.

Michael W. Ross studied in New Zealand, Australia, Sweden, Finland and the United States. The author of 10 books and over 200 published scientific papers on topics including sexuality, STDs and AIDS, he is a Professor of Public Health at the University of Texas.

Contents

Foreword

CONTROVERSY has emerged in the AIDS behavioural literature regarding the link between alcohol and/or drug use and high risk sexual activity (1), a disagreement that nonetheless does not exist in the HIV seroconversion literature conducted among gay men (2-5). Until such time that we develop new ways of measuring the association between drug/alcohol use and concurrent sexual behaviour, we may have reached the working limits of quantitative behavioural methodologies in studying the relationship between substance use and high risk sexual behaviours for HIV transmission.

Given the methodological limitations of quantitative research in this area, it is remarkable that this book is the first in which qualitative methods have been used to study the social and cultural contexts where high risk sexual behaviour and drug or alcohol use intersect among gay men. This innovation begs a question: How can qualitative methods best be used to continue to expand this area of investigation? It takes little reflection to conclude that qualitative investigators are in a position to open this field to many new areas of study regarding the intersections between gay substance use, sexual practices and the socio-cultural contexts of these behaviours.

First, a comparison of Lewis and Ross' account of the rise of dance parties in Sydney with historical account with that from other cities that have large gay communities would be of great interest, and particularly how the HIV/AIDS epidemic has changed what have by now become time-honoured institutions in many gay communities. In addition, it would also be of great interest to see a comparative qualitative description of the circumstances of gay men for whom dance parties and/or drug use are and are not prominent. How are gay men who ignore the dance club scene different from those men who use dance clubs as a central recreational activity? How are they the same? Do they differ in respect to their experience with the AIDS epidemic?

It has become commonplace to note that gay bars have a nearly unique place for gay men in many (most?) cities, serving *de facto* community centers, since bars are one of the few places where gay men can safely assemble in public. Urban gay bars were a prominent setting in which gay culture first formed and they continue to exert an indelible influence on the evolution of the gay community. This circumstance accounts for the widespread perception that gay culture is quite 'wet' (i.e. alcohol- and/or drug-positive) and that gay men drink more and use more drugs than straight men do. The prominence of the gay bar raises some interesting questions regarding the socialization, and specifically the sexual socialization, of gay men. What is the effect of the gay bar scene on the way that gay men are socialized to meet each other, flirt with each other, have sex, fall in love and have relationships? Would these centrally-important themes in gay men's lives be different if other widely-accepted institutions existed besides bars/dance clubs for gay men to meet? In short, to what extent is the gay scene, in fact, a *bar* scene? Although the prominence of the gay bar still makes this a difficult question to answer, the continuing development of 'alternative' social settings for gay men to meet aside from bars makes it possible for ethnographers to speculate about this question.

Drug use is a dangerous business. To be a successful drug user, one needs to purchase one's favourite inebrient from vendors who are obviously outlaws, and yet be relatively sure that one has not purchased a substance that is poisonous. It goes without saying that dosage and/or purity of the drug can only be guessed at by users, which (depending on the drug) can lead to serious medical complications. The potential for addiction to the drug also needs to be carefully self-monitored after the drug kicks in, one needs to comport oneself in a manner that does not add to the usual dangers of urban life, among them gay-bashing in darkened urban centers in the wee hours of the morning. If sex is a goal of the evening, one needs to navigate not only the social nuances of flirting but also the more serious complexities of avoiding HIV transmission (or any other STD), all while having one's judgement impaired, however pleasantly. The fact that men who frequent the dance clubs are accomplished at juggling these risks – indeed undertake them as a recreational activity – raises some interesting questions. Do they, in fact, perceive these risks to be dangerous? If so, do they regard them as avoidable dangers or yet another of the risks that accompany being a gay man in a big city? How is gay male drug use different from heterosexual patterns, and is drunken/drugged comportment different across gay and straight cultures? Is sex regarded by the dance club patrons as an expected part of the drug-using experience? To what extent is drug or alcohol use an expected part of sex? How are gay men socialized so that they are able to purchase drugs, use drugs, navigate urban settings while drugged and/or have sex under the influence so that they experience only a minimum of social problems? Or is the assumption that gay men have 'only a minimum of social problems' associated with drug use, in fact, incorrect?

To an outisder, the gay dance scene might be most memorable for its collection of hundreds (and sometimes thousands) of strikingly handsome young men. The gay dance club scene is one that is dominated by youth – and, in fact, may be the *only* social scene where young gay men are dominant. This consistent quality of the dance club scene for (at least) the past few decades raises several additional points for consideration. How do gay men 'age out' of the dance club scene, or, put more broadly, what are the social and cultural processes that govern ageing in the gay community? Do dance club participants expect to become old? What is their view of becoming old themselves? Do they think that it is possible for older gay men to have happy lives? If the dance clubs help socialize young gay men, how are middle aged or old gay men socialized to their new age statuses? What do older gay men have to teach young gay men and what could young gay men teach their elders?

The dance club scene is also about beauty, but not all gay men are considered to be beautiful. How has 'beauty' been constructed among gay men and where did the components of beauty come from? How has beauty changed over time, and why? How do gay men who are not thought to be graced with a model's face or a great body experience the gay community? Is beauty a burden – not only to the men that do not have it, but also to the men who must try to keep it? To what extent do issues around looks divide the gay male world? To what extent do looks govern the esteem that gay men receive within gay culture, and what are the other variables that contribute to receiving social support within the gay male world? Does a fascination with looks and beauty mean that gay men relate to each other as objects? If so, how would this affect the formation of community within an urban environment among gay men? For gay men not perceived to be blessed with beauty, which is more hurtful – the stigma associated with being gay in the dominant culture or being ignored by other gay men?

The dance club scene is a recreational activity, and its prominence within the gay male world raises other interesting questions. First, what other 'time out' activities exist within the gay male community? Is participation in the gay dance world a dominant force in gay male life, or is it one of many alternatives? To what extent do gay men organize themselves into associations or cliques around specific recreational activities? Are the men who use gay dance clubs as a central recreational activity also found among the social networks of gay men who have organized around other recreational activities? If these are intersecting social networks, do they constitute a community?

I hope that this small foreword has supported the idea that the study of gay dance clubs is a very interesting thread to follow in the tapestry of gay men's lives. Lynette Lewis and Michael Ross' innovative study has set us on the beginning of a valuable course of study, one that it is to be hoped will be followed by others. They are to be congratulated for their innovation and their contribution.

Ron Stall, PhD., MPH
University of California
San Francisco

Notes

1.   Leigh, B. and Stall, R. (1993) Substance use and risky sexual behaviour for exposure to HIV: Issues in methodology, interpretation, and prevention, *American Psychologist,* 48(10), pp. 1035–1045.

2. Burcham, J., Tindall, B., Marmor, M., Cooper, D., Berry, G. and Penny, R. (1939) Incidence and risk factors for human immunodeficiency virus seroconversion in a cohort of Sydney homosexual men, *The Medical Journal of Australia,* 150, pp. 634–639.
3. Silvestre, A., Lyter, D., Valdiserri, R., Huggins, J. and Rinaldo, C. (1989) Factors related to seroconversion among homo- and bisexual men after attending a risk-reduction educational session, *AIDS,* 3, pp. 647–650.
4. Penkower, L., Dew, M., Kingsley, L., Becker, J., Satz, P., Schaerf, F. and Sheridan, K. (1991) Behavioral health and psychosocial factors and risk for HIV infection among sexually active homosexual men. The Multicenter AIDS Cohort Study, *American Journal of Public Health,* 81, pp. 194–196.
5. Ostrow, D., DiFranceisco, W., Schmiel, J., Chmiel, J., Joseph, J. and Wesch, J. (in press) Behavioral factors associated with HIV-1 seroconversion among members of the Chicago Multicenter AIDS Cohort Study/Coping and Change Study Cohort, 1984-92. *American Journal of Epidemiology.*

Acknowledgements

WE would like to acknowledge the tremendous support by numerous people and institutions during and after the study. This work was carried out by the first author as her PhD research in the National Centre in HIV Social Research, School of Community Medicine, University of New South Wales, Sydney, under the supervision of the second author. It was made possible by a scholarship from the Australian Commonwealth AIDS Research Grants Committee, 1991–94. We especially wish to thank Michael Drury for his invaluable introductions, assistance and support during the major part of this investigation, Professor Wayne Hall for his co-supervision of the research, and Professor Peter Baume for his support of this research project. We also thank Douglas Cornford and Associate Professor Don Mixon of the University of Wollongong, David Wain, James Skelton, Jin Jiang, and the organizers of the Bacchanalia Dance Parties. Dr Lewis particularly acknowledges the support of her brother, Dr Milton Lewis, her daughters Christine, Julie and Raechel, and her husband Aaldrik Arnoldus. The three cartoons are reproduced by kind permission of Jeff Allan, creator of the series 'Living with Adam' in the *Sydney Star Observer*. Parts of these data were presented at the International Conference on Biopsychosocial Aspects of HIV Infection, Amsterdam, in September 1991, and we are indebted to our friends and colleagues both locally and internationally who provided valuable criticism and feedback throughout.

Last but certainly not least, we thank the sixty-three men who made this study possible by allowing us to interview them: they shared their laughter and their pain. Many of them have become close friends, and six of them have since died from HIV-related disease. The data from this study were presented at seminars at St George's Hospital, Sydney University of Technology, and the National Drug and Alcohol Research Centre, University of New South Wales; some of the men interviewed attended and supported the findings, as did those dance party organizers and patrons who read the manuscript in its final form.

Other books in Cassell's AIDS Awareness Series include:

The Economic and Social Impact of AIDS in Europe
(David FitzSimons, Vanessa Hardy and Keith Tolley)

Fighting Back Against HIV: Self-Help for the Newly-Diagnosed
(Peter Tatchell)

Positive Lives: Responses to HIV – A Photodocumentary
(Stephen Mayes and Lyndall Stein)

Reports from the Holocaust: The Making of an AIDS Activist
(Larry Kramer)

Rubber Up!: Every Gay Man's Guide to Condoms
(Edward King and Chris Markham)

Safer Sexy: The Guide to Gay Sex Safely
(Peter Tatchell)

Safety in Numbers: Safer Sex and Gay Men
(Edward King)

It is dangerous to let the public behind the scenes. They are easily disillusioned and then they are angry with you, for it was the illusion they loved.

W. Somerset Maugham, *The Summing Up*

The visible universe was an illusion of, more precisely, a sophism. Mirrors and fatherhood are abominable because they multiply it and extend it.

Jorge Luis Borges, 'Tion, Uqbar, Orbis, Tertius' (1976)

My whole life becomes this exquisite dance of being in one role after another where we do our on-stage routine.

Ram Dass, *The Only Dance There Is* (1976)

A nation is a society united by a delusion about its ancestry and by a common hatred of its neighbours.

W.R. Inge: Dean of St Paul's

Chapter one

Overview of the Inner-City Gay Dance Party Culture

MOST research into the set and setting of the social and sexual interactions of gay men has examined the traditional bars and cruising areas. ('Set' refers to the mind-set of the individual and 'setting' describes the social and physical context.) However, there have been significant temporal changes in the gay subcultures in the past two decades, many of which reflect social and psychological changes in the construction of homosexuality and gay identity (we refer to sex between men as homosexual behaviour, and the identification of the self as a homosexual person as gay). Many of these are inextricably bound up with the HIV/AIDS pandemic and the redefinition of same-gender sexual contact in terms of HIV infection risk. Study of the new gay subcultures, and their development in the age of HIV/AIDS, is well overdue, particularly as these subcultures will contain elements that impact both HIV risk and HIV prevention, as well as itself being a product of the HIV pandemic. This work pioneers investigation of the norms, values, belief systems and set and setting of some inner-Sydney gay dance party patrons and how the social world or reality of the dance party milieu may contribute to increased risky sexual behaviour among this population. The findings that emerge from this investigation should have important implications for future research and public health interventions to prevent HIV infection, as well as for the understanding of gay culture in the last decade of the twentieth century. It is interesting that the gay dance party phenomenon has received so little serious attention in Australia or internationally, since it is a unique social phenomenon within the inner-Sydney gay subculture linking directly with the HIV pandemic. Reasons for the total absence of theoretical analysis and empirical research of the dance party institution (including drug use and its impact on the risk of HIV infection) are not clear, although there is an abundance of empirical literature indicating that recalcitrant risky sexual behaviour occurs in young gay drug-using subpopulations (Stall *et al.*, 1986; Stall and Ostrow, 1989) similar to the inner-Sydney gay dance party subpopulation. The terms 'young' or 'youthful' are used in this book to define a specific age range (from eighteen to thirty-five years) of gay dance party patrons and similar samples of recreational drug users.

The gay dance party is a social institution with situational and structural dynamics which may affect some of its patrons' lifestyles in ways that may have significant implications for future research on minorities and their subcultures, health education interventions, and public health policy. Since the early 1980s, these inner-city gay social events have emerged as a significant gay subcultural institution (including Mardi Gras Party and Sleaze Ball, their annual celebrations, and other private dance parties) attracting thousands of young gay recreational drug-using party patrons, who dance through the night to loud frenetic music (on an almost weekly basis). The phrase 'recreational drug' is used in this book to describe the combined use of psychoactive substances in specific social- or leisure-oriented contexts (of which the inner-city gay dance party milieu is an example). The use of alcohol at football fixtures, other sporting activities and licensed social clubs in Australia is a similar form of recreational or context-specific drug use.

Research literature has revealed a strong association between recreational drug use and increased risk of HIV infection in a growing number of younger gay-oriented subpopulations in specific gay social contexts (Paul *et al.*, 1993; Plant, 1990; Room and Collins, 1983; Siegel, 1986; Soloman and Andrews, 1973; Stall and Ostrow, 1989; Stall and Wiley, 1988; Stall *et al.*, 1986; Trocki and

Leigh, 1991). These data also indicate that whilst previous intervention programmes were successful in imparting safer-sexual and drug-related information to a large proportion of gay men, they have been less efficacious in changing these risky behaviours among a minority of younger gay men.

One of the major research problems examined in this book is the reason for the incongruity between safer-sexual knowledge and the failure to comply with these safer-sexual guidelines. What factors other than lack of knowledge account for this recalcitrant risky sexual behaviour? Perhaps these educational messages (including their content, argot and symbolic language) are too general, or do not address the dominant attitudes or belief systems that underpin risky sexual behaviour that occurs among younger gay men in specific social contexts. The relative importance of developing effective and closely targeted safer-sexual educational strategies for the inner-city gay dance party subpopulation is emphasized by the continuing number of recently diagnosed HIV seroconversions and the failure of science and medicine to develop an HIV vaccine or cure.

This book emerged in accordance with Glaser and Strauss's (1967) Grounded Theory model which proved to be the model best fitted to researching this previously unresearched inner-city gay dance party subpopulation. Its flexibility and robustness allowed the naive researcher to become familiar with, and sensitized to, the social context (including sexual and drug-related attitudes, belief systems and behaviours) during the participant-observation stage of this investigation. The data from this stage provided a foundation for the development of honest and open rapport with the respondents during the interviews, and for the subsequent formulation and refinement of open-ended questions on the interview schedules. The chapter topics and their location in this book also reflect the way in which each chapter emerged out of the core categories and data generated by the previous interview segments, as described by Glaser and Strauss. In this book most of the information or supporting data relating to the origins and development of the inner-city gay dance party institution was reported in local gay newspapers (*Capital Q* and the *Sydney Star Observer*), glossy magazines (*Campaign* and *Rolling Stone*), an inner-Sydney radio station (Triple J), the mass media (press and television) and party advertisements (displayed on bulletin-boards or buildings in the inner-Sydney area, and in the annual *Gay and Lesbian Mardi Gras Guide*).

Chapter Two provides a review of the current literature on the widespread use of recreational drugs among young gay men, the increased likelihood of risky sexual behaviour among these men and the emergence of a dominant recreational drug-using youth culture across a wide range of geographical and cultural contexts. For those interested in the methodological detail, the full methodology is contained in the Appendix, which explores the appropriateness of the theoretical model used in this book, and the procedural variations between the six research segments, the sample characteristics, including the social worlds and roles of the organizers, the patrons and the drug dealers who constituted the sample interviewed. The use of Glaser and Strauss's model limited the size of the sample interviewed because it requires strong personal commitment from the researcher during the emerging stages. These included the participant-observation stage, interviews, continuous analyses of transcripts, generation of data, the inclusion of new items on the interview schedule and the final analysis and writing up of the book which occurred over a period of three years. This evolutionary process not only provides the researcher with invaluable data, but it also heightens awareness of the idiosyncratic characteristics (including attitudes, belief systems and behaviours) of the social worlds under examination. The ethical conditions of subject participation, such as anonymity, confidentiality and debriefing, and the overall integrity of this investigation, are also described in the Appendix.

Chapters Three and Four examine the complex and diverse socio-political dynamics that contributed to the historical evolution of this dominant gay youth-oriented social institution and the inner-city gay.subculture. They were drawn together to help define and understand the significant influence this major gay social institution has had on its members' sexual and drug-related attitudes, belief systems and behaviours within the context of the HIV/AIDS pandemic. The gay dance party institution (including the Gay and Lesbian Mardi Gras parties) both reflects and amplifies the recent political legitimation of the gay identity in the state of New South Wales (of which Sydney is the capital), the increased availability of psychoactive stimulants (including Ecstasy [3,4 Methylenedioxyme-thamphetamine, known also as MDMA]) and the impact of the HIV/AIDS pandemic on the inner-city gay dance party patrons.

Chapters Five and Six look at the attitudes and belief systems that determine the use, popularity and effects of particular dance party drugs, such as Ecstasy and Ice (d-methamphetamine hydro-chloride), and the implications for risky sexual behaviour and future intervention programmes. Ice, unlike Ecstasy, remained popular for only an extremely brief period in the gay dance party context according to our data. Its short-lived popularity was probably due to a growing concern among dance party patrons about their potential dependency, overuse, loss of control and increased risky sexual behaviour following its use. These prevalent attitudes and belief systems may have been fuelled or biased by negative reports in the popular press and glossy magazines prior to the arrival of Ice in Australia and its distribution through the inner-Sydney illicit drug market. The terms 'overuse' and 'dependency' are used in preference to 'abuse' and 'addiction' because of the negative connotations of these latter terms, which imply that the user has effectively little or no personal choice, control or responsibility for their behaviour. Chapters Five and Six also examine the hypothesis that memory impairment while intoxicated or state-dependent learning may explain the widely reported incongruity between a person's knowl-edge of safer-sexual guidelines and their subsequent sexual behaviour risks.

As this study evolved, the need was recognized for an in-depth pilot investigation of the possible communication and belief systems and the ritualized behaviours that appeared to sustain the use of drugs and risky sexual behaviour within the context of the inner-city gay dance party milieu. Chapter Seven examines the similarities and differences between these responses to the HIV/AIDS pandemic, growing homonegativity (internal and external), and the similar reactions in other times and places to similar life-threatening crises that have defied the collective knowledge of the dominant paradigm (including church and science), such as the Black Plague which destroyed up to 25 per cent of the European population in epidemics over a number of past centuries.

Chapter Eight deals with the social and sexual significance of the dance party communication symbols ('argot') in the context of safer-sex negotiations between dance party patrons. It also examines the durability, reliability or fragility of these symbols in the evaluation of the HIV/AIDS status of a potential sexual partner, and decisions on whether to participate in unprotected anal intercourse. The idiosyncratic characteristics of the dance party environment, such as the loud music, subdued stroboscopic lighting shows and the widespread use of psychoactive substances necessitated the development of non-verbal communication media and argot. The efficacy of safer-sexual and drug-related educational programmes may depend on the successful incorporation and bonding of this argot with appropriate safer-sexual messages.

In conclusion, Chapter Nine synthesizes, clarifies and analyzes the specific questions asked about the ways in which the attitudes and belief systems of gay dance party patrons may contribute to an increased risk of unprotected anal intercourse in the social contexts of the inner-city gay dance party institution. Further studies, preferably of representative random samples of dance party patrons are needed to assess the generalizability of these findings, which are limited by the small sample sizes and the pilot characteristics of these qualitative investigations. However, these data provide a rich source of conceptual categories from which hypotheses and research questions may be generated for future research. They thus help to deepen understanding of the reasons for increased risk of HIV infection among inner-city gay dance party patrons as well as a better understanding of the development of the gay dance party institution and the role of the HIV pandemic in its structure.

Chapter two

Sex and Drugs: A Review of the Literature

ANOTHER researcher who has reported on ethnographic work in drug-using and dealing communities, although before the AIDS pandemic, is Adler (1985). Her work is theoretically important in that she describes hedonism as a primary motivation, with the thrills, sexual opportunities, and deviant lifestyles as all equal in their attractions and rewards as materialistic compensations (p. 98). Similar to the dealers in the gay dance party scene, she also notes that the early rationalism of the dealers gave way to heavy partying, impulsive behaviour, and 'present-orientation' in what she terms 'subculture of hedonism' (p. 118). Peer relations in this subculture were characterized by provision of the necessary skills, ideology for dealing (p. 145) and functions for its members. These functions increased members' social solidarity, and were instrumental in the recruitment and socialization of new members, and in transmitting the jargon, norms and values surrounding both business and social relations, similar to the gay dance party situation. Adler notes that deviant behaviour has only recently been conceptualized by sociologists as pleasure-motivated – usually, it has been viewed as rebellion against the establishment, rejection of society's norms and values, and a mode of escape. In the gay dance party situation, all these variables may be seen in operation, with the pleasure often counterbalanced against the painful impact of the HIV pandemic and the homonegative attitudes of society. Indeed, Adler suggests that the dealers and smugglers she studied 'pursued deviance to live freely and wildly, to make their hedonistic way of life possible. This was the domain in which their existential selves were lodged. Their entry into the drug world represented their rejection of conventional society so they could find satisfaction for their brute inner drives in the subculture of hedonism' (p. 151). This description is probably more accurate for the gay subculture before the advent of HIV/AIDS, as described by Ringdal (1991), although Adler collected her data in the late 1970s. But Adler also notes that many outsiders (like the heterosexual invaders of gay dance parties) found the passion for indulgence inherently attractive, and freely welcomed the feelings of excitement, spontaneity, glamour, and self-importance they derived from the drug-related lifestyle. These findings provide an important existential context for looking at the gay dance party.

In order to examine the gay dance party phenomenon, and specifically its impact and interaction with HIV risks, it is also necessary to look at related previous research findings. Empirical literature has revealed growing evidence of a relationship between increased risky sexual behaviour and the use or overuse of psychoactive substances among a diverse range of gay subpopulations, particularly within traditional gay social contexts, such as bars, nightclubs, saunas or bathhouses (Butt, 1989; Cabaj, 1989; Ekstrand and Coates, 1990; Gold, 1989; Gold et al., 1994; Hays et al., 1990; McKirnan and Peterson, 1989; McCusker et al., 1990; Ostrow, 1986; Paul et al., 1993; Sittitrai et al., 1990; Stall and Ostrow, 1989; Stall et al., 1986; Stall and Wiley, 1988; Trocki and Leigh, 1991). The robustness of this relationship is reflected in its being consistently reported by inter-disciplinary studies varying in methodological approach (including qualitative and statistical studies, case histories, biographical data, pathology or HIV serological serum tests, longitudinal or cross-sectional samples), and conducted in different historical settings or social contexts.

Evidence of modified risky behaviour

Several of these studies and others in Australia (Gold and Skinner, 1992; Gold et al., 1994) also reported strong evidence that gay men have adopted safer-sexual and drug-related behaviours since the advent of the HIV/AIDS pandemic. McCusker *et al.* (1990), also noted a significant decline in the frequency of self-reported risky sexual incidences following the reduction of, or abstinence from, drug use, in both their longitudinal and cross-sectional investigations (in Boston) of HIV-seronegative gay men in treatment for drug overuse. Martin (1990) also reported similar reductions in drug use and risky sexual behaviour, in both his longitudinal and cross-sectional investigations of HIV-seronegative gay drug users from New York City. He also found, in an earlier study (1987), similar encouraging trends among 745 gay New York men.

The major benefit of conducting a longitudinal investigation by contrast to cross-sectional or retrospective analyses is that researchers are able to differentiate between the possible causal and correlational effects of drug use and risky sexual behaviour. None of these studies, however, was able to establish a causal link between increased or decreased frequency of sexual activity and a reduction in use of, or abstinence from, psychoactive substances.

A significant minority participate in unsafe sex

Martin (1987) found only an 11 per cent reduction in high-risk sexual behaviour at the second stage of data-gathering in his longitudinal investigation. In their review of these findings, Ross and Rosser (1989) suggested that these unpredictable and 'disturbing' results were 'not necessarily' a good measure of permanent behaviour change but were more likely to be artifacts of the 'dynamic process' of change. The relevance of this instability in risk behaviour was reflected in the growing evidence of increased risky sexual behaviour, particularly among a wide range of younger gay drug-using subpopulations (Hays *et al.*, 1990; Ross *et al.*, 1992; Stall *et al.*, 1991; Temple and Leigh, 1992).

Multi-factorial explanations for risky behaviour

A plethora of investigations has generated various possible explanations for the failure of educational programmes to reduce effectively this potentially risk-laden sexual and drug-related behaviour among a growing minority of young gay men (Beck *et al.*, 1989;

Cabaj, 1989; Gold *et al.*, 1994; McCusker *et al.*, 1990; McKirnan and Peterson, 1989; Paul *et al.*, 1993; Stall and Ostrow, 1989; Stall and Wiley, 1988; Stall *et al.*, 1986). Stall *et al.* (1986) suggested several competing hypotheses to explain the associations between increased risky sexual activity and use of psychoactive substances. Ostrow (1986) defined these hypotheses in accordance with a variety of biopsychosocial dimensions which might explain this risky sexual behaviour. He suggested that they be labelled 'disinhibitory', 'aphrodisiacal', 'social context', 'personality traits' and 'multi-factorial'. Stall *et al.* hypothesized that the disinhibitory and aphrodisiacal effects of drugs, including hyper-sexuality and high-risk sexual activity within specific gay male contexts, are often culturally or subculturally determined.

Room (1983) also argued earlier that the disinhibitory effects of the drugs were largely determined by, or causally related to the culture, the environment or social context in which they were used, rather than an artifact of the biochemical interaction within the physical organism. The social context hypothesis also explains the combined use of drugs and risky sexual behaviour in terms of learned social rituals or sanctioned behaviour in specific gay sub-groups. By comparison, the personality hypothesis assumes a deterministic model in which these risky behaviours are attributed to underlying personality needs or traits.

The multifactorial hypothesis suggests that all of these factors and other undiscovered elements may independently or interrelatedly (to varying degrees) account for this risky sexual behaviour. Although there is no conclusive demonstration of a causal relationship between these psychosocial variables and risky sexual behaviour, there were a number of investigations into these hypotheses. These studies used a variety of data-gathering procedures, such as self-reports, HIV serological tests (Paul *et al.*, 1993), or other reported STD tests (Siegel, 1986), to test these hypotheses. Collectively, their results provided support for a causal link in several of the hypotheses of Stall *et al.*

Age-related findings

Youth was the most consistent and reliable predictor of risky sexual and drug-related behaviour, irrespective of the discipline, methodological approach, historical period, geographical location, social or cultural context of the study (Hingson *et al.*, 1990; Ross *et al.*, 1992; Stall and Wiley, 1988). A retrospective cross-sectional analysis of data from the San Francisco Men's Health Study by Stall *et al.* (1986) also showed age-biased findings strongly associated with increased frequency of risky sexual behaviour. Butt (1989) argued that 'many young people, although agreeing with the philosophy of, and need for, safe sex still do not practise it for various reasons including the idea that "it [HIV infection] can't happen to me" ' (p. 9). Several studies across a wide range of cultural locations found similar patterns of age-related perceptual biases of personal risk (Hall and Hando, 1993; Kaplan *et al.*, 1992; Korf *et al.*, 1991), or vulnerability to HIV infection (Beck *et al.*, 1989; Klee, 1991a, 1991b).

Reilly and Homel (1987) also found that only 27 per cent of their heterogenous drug-using sample (n = 1071), aged fifteen to eighteen years in Sydney, thought that they were at risk of contracting HIV. Most of these investigations found a consistent pattern of age-related sociopsychological dynamics that contributed to a person's distorted perception of the risk of HIV infection. These included: social modelling, peer-group conformity, friendship networks, thrill-seeking, experimentation, rebellion against cultural norms or authority, loss of control, inexperience, avoidance of responsibility for safe sexual negotiations and impaired judgement.

Social systems or friendship networks

Trocki and Leigh (1991) found that many young people continued to have unprotected intercourse with friends or other members of their social group or context because they believed they would be less likely to be HIV seropositive. These social networks were also the main agents for the introduction and supply of drugs (Beck *et al.*, 1989; Klee, 1991a; Korf *et al.*, 1991; Newcombe, 1992; Paul *et al.*, 1993; Solowij *et al.*, 1992).

In Australia, Solowij *et al.* (1992) recently reported that the majority (60 per cent) of their sample of MDMA users were introduced to the drug through friendship networks, usually within a specific social context (such as dance parties, nightclubs and private parties). Similar findings were reported among young drug-using samples in Britain (Newcombe, 1992), Europe (Korf et al., 1991), and the USA (Beck et al., 1989). They found a significant relationship between social networks (such as friends or acquaintances) and the drug users' subsequent risky sexual behaviour (Paul et al., 1993; Trocki and Leigh, 1991). The importance of context in gay drug-using populations has not been extensively studied.

Traditional gay social contexts and behaviour

Gold and Skinner (1992) found that risky sexual behaviour occurred more frequently in gay social venues that promoted the use of intoxicants (including alcohol) and 'sex-on-premises'. Trocki and Leigh (1991) found that this risky sexual behaviour was often an 'idiosyncratic' artifact of these gay social systems (including friendship networks or contexts) and of the combining of drug use with sexual activity.

Several investigations found that the use of psychoactive substances while engaging in sexual activity was culturally sanctioned within many traditional gay social venues (Achilles, 1967; Dank, 1971; McKirnan and Peterson, 1989; Read, 1980; Stall and Wiley, 1988). Seigel et al. (1989) concluded that these gay conventions strongly contributed to increased 'high-risk sexual behaviours' in gay subpopulations or social contexts similar to those in their New York longitudinal study. McKirnan and Peterson (1989), also found that these cultural prescriptions contributed to a large proportion of their 'high-risk' group's over-use of psychoactive substances (including alcohol), in this heavily class- and gender-weighted sample of 3400 middle- to upper-class 'homosexual' men (n = 2603) and women (n = 748), in Chicago. The term 'homosexual' is used here to refer to behaviour rather than identity.

Many other researchers also provided evidence to support the powerful influence these social prescriptions of conformity have on the sexual and drug-related behaviour of their gay samples, within these social worlds or contexts (Buffum, 1988; Butt, 1989; Cabaj, 1989; Paul et al., 1993; Stall et al., 1986; Trocki and Leigh, 1991; Ziebold and Mongeon, 1982).

Frequency of drug use

Wills and Shiffman (1985) predicted that patterns of frequent drug overuse would generally lead to increased stress and dependency on drugs. These predictions were supported by several studies which found significantly higher (up to one third) prevalences of overuse and dependency on alcohol and other psychoactive substances among gay men than among the general population (Cabaj, 1989; Fiefield *et al.*, 1977; McKirnan and Peterson, 1989; Stall and Wiley, 1988; Ziebold and Mongeon, 1982). Thirty per cent of the gay men reported some 'type of chemical dependency' by contrast to the general population's range of 10 per cent to 12 per cent in Cabaj's (1989) study. Paul *et al.* (1993) recently reported a 32 per cent increase in frequency of unprotected insertive and receptive anal intercourse during the previous three months among their clinical sample (n = 314) of gay and bisexual outpatient 'substance-abusers' in San Francisco (58 per cent of whom tested HIV-positive). This was a considerable increase to the 22 per cent of risky sexual incidences reported by Stall *et al.* (1986) among an earlier more representative sample of gay men in the same area.

Paul *et al.* also found 66.7 per cent of their sample were 'always' intoxicated when they performed unprotected anal intercourse. These findings were supported by similar data from their qualitative investigation involving three focus groups (n = 18). According to Stall *et al.* (1986) people who used three or more drugs during sexual activity were 4.3 times more likely to engage in risky sexual behaviour in a gay bathhouse or bar setting than the 'lowest-risk' group who did not combine these behaviours. Their findings showed that this high incidence of risky behaviour was not attributable to the sample's ignorance about safer sexual guidelines, as 90 per cent of the sample were well-informed. The data from this retrospective study provided a baseline for more recent investigations (Paul *et al.*, 1993) to measure the efficacy of safer-sexual and drug-related educational intervention programmes in reducing the strength of the association between sexual behaviours and drug use. However, Gold and Skinner (1992) indicated that this safer-sexual and drug-related knowledge was not sufficient to control or change risky behaviour among 'the majority of urban gay men', in Australia.

Stigmatized lifestyles and overuse of drugs

Many studies (previously mentioned) have attributed recalcitrant risky behaviour among gay men to the psychosocial stresses of belonging to a stigmatized subculture (McKirnan and Peterson, 1989), the accumulated anxiety of HIV-related issues, including the proximity of death (Cabaj, 1989), and the centrality of substance use in many gay social contexts (Linn *et al.*, 1989). These multi-faceted social institutions 'have traditionally served an important cultural function as havens where people can be explicitly homosexual and not suffer stigmatization or exclusion' (McKirnan and Peterson, 1989, p. 557). Siegel (1970) suggested that stigmatized identities often developed their own 'defensive structures' (including social boundaries, contexts or prescriptions) in response to an external threat to their survival.

Herek and Glunt (1988) found that gay social venues have become increasingly important for many gay men in the USA, particularly since 'AIDS was equated with homosexual behaviour' (p. 888), and there was an escalation in the dominant culture's (including the media's) homonegative attitudes and discrimination. Many researchers have also found that the use or overuse of alcohol and other psychoactive substances within these contexts was often due to the dual stress of external and internalized homonegativity (Bell and Weinberg, 1978; Cabaj, 1989; Finnegan and McNally, 1987; Hammersmith and Weinberg, 1973; Herek and Glunt, 1988).

Low self-esteem and overuse of drugs

Paul *et al.* (1993) also identified low self-esteem as one of the major contributory factors to increased risk of HIV infection in their inductive and qualitative segment of this mixed methodological study (comprising qualitative and quantitative data). Stall and Ostrow (1989) suggested that one of the main reasons for the use or overuse of drugs was the alleviation of accumulated 'tension, anxiety, depression and guilt' from this unresolved homonegativity or self-hatred in the gay subpopulation they studied. Paradoxically, the literature also revealed that many of these homophobic gay men also reported increased self-loathing, denial, fear, guilt, self-pity, depression, isolation and fragmentation during the post-intoxication or withdrawal phase of drug use or overuse. Cabaj (1989) argued that 'all gay men' were 'homophobic' because of their cultural conditioning in a homonegative dominant culture. Stall and Ostrow (1989) noted that this widespread homonegativity was a major barrier to the treatment of chemical dependency and to the provision of adequate care and prevention of HIV transmission among gay subpopulations. Cabaj (1989) also suggested that many homophobic gay men were unable to enter gay social contexts or participate in homosexual behaviour without the use or overuse of drugs. He suggested that this combination of drugs and sexual behaviour became increasingly difficult to change the longer it was associated with risky sexual behaviour.

HIV/AIDS stress and use of drugs

The literature also disclosed that, historically, higher rates of psychoactive substance overuse and risk-related behaviour have been found among stigmatized minorities or groups facing social turmoil, such as life-threatening epidemics, chronic diseases or natural disasters (Cabaj, 1989; Cassel, 1976; Douglas, 1986; Hanna, 1989; Helman, 1990; Vaillant, 1983; Zoja, 1989). This phenomenon was reflected in Siegel's (1986) observations in the early stages of the HIV/AIDS pandemic when at least 80 per cent of gay men who were HIV-seropositive had used alcohol or drugs, whilst 65 per cent of gay people combined the use of recreational drugs with sexual activity. Many studies showed that correct information about safer-sexual and drug-related behaviour, although necessary, was not always sufficient to change this risky sexual behaviour (Beck et al., 1989; Linn et al., 1989; Paul et al., 1993). The majority of gay men in these studies were well-informed or aware of their increased risk or 'susceptibility to AIDS' infection following their use of psychoactive substances but few felt able personally to change or control this risk-laden behaviour. In summary, this concept of cognitive or sexual 'control' (including 'lack of control', 'impaired' psychophysiological functions and 'need for control') whilst intoxicated on psychoactive drugs was one of the most consistently reported findings.

Loss of control and impaired cognition

Linn *et al.* (1989) revealed in their study that gay 'men who engaged in riskier sexual activity also felt they had less control over their sex lives' (p. 2689). They also found that drug users who frequently combined drugs with sexual activity were less likely to negotiate safe sex with partners and were less in control of their behaviour. McCusker *et al.* (1990) also found a higher frequency of risky sexual behaviour among gay men who reported loss of control and impaired judgement during sexual activity. Many researchers also showed that this 'subjective intoxication' (Trocki and Leigh, 1991) often overwhelmed the user's capacity to judge the relevance of safer sexual behaviour (Butt, 1989; Cvetkovich and Grote, 1983; Martin, 1990; Reilly and Homel, 1987; Smith, 1988; Stall *et al.*, 1986). Liester *et al.* (1992) recently found that 90 per cent of their sample of MDMA-using psychiatrists (n = 20) in the USA reported impaired cognition or perceptual biases including altered reality, time, space and speech. Most of the sample studied by Paul *et al.* (1993) considered that there was a greater risk of their engaging in unsafe sexual behaviour because of their impaired judgement following the use of intoxicating substances. Zapka *et al.* (1988) found a strong association between this drug-related cognitive impairment and unsafe sexual behaviour.

The concept of control determining the popularity of a drug

The significant meaning of this cognitive or physical control was reflected in the growing popularity of the illegal substance MDMA (Ecstasy) among young recreational drug-using subpopulations in similar social contexts or settings by several researchers in Australia (Hall and Hando, 1993; Solowij *et al.*, 1993), Britain (Mansfield and Owen, 1993; Newcombe, 1992), Europe (Kaplan *et al.*, 1992; Korf *et al.*, 1991) and the USA (Beck *et al.*, 1989).

The widespread popularity of Ecstasy was partly due to its quality of enhancing social situations and environments, according to numerous researchers (Beck *et al.*, 1989; Chesher, 1990; Newcombe, 1992; Solowij *et al.*, 1992). This was confirmed in the investigation of Liester *et al.* (1992), in which 80 per cent of their professional sample specifically used MDMA to enhance or manipulate their external or internal environments (effects including increased self-confidence, self-acceptance and disinhibition).

Solowij *et al.* (1992) suggested that it was mainly Ecstasy's 'easily controlled' (cognitive and behavioural) intoxication phase that accounted for its popularity in different social contexts among their relatively young (mean age of twenty-seven years) sample (n = 100). Siegel (1986) suggested that this specificity of drug use within a specific social context often led to 'more frequent and "dangerous" exposure to the probable causative virus of AIDS ... ' (p. 272). This suggestion was supported by McKirnan and Peterson (1989), with gay men in their study being two to three-and-a-half times more likely to perform unsafe sexual acts following intentional use of a drug for its specific biopsychosocial effects. Amphetamines ranked second to marijuana in the scale of popularity among a wide range of drug-using subpopulations in the United States (Paul *et al.*, 1993), Britain (Klee, 1991b; Newcombe, 1992) and Australia (Hall and Hando, 1993).

A recent study by Hall and Hando (1993) showed an increased frequency of amphetamine use and its analogue (including 'speed' or methamphetamine) in a heterogeneous subpopulation of relatively young (median age of twenty-five years) illicit drug users (n = 231). Paul *et al.* (1993) found that the use of amphetamine tripled the likelihood of risky sexual behaviour by contrast to people who did not use it.

Klee (1991b) reported similar patterns of risky sexual and drug-related activity (including sharing contaminated injecting equipment) among a growing number of young injecting amphetamine users in Britain. She also suggested that there was a strong association between the growing popularity of amphetamine, its sexually enhancing characteristics, and increased risk of HIV transmission. Previous research showed that injecting amphetamine users reported both the highest frequency of sexual arousal or activity (Käll and Olin, 1990) and the highest number of cases of HIV-seropositivity (Harris *et al.*, 1991). Beck *et al.* (1989) suggested that drug use during or in anticipation of sexual activity was one of the strongest predictors of unsafe sexual activity among their predominantly middle-class, heterosexual (85 per cent), white (95 per cent) sample (n = 100) of Ecstasy users in the USA.

A comparison of heterosexual and gay drug users

In Stall and Wiley's (1988) comparative cross-sectional investigation (drawn from the prospective San Francisco Men's Health Study sample), gay men under thirty-five years of age were significantly more likely to use a wider range of specific drugs (including marijuana, poppers or amyl nitrite, MDA (methylenedioxyamphetamine) and other amphetamines) for their idiosyncratic or disinhibitory effects, than were heterosexual men or older gay men. They also found that these gay men were seven times more likely to use five or more drugs, and more frequently, than were heterosexual men of the same age (over the previous six month period).

Reilly and Homel (1987) also found that a third of their heterogeneous sample had 'no control' over their sexual behaviour following their use of drugs. Beck *et al.* (1989) reported a similar strong association between the use of psychoactive substances and impaired judgement, lowered inhibitions, loss of control and frequent participation in risky sexual behaviour. Paradoxically, many studies showed that people often used the drugs to manipulate or control their personality, moods and environment (Butt, 1989; Paul *et al.*, 1993; Solowij *et al.*, 1993).

The growing popularity of drug use and youth-oriented social institutions

The youth-oriented social contexts were known by a variety of names (including dance parties, raves, house parties, discos and acid house parties) in different geographical and subcultural studies. Solowij *et al.* found that 72 per cent of their sample preferred to use Ecstasy at inner-Sydney dance party venues.

Beck *et al.* (1989) reported MDMA use among a broader taxonomy of social worlds in the USA than in Australia or Britain.

These included: 'gays', 'New Age/spiritual seekers', 'college students' and 'deadheads' who were followers of the rock band the Grateful Dead. Solowij *et al.* (1992) suggested that these differences were partly due to the sampling composition or focus of their study, primarily drawing on the inner-Sydney area, by contrast to the broader-based American study.

Several European researchers (Kaplan *et al.*, 1992), found similar profiles of MDMA use, social contexts (including house parties and discos) and subpopulations of relatively young recreational drug users in the Netherlands, Belgium, Germany and Britain. By contrast, Korf *et al.* (1991) did not find this specificity or intensity of MDMA use in their earlier investigation in Amsterdam. In Britain, Newcombe (1992) found Ecstasy's widespread popularity commensurate with the rapid growth of the rave scene or the 'dominant youth sub-culture of the 1990s'. He reported that tens of thousands of relatively young ravers attended these social events (of 'varying legality') every weekend in north-west England. A similar phenomenon has been reported in Australia in the inner-Sydney gay media (*Sydney Star Observer* and *Capital Q*), popular gay-empathic magazines (*Campaign* and *Rolling Stone*), local radio station (Triple J), television reports and major newspapers (*Sydney Morning Herald*, *The Daily Telegraph Mirror* and others), and advertised on inner-city bulletin-boards or buildings.

Ecstasy's high media profile (since the mid-1980s) in youth-oriented magazines, television specials, radio programmes and video clips also promoted its popularity among these youth-oriented sub-cultures, according to numerous researchers (Beck *et al.*, 1989; Chesher, 1990; Newcombe, 1991). For example, Kaplan *et al.* (1992) also found that this public broadcasting played a significant role in the promotion and spread of MDMA use in Europe.

The degree of popularity was also reflected in the British Home Office's statistical records of MDMA seizures and convictions, as Newcombe (1992) noted. They were from zero convictions in 1981 to 1735 seizures (of 365,000 doses) and 559 convictions in 1991. Mansfield and Owen (1993) also found that Ecstasy was widely used as a recreational drug in London gay subculture. A dual-stage (nomothetic and idiographic) model was developed to measure the levels of increased risky sexual behaviour in their gay clinical sample following their use of recreational drugs (including Ecstasy). An intervention workshop component was designed to educate and empower the participants in the negotiation and implementation of safer-sexual and drug-related guidelines. Ross (1993) also noted that these findings were part of a 'dominant theme' of association between the use of psychoactive substances and risky sexual behaviour in his recent review of the literature from the 1993 Berlin IXth International Conference on AIDS.

Conclusion

Researchers have warned that these findings are not representative of all men who have sex with other men (Cabaj, 1989; Gold *et al.*, 1994; Miller, 1989; Paul *et al.*, 1993) because not all of these men live in large conurbations (such as Los Angeles, San Francisco and Sydney), which is where most of these studies have been conducted. Nor do all gay men necessarily use psychoactive substances, or overuse drugs, or participate in anal sexual intercourse, or perform unsafe sexual acts, or identify with any gay subpopulation, or self-identify as gay (Bell and Weinberg, 1978; Weinberg and Williams, 1974) or frequent gay social institutions (such as bars, nightclubs, saunas and parties). Nonetheless, these data from the research literature suggest a strong association between the use of psychoactive substances and increased risk of HIV infection within specific social contexts or subcultures. There was little or no empirical information beyond anecdotal and media reports on this phenomenon at the time this study commenced in terms of the social and cultural factors surrounding drug use, among the inner-Sydney gay dance party institution.

The aim of this series of qualitative studies has been to identify some of the possible subcultural and psychosocial factors that have contributed (by either increasing or decreasing risk) to the context-specific risky sexual behaviour that occurs within the social worlds of the inner city gay dance party institution, as well as the interactions between the development of the gay dance parties and the HIV pandemic.

Chapter three

The Evolution of the Gay Dance Party Culture in Sydney

SINCE the early 1980s thousands of gay men have gathered together at large inner-city Sydney venues to dance and use illegal drugs on an almost weekly basis (Safe and Sager, 1990). The aim of this qualitative analysis is to investigate some of the cultural, social and psychological dimensions (including setting, attitudes and belief systems) that may have contributed to the evolution of these social institutions.

According to Wotherspoon (1991) gay social institutions (such as Mardi Gras, Sleaze Ball and other large-scale gala events) evolved out of a specific set of social, political and economic determinants dating back to the 1950s and 60s. He suggested that these elements were mainly responsible for the current demographic characteristics (such as size, density and location) of both the wider society and the gay inner-city subculture. First, Sydney had to reach a critical population mass before it was large and dynamic enough to tolerate a diverse range of subcultures (Fischer, 1975), such as the gay subculture and its social institutions. Moreover, two important gay legal reforms relating to anti-discrimination and decriminalization of homosexuality needed to be enacted before gay men were more at liberty to 'come out' of their traditional covert social venues (such as bars, nightclubs and private parties) and interact at large-scale public venues. Humphreys (1979) has distinguished between gay subcultures and satellite cultures, where the satellite culture is the publicly visible culture. The gay dance parties span the range from subculture to satellite culture, with the Mardi Gras and Sleaze Ball more of a satellite culture than a subculture. The legal reforms made the growth of the satellite culture possible.

The Mardi Gras' official social 'debut' in 1978 heralded the birth and subsequent political legitimation of Sydney's gay subculture (Wotherspoon, 1991), along with its prodigious satellite culture, the inner-city large-scale gay dance parties. Five hundred gay men and lesbians gathered in the inner-Sydney city for the inaugural Mardi Gras march down Oxford Street, according to North (1992). This march was disrupted by the police following the arrest of fifty-three demonstrators and the withdrawal of their march permit. Ironically, Gailbraith (1991) noted that the 'initial party was held at police request to help clear the crowds off the streets after the Parade' (p. 9). Wotherspoon (1991) also concluded that it was 'particularly ironic that Sydney's Gay Mardi Gras has now become one of the city's major public events . . . ' (p. 210). The growing significance of this gay annual festival (including the parade, party and other related events) was reflected in its national and international reputation, and patronage which attracted in February 1993 an estimated crowd of half-a-million people ('500,000: Biggest Mardi . . . ', 1993, p. 1).

Gailbraith (1991) argued that Mardi Gras pioneered large-scale dance parties in 1982 at the Hordern Pavilion, located at the Sydney Showground and within walking distance of the inner-city suburbs (Waingarten, 1989). The acquisition of this major public venue was premised by the enactment of the Anti-discrimination Act earlier in the same year in New South Wales. Coincidentally, the first reported case of HIV/AIDS in Australia was also diagnosed in November 1982 at St Vincent's Hospital, which is located in the inner-city Sydney area (Penny *et al.*, 1983). Duffin (1992) noted that the 'community initially responded [to the HIV/AIDS crisis] by using Mardi Gras events as a vehicle for preventive education'.

In 1984 the gay subcultural identity was finally granted political enfranchisement following the decriminalization of homosexuality in New South Wales. However, this transformation of status did not bring about the social legitimation of the gay identity. In discussing this inequitable enfranchisement, O'Sullivan (1992) pointed out that 'it is easier to make something legal than to make it legitimate' (p. 73). Nevertheless, Wotherspoon (1991) predicted that there would be a significant relationship between the survival (and continuing growth) of these gay institutions (including Mardi Gras) and the future social legitimation of the inner-city gay subculture.

Gailbraith (1991) supported this prediction with his estimated crowd of 200,000 people attending the gay subculture's major annual celebration in 1991. The transformed status of the inner-city gay subculture, according to O'Sullivan (1992), is reflected in the 'Mardi Gras' relationship with the police [which] changed as it became clear that the outrageous celebration was going to continue every year . . . it was going to get bigger and bigger' (p. 75). Wotherspoon (1991) suggested that 'Mardi Gras should be seen as something more – as a symbol of the new situation of Sydney's gay community and gay subculture: more than merely tolerated . . . to being accepted on their own terms' (p. 210).

The growing popularity of these gay institutions (including Mardi Gras and Sleaze Ball) enabled people, both inside and outside the gay subculture, to appreciate the potential size, diversity and political power of this previously disenfranchised subculture. Wotherspoon (1991) suggested that many gay entrepreneurs also recognized this 'instant' market and established a wide range of social institutions (such as the dance parties) to cater for this previously 'closeted' gay population. These gay dance parties at the Hordern Pavilion proved to be a formula for success with crowds in excess of 7000 people almost every weekend (Safe and Sager, 1990). Consequently many organizers decided to expand their enterprises by soliciting party patrons from outside the inner-city gay subculture (Waingarten, 1989).

In analyzing the origin and exceptional growth of the dance party phenomenon it is important not to neglect the biopsychosocial impact the HIV/AIDS pandemic has had on the inner-city gay subculture. To start with, the gay subculture and the popular press were becoming increasingly aware of the prevalence of HIV/AIDS cases among western gay men. But early media reports were often inaccurate and sensational and only added confusion and fear to an already frightening situation among the gay communities and wider cultures (Davenport-Hines, 1990). A growing number of inner-city Sydney gay men were being confronted with continuing shock-waves related to the stark reality of the virulence of the HIV/AIDS virus among their subculture (which often included acquaintances, significant others, or themselves being diagnosed with this intimidating disease) and internationally. The confusion, frustration and accumulative fear during this period were compounded by the absence of a vaccine or cure for HIV/AIDS (Davenport-Hines, 1990). According to Sartre (1977), individuals who are constantly enmeshed in unrelenting life-threatening experiences often seek out other people (who identify with their fears and lifestyles) to help them cope with their escalating anxiety.

A major concern of this research was the dance party patrons' social, sexual and drug-related behaviours within the context of the dance party institution (Lansing, 1992; Solowij *et al.*, 1992), and their possible altered risk of HIV infection (Butt, 1989; Stall *et al.*, 1986). According to Stall *et al.*, the use of recreational drugs may alter the discriminative perception of the user and result in an increase in HIV infection.

The quotes reproduced here are verbatim extracts from the transcript of sixteen respondents and one organizer. These statements are expressions of their individual social constructions (perceptions) of the inner-city gay dance party reality and the wider gay subculture, and therefore are perspectives on 'a truth' and not necessarily 'the truth', as noted by Berger and Luckmann (1975).

The criterion for selection or inclusion of each statement was based on their representativeness of the sample's responses to the phenomenon under examination (Glaser and Strauss's theory, 1967). The data in these sections have been reported in a sequential format, to allow the qualitative analysis to emerge chronologically and contextually. Full details of the research methodology and approach are provided in the Appendix.

History of the dance parties

The organizer and the respondents described some of the social and economic factors that partly contributed to the inception, rapid growth and evolution of the current inner-Sydney dance parties as a gay social institution. The organizer described the origin of his dance party organization:

> The parties grew out of my participation, I used to have parties at home.

These private parties were ideal venues for gay men to expand their network of contacts with men who shared a similar lifestyle. Wotherspoon (1991) suggested that these early inner-city gay social activities were held in secret underground venues because homosexuality was a felony in New South Wales until 1984. Respondent 6 described some of the social characteristics of these earlier covert venues:

> The parties were underground and they weren't very well known ... 90 per cent of the people plus would take drugs. It was all very well understood and very expected, not only by the people that go, but by the organizers ... they're all generally inner-city residents.

Because of the growing popularity of these social events the organizers were motivated to find a convenient venue large enough to accommodate the thousands of potential party patrons. The Hordern Pavilion met the organizers' criteria on both size and location, being only minutes from the densely gay-populated inner-city suburbs, such as Darlinghurst, Kings Cross, Paddington and Surry Hills. The organizer claimed that the unprecedented success of his organization was responsible for a new gay social institution:

> Our first party in '83 [was] ... at the Hordern for over two thousand people ... it really exploded after this first major success ... everybody said here's a way to make dollars or here's a way we can express our creativity.

He also suggested that the Hordern's unrestricted alcohol licence was one of the main reasons for the unprecedented success of the dance party organizations:

> Sydney's licencing laws at the time [1983], combined with not many venues that are open all night ... it was perfect.

The Hordern's 24 hour alcohol licence meant that the venue there was ... perfect.

Ironically, the leasing arrangements were conditional on the liquor licensing regulations, which provided the patrons with a 'perfect' venue for the use of illegal intoxicants. During this period, most licensed premises in New South Wales traded till 10 p.m. with only a few exceptions (Lewis, 1992).

According to many of the respondents, the Hordern Pavilion had a capacity to accommodate approximately 7000 party patrons. They also said that the Mardi Gras and Sleaze Ball committee leased several adjacent venues (including the Royal Hall of Industries) to accommodate the growing number of party patrons (with a record crowd of 17,000 in 1993).

One of the main reasons for the party's instant success was that gay men in New South Wales (of which Sydney, with a population in the greater urban area of 3.2 million, is the capital) were experiencing increasing legal and social liberation which enabled them to socialize in public arenas, as discussed by Wotherspoon (1991). These political and social gains gave many people a unique opportunity to see and experience the diversity and potential size of their subculture.

The impact of socio-political and economic factors

According to Wotherspoon (1991), from the 1950s on the inner-city suburbs (including Darlinghurst, Kings Cross, Paddington and Surry Hills) were rapidly populated by the influx of young men. For decades the Kings Cross area had a libertarian reputation attracting many marginalized individuals or groups. The postwar economic growth in Australia contributed to the increased ownership of private vehicles and migration of many young (previously dependent) males to large cities with the ensuing growth of the inner-Sydney gay subculture, as Wotherspoon (1991) notes.

Once the large dance party scene flourished it attracted the interest of gay men who recognized the financial and personal benefits of these enterprises. Respondent 11 was offended by the preoccupation of some organizers with financial self-interests, whereas others he commended for their social conscience:

> Some are purely avaricious, they just want to make as much money as they can ... and they want people to come back the next time ... and there are those who are supporting the gay community by putting money back into the gay community ... such as Pride or Bacchanalia.

According to some respondents the inner-city gay subculture had also developed a sense of community identity. Respondent 10 said:

> When you're gay you're always part of the scene ... there is a set community.

Sorrels and Kelley (1984a, 1984b) suggested that commitments to a social identity generally involved prescribed lifestyles including norms and values, such as those adhered to by the gay dance party patrons. According to the organizer the gay dance parties reflected the social status and lifestyle of the party patrons:

> They are too expensive for the poor kids, so they're mostly middle class.

Respondent 16 summarized the basic cost of attending the dance parties:

> It is quite expensive: it can cost you, say, one hundred and fifty dollars to two hundred, to get everything together for the dance party.

The gay dance party milieu was undermined by the infiltration of marginal outsiders who attended the parties despite the financial costs. Respondent 6 said:

> The very hip crowd who go to the very hip clubs ... has changed, with lots of people from further out. It's far less drug involved, it's far less fashionable, it's far more ordinary people coming in.

The respondents suggested that there was a definite class difference between the 'very hip' (culturally aware) inner-city gay dance party group and the 'ordinary' outsiders whose presence had a degenerative effect on the ambience of the party scene. Feather (1985) suggested that group members often increased inter-group cohesion by attributing negative characteristics to outsiders. Many of the respondents may have derived increased self-esteem and group identity by attributing negative characteristics to these unwanted outsiders.

Some social and demographic characteristics

Age

The age of the party patrons varied from mid-teens to mid-forties, according to the respondents and the organizer. Respondent 9 suggested that party patrons were getting younger with the infiltration of outsiders:

> The patrons are definitely getting younger. I think this accounts for the police interest or renewed interest. The age ranges from quite young because there is not strict rules . . . you're not talking about alcohol.

The organizer described the age range of the dance party patrons as

> Fourteen to forty-six years . . . with a concentration in the early twenties.

The purchasing of tickets

The cost of most dance party tickets ranged in price from A\$30 to 35 (A\$1 is about 50p) and were mainly available from established gay distribution outlets, according to the respondents. The gay subcultural dance parties (including Mardi Gras and Sleaze Ball) sold their tickets from only established gay distribution outlets exclusively to members of the gay subculture. Respondent 2 said:

> The parties are only advertised in the gay circle and the tickets are only available from gay ticket outlets.

Time span

According to respondents the parties generally started at 11 p.m. and ended around 8 a.m. the following morning. The parties usually climaxed between 1 a.m. to 2 a.m.; this coincided with the reported peak-phase of the drugs for most of the patrons.

Male to female ratio

The male to female ratio of the party patrons varied in accordance with whether or not they were promoted as more exclusively (male) gay social events. As Respondent 8 said:

> There are some gay underground parties where women are not invited ... you have to be on an exclusively gay mailing list to attend.

The increasing number of young heterosexual party patrons (some as young as fourteen) were not deterred by the considerable cost of attending the dance parties. Many of these patrons also seemed to be at liberty to dance through the night whilst intoxicated on illegal drugs, even though they were under the legal age (of eighteen years; Lewis, 1992) to purchase or consume alcohol in New South Wales.

The role of the organizer

The organizer suggested that part of the role as organizer was a commitment to a safe-sexual and drug-related policy within the context of the dance party milieu. He also indicated a willingness on behalf of both himself and the dance party industry to co-operate in future intervention programmes:

> Our responsibility as organizers of the dance parties [is to] provide an excuse for drug use and sexual behavior ... but we certainly didn't design it that way. We have a responsibility to do something about it. The best approach is education and signage about safe behaviour in relation to HIV and the availability of condoms at the parties. I don't know what else we can do.

The organizer suggested that his role, gay identity and charismatic personality legitimized his authority (Weber, 1964) within the context of the gay dance party institution:

> Coming from the position that I am ... I believe I can
> actually make a difference what people say ... because I
> influence people through what I create and produce.

He was convinced that his dance party organization was a potent medium for conditioning party patrons' attitudes and behaviours. These commitments may be important considerations for the efficacy of future safe sexual and drug-related educational programmes at the dance parties, because of his knowledge about the party scene, his self-identified leadership role and the researcher's access to the target population.

The role of media

Most of the sample indicated that the media's scrutiny of the large scale dance parties at the Hordern Pavilion was partly responsible for their dismantling at this venue. In the words of Respondent 9:

> The recent media exposure is something to do with the
> dance parties attracting a younger crowd, and from a
> broader section of society ... and for some reason all these
> things are starting to happen, and the Hordern is closed
> down.

The infiltration of these outsiders, the state authorities' growing presence and the media's sensational reporting of the large-scale dance parties at the Hordern Pavilion contributed to their demise and the resumption of more exclusively gay dance parties held in vacant inner-Sydney warehouses or other smaller venues.

State authorities at the parties

The State authorities, using plain-clothed police, had increased their presence and intervention at the dance parties, according to the organizer and the respondents. Respondent 1 said:

There are more cops ... people have been detained and given the opportunity of identifying dealers, or users.

Organizer 1 endorsed this observation, saying:

The police have had their undercover people in there for months.

Respondent 6 said:

I was searched by a policeman on the way to a party a couple of months ago.

Respondent 8 outlined the magnitude of the problem faced by the authorities in policing the use of illegal drugs at the dance parties:

When you're faced with five thousand people who've ingested something, you can't give them all a urine test.

The New South Wales Minister for Police verified the impossible logistics of enforcing the laws related to the use of illegal substances within these dance party venues. In a recent media report he said: 'we're up against sheer weight of numbers – you can't individually search 5000 people before they enter a venue' (Safe and Sager, 1990, p.12). Prohibiting the leasing of the Hordern Pavilion and adjacent buildings to privately owned dance party organizers was, perhaps, an attempt to control the growth of the large-scale gay dance party industry and the increased use of illegal substances (in a public facility).

Infiltration of outsiders

Respondent 1 suggested that these heterosexual outsiders were disrupting the ambience of the parties with their aggression and lack of respect for the gay dance party patrons' norms and values:

The straights are coming into the parties and they are bringing aggression. They do not know the social etiquette of the scene and they are using alcohol.

Taylor and Leonard (1983) suggested that alcohol was one of the main contributory factors in the frequency of overt aggression.

Many of the respondents withdrew from social interaction with heterosexual dance party patrons because of their overt aggressive attitudes and behaviours. As suggested by Respondent 13:

> I stopped going to straight parties: too much aggro, too much alcohol ... straight guys don't know how to handle the drugs.

According to Respondent 8 gay dance party patrons became increasingly discriminating in their choice of dance parties:

> There were some parties we just didn't go to, because we knew there'd be a lot of B & T people there.

The label 'B & T' (bus and train) was used pejoratively by some of the respondents to describe these unwanted outsiders and their main modes of transport to the inner-city dance parties. Many of the outsiders violated the norms and values of the dance party milieu because they were not familiar with the possible dangers of not adhering to them. Respondent 8 described some of these violations:

> The new wave of people from the outer city limits do not know the party format of purchasing their drugs before the event. The etiquette involves getting your act together before you go to the party so you don't draw attention.

Some of these norms and values were developed to ensure the survival of the dance party institution. They created a cohesive front against their common enemy: the drug enforcement authorities. The social structure of the original gay dance party institution had evolved into a hostile environment for many gay patrons with the infiltration of these heterosexual outsiders. In response to this aggressive coup many of the gay party veterans abandoned the large-scale semi-public party scene and attended smaller gay-oriented underground venues. Respondent 8 described this phenomenon:

> The underground parties have sprung up as a reaction against the widening group of people who have come to the Hordern parties. The underground parties are usually more exclusive, they're gay or inner-city type people.

Respondent 4 suggested that the intimidating presence of these outsiders was responsible for the dismantling of the large-scale gay dance party institution, for example:

> When they see us they say 'fags' and other things ... the gays are the ones that started off the parties ... they like fucked it up.

A form of heterophobia may have developed among this traditionally repressed group (Evans, 1988) with the possible threat of their parties being overwhelmed by these outsiders. The semi-public gay dance party institution became so unbalanced with representatives of the dominant culture (heterosexuals) that most gay men resumed their pattern of attending 'closeted' dance party venues. Festinger and Carlsmith (1959) suggested that groups often reverted to familiar patterns of behaviour to reduce ambiguities and incongruencies between conflicting groups, which in turn usually increased within-group cohesiveness or solidarity.

Closure of the Hordern Pavilion

The large-scale gay entrepreneurial dance party organizations reverted to smaller, less accessible underground gay-identified social venues following the closure of the Hordern Pavilion (in late 1990). This development was perceived by the respondents as an unfortunate and retrograde social phenomenon for both the gay subculture and the wider society. As described by Respondents 2 and 8 respectively:

> If you stop the dance parties and the drugs, it all peters out, and they spread out. It's now veering back towards going out every Saturday night to Oxford Street ... to more exclusive gay venues.

Oxford Street was the social and commercial centre of the gay subculture where many gay men traditionally met with other men in gay-oriented venues, including bars, coffee shops, gyms, saunas, restaurants and nightclubs. The large-scale dance parties had the potential to afford many impressionable young adults the opportunity respectfully to socialize (which was rare in this culture) with other party patrons irrespective of sexual orientation or lifestyle.

Conclusion

A rich set of alternative hypotheses related to gay social organization, stress reduction, and drug use patterns were generated from these transcripts. These data may not generalize because of the small number of people interviewed and the pilot nature of the study, although there is a tradition of ethnographic work with small numbers of respondents (e.g. Pronger, 1992; Read, 1980; Ringdal, 1991) to describe the styles of interaction and the function of social structures in the homosexual subculture.

Further, there was occasional evidence of contradictory statements reflecting, perhaps, a wish to make more socially desirable comments. This must be taken into account in the interpretation of these data. However, the data in themselves are important for the generation of future empirical research and an understanding of the structure, function and context of the gay dance party milieu.

The dance party scene serves an important social and personal function for a significant subset of inner-city young gay men. The benefits are numerous and are enjoyed not only by patrons who attend the dance parties, but also by the larger gay subculture. The scene also provides many patrons with a satisfactory alternative social structure and enhances their sense of pride in belonging to a minority group.

The parties attracted the curiosity and attendance of outsiders (mainly outer suburban Sydney heterosexuals) who did not have the same vested interest or ideological commitment to the gay subculture or the dance party milieu. They were not part of the inner-city gay subculture, nor did they share the same pattern of recreational drug use (Solowij *et al.*, 1992); they preferred to use alcohol. These ideological, social and psychological differences have mainly been responsible for the reported covert and overt hostility between these two factions ('Yobs Out!', 1991, p.1). The conflict between the 'new' and 'old' groups at the inner-city gay dance party scene, combined with the recent closure of the Hordern Pavilion has effectively led to the dissolution of the large-scale dance parties, with the exception of Mardi Gras and Sleaze Ball. The predominantly gay-oriented group of patrons appear to have reverted to smaller more exclusive underground party venues.

These young gay men represent the 'new' generation of gay men, and the parties are also a public declaration of their recent political enfranchisement. Gagnon and Simon (1974) suggest that, previously, many gay men over-reacted to the social and legal constraints imposed upon them, by presenting an ultra-conservative 'facade' to the wider society endeavouring to avoid discrimination in the workplace and in their private life by assimilating or being invisible among the dominant culture. They chose to socialize within the framework of the 'underground' gay bars and nightclubs because they were not free to display or publicly acclaim their gay identity, as Wotherspoon (1991) also suggests. As Read (1980) found, these exclusively gay venues enabled patrons to mix safely socially and sexually with other men.

By contrast the new generation of young gay party patrons have been able to 'come out' to a network of social support systems within the gay subculture (including the dance party institution) which helps validate their gay identity by being with people who share a similar lifestyle (Wotherspoon, 1991). The dance parties offer many young gay men the opportunity to experience a sense of pride from belonging to a significant subculture, even though discrimination and negative attitudes towards gay men are still a serious social reality within the wider culture.

The gay subculture has become more organized and politically powerful since the decriminalization of homosexuality and the current HIV/AIDS crisis. The gay dance party patrons are making a powerful political statement by gathering in large numbers using illegal substances on a regular basis in semi-public venues under the scrutiny of the very social and legal system that traditionally ostracized and, until recently, punished them for their lifestyle.

The gay dance party phenomenon contrasts with the style of the suburban homosexual tavern described by Read (1980). Whereas Read described a working-class tavern in a small city, the dance party phenomenon is set in a large conurbation and among predominantly middle class and young gay men. Although altered in time, country and setting, the common components of the milieu described by Read are similar to those of the inner-city dance party milieu. But to these have been added a more 'public' but still safe context and one psychoactive substance (alcohol) has been replaced with a range of others (including Ecstasy, LSD and Speed).

The difference between the findings of Read and the present study revolves around the fact that the inner-Sydney gay subculture has become more politically powerful, and gay men have become more confident in expressing their gay identity since Read carried out his research more than ten years ago. However, the dance party, while still retaining many of the sociopsychological characteristics of the tavern, should be seen as a development beyond the homosexual tavern that until recently was the most commonly favoured meeting place for gay men (Bell and Weinberg, 1978; Read, 1980). Further research into the diversification of the gay social scene, which describes and analyzes the similarities and differences to earlier settings, is warranted, and the dance party is one example of this diversification which is a response to set and setting within a legal and social context.

The data in this chapter suggested that the inner-city gay dance party institution reflected and often amplified the same social and political issues, including the legitimation of the gay subcultural identity and the HIV/AIDS pandemic, that contributed to the evolution of the inner-city gay subculture. Chapter Four describes and analyses the effects these social and political issues have had on the structure, function and meaning of the dance party institution in the context of the HIV/AIDS pandemic.

Chapter four

The Impact of Political Legitimation and the HIV/AIDS Pandemic

THE inner-Sydney gay social institutions (including Mardi Gras, Sleaze Ball and commercial organizations) emerged in reaction to the dominant culture's negative framing of their gay identity (Wotherspoon, 1991), and the predominance of HIV/AIDS-related issues among this subculture. There are now numerous gay subcultural and entrepreneurial organizations under the taxonomy of the inner-city gay social institution. The major foci of this book are the reported use of psychoactive substances among the inner-city gay dance party patrons (Lansing, 1992; Safe and Sager, 1990) and the associated risk of HIV infection (Butt, 1989; Stall and Ostrow, 1989) within these social contexts (Stall *et al.*, 1986).

Many of these social venues, such as bars, hotels, nightclubs and saunas, are traditional gay habitats where gay men continue to meet other men for social and sexual interactions (Bell and Weinberg, 1978; Read, 1980; Ringdal, 1991). Wotherspoon (1991) argued that these 'privatised ways of meeting other people were important in the homosexual world . . . ' (p. 72), particularly prior to the legitimation of the gay subculture.

The large-scale inner-city gay dance party institution is an extension of these traditional gay social patterns of behaviour. The major differences between the inner-city gay dance parties and their predecessors are their high public profile, the size of venues, and the significance of HIV/AIDS among the dance party subculture. The first two differences were determined by the social and legal systems that previously stigmatized the gay identity (Goffman, 1963) both as a psychological disorder and as a criminal act. Hanna (1987) suggests that 'a society's dance conventions may be elaborations of, or reactions against, earlier rules' (p. 33) and that such conventions are often adopted by marginal groups in urban areas as a political statement. All these social and political elements heightened the inner-city gay subculture's public profile and verified its substantial presence.

Festivals, celebrations and dance have traditionally provided social, political and psychological safety-nets for subcultures, similar to the inner-city gay community, in crisis (Evans, 1988; Hanna, 1989). Nohl (1971) supports these findings in his comprehensive analysis of people's reactions to the deadly plagues which annihilated more than 25 per cent of the European population from the fourteenth to the eighteenth century.

According to Gough (1992), Mardi Gras provides the inner-city gay community with a medium to communicate 'just how strong and imaginative we are in the face of adversity' (p. 66). Gailbraith (1991) also acknowledges the importance and durability of the Mardi Gras Festival for this traditionally repressed subculture; as 'survive and grow it will after all, on that magical night in February each year, Mardi Gras and the gay and lesbian communities become one' (p. 10). The inner-city gay subculture's solidarity and pride emerged out of their concerted efforts to redress their social and political status and their battle against a life-threatening disease for over a decade. Gailbraith goes on to suggest that the survival of the Mardi Gras celebration exemplifies the 'challenges ... [which] have been many and those 13 years are a testament to our strength and determination' (p. 9).

Wotherspoon (1991) argues that Mardi Gras 'serves the function of creating a sense of "gay" identity for thousands of homosexuality [sic]-inclined [persons] ... ' (p. 210). Phillips (1991) suggests that the Mardi Gras 'Festival gives us the opportunity to define and develop our own culture on our own terms ... we are in a unique and powerful position to hold on to our own vision of how we see the world and our relationship with it' (p. 8). Further, Redhead (1990) argues that youth-oriented or 'pop' culture, similar to the inner-city dance party institution, lends itself to the exploration of sexual expression and politics: 'it is in its relations to sexuality and gender that the politically deviant character of pop has been most pronounced' (p. 27).

Duffin (1992) points out that Mardi Gras has provided the gay community with a body politic for the expression of their social, psychological and political issues: 'Mardi Gras has always been emotionally important ... as a tribal celebration of being gay, of community ... a celebration of life going on, a recognition of the community's response to this challenge and a remembrance of the many people who aren't here any more' (p. 70). Gough (1992) also comments that the Mardi Gras organization is ideologically committed to providing a social and political forum for the communication, confirmation and celebration of the gay subculture's identity. These social prescriptions are similar to the religious canons of most ancient belief systems, including the Judeo-Christian tradition (particularly the teachings of Christ and his church), as Eliade (1977) notes. Gough adds that Mardi Gras is 'the public face of all the individuals who are part of our community ... [and it] has grown in strength and stature to become one of Australia's premier events. People from all over the globe come together to experience the pride and diversity of community as we celebrate' (p. 69).

Ironically, the outstanding success of these gay social institutions attracted the patronage of an increasing number of homophobic heterosexuals. The Mardi Gras committee suggested that most of these heterosexual outsiders 'proved to be a concern to many gay men.' ('Keeping the gay', 1992, p. 77). They decided to implement a 'members only' ticketing policy, following unsuccessful attempts to negotiate acceptable terms with these outsiders. This social filtering system increased the degree of control the Mardi Gras committee had over their social institution's patrons. Merton (1957) suggests that successful marginal groups, similar to the inner-city gay subculture and their social institutions, were at high risk of being eliminated or significantly modified through this process of assimiliation. Hanna (1987) notes that social institutions such as dance 'may release and neutralize socially produced tensions and thereby perform a politically stabilizing function ... dance may often be a vehicle of self-assertion symbolically establishing identity as a counter to ... a dominating power' (p. 142). This preliminary investigation mainly concerns the structure, function and meaning of the inner-city dance party institution and how these aspects of it relate to possible increased risky sexual behaviour, a relationship suggested by previous research within similar contexts (Butt, 1989; Stall *et al.*, 1986).

The thirty-four respondents and the organizer suggested that there was a taxonomy of parties catering for different categories of patrons and organizers. These parties fall into two core categories (Glaser and Strauss's theory, 1967): (1) the community-based dance parties and (2) the privately organized parties. The properties of these core categories were: (1) the Mardi Gras, Sleaze Ball and gay fund-raising organizations and (2) the private dance parties, post-party recovery parties, sauna and private venues. The heterosexual rave dance parties, which had similar counterparts in northern England (Newcombe, 1991) were also included in this analysis because of their high significance to the inner-city gay dance party milieu, despite there being only marginal interactions between the two types of party.

All the respondents acknowledged the important contributions this wide range of social institutions, particularly Mardi Gras, had made to their subculture's continuing struggle for social legitimation.

The structure and function of the dance party institution

Respondent 10 described the symbiotic relationship between the gay community and its major social institutions in this way:

> The Mardi Gras and Sleaze Ball are run by the gay
> community for the gay community. They were considered
> the premier gay activities.

These two annual gay events were extremely significant celebrations for the majority of respondents. The degree of this significance was encapsulated in Respondent 11's symbolic analogy:

> They are very special. . . . To draw an analogy to see the significance [they are] like Christmas and Easter.

These two Christian celebrations may be seen as the core elements of their members' religious identity, in a similar way to Mardi Gras and Sleaze Ball for the gay community. The majority of respondents organized their social calendar around these important annual social celebrations. These grand-scale celebrations also had significant meaning for many gay-sensitive people outside the inner-city gay subculture. As Respondent 11 described:

> I've got friends who visit from overseas and they always come back because they think that's a great time to be here where there is a lot of gay people around, especially around February, and I always invite them to come around that period.

[It should be noted that February is the height of *summer* in the southern hemisphere.]

According to Respondent 4, Mardi Gras and Sleaze Ball epitomized the diversity and complexity of the gay subcultural identity:

> Mardi Gras has the whole festival with it and the parade that leads right up to the door and it's a real feeling of celebration . . . Sleaze is more . . . a dirty kind of thing, being naughty . . . celebration of different kinds of sexuality . . . whereas Mardi Gras . . . is the glitz and the glamour.

Most of the respondents suggested that the commercial gay dance party organizations varied in their commitment to the inner-city gay subculture. The Bacchanalia dance party organization was considered the most representative of the gay inner-city subculture by 90 per cent (n = 25) of the respondents. Respondent 11 attributed Bacchanalia's market leadership to their strong gay orientation:

Bacchanalia stands out as being more open to the gay scene, and gay groups organize them.

Most people according to Tajfel and Turner (1979), endeavoured to reduce intergroup ambiguities by dividing their social world into 'them' and 'us'. These social distinctions generally involved an intergroup evaluation process of the positive and negative attributions of the opposing group. This group dynamic often involves focusing on the negative attributes (or differences) between the opposing groups, rather than their positive characteristics (or similarities). Most of the respondents were critical of the rave dance party group's norms, values and behaviour by contrast to their own, as described by Respondent 1:

> A rave is very much heterosexual ... they're ninety per cent English ... about 1,500 [patrons attend] and they have them every weekend ... I absolutely hated it.

The respondents' negative evaluation of the rave scene may have been biased by their unpleasant experiences with hostile heterosexual party patrons within the context of their parties. Ironically, these rave parties had their origin in gay social venues, according to Redhead (1990). The respondents suggested that the community-organized parties afforded them the opportunity to publicly communicate the diversity of their gay subcultural identity and the complexity of its social and political issues.

Parties target different groups

According to the respondents there was a plethora of dance party organizations catering for different subgroups in the gay inner-city dance party subculture. These reports were supported by the large number of dance party advertisements in the gay media. Some of the respondents suggested that there was a strong association between the healthy libertarian attitudes of the dominant culture and the autonomy of these dance party subcultures. Respondent 29 described this phenomenon:

> In its totality it's an expression of how healthy our city is to how much democracy these groups have got.

Respondent 24 summarized the complex social substructure of the gay subculture:

> There are different tribes ... which are subcultures within the gay community or within the dance party community.

Ringdal (1991) noted a similar pattern of social organization among a group of gay patrons in a New York discotheque where the 'true members of the "tribe" could be recognized by their "steps" [dance] and by the subtle code of dress' (p. 67). According to Respondent 31 a similar group dynamic was operative on the dance floor among the gay party patrons:

> Dance parties can be a bit like an arena or a sports field and you can see quite clearly the different groups on the dance floor.

Respondent 1 also described the efficacy of some of the non-verbal communication symbols used within the gay dance party subculture that signify a patron's subgroup membership:

> You can delineate between groups by their body language ... like this [party] called Attitude ... it will be full of what we call 'A' grade gay men full of attitude and muscles.

Respondent 20 described the rigidity and distinctiveness of these social boundaries or symbols which defined the social composition of the inner-city gay dance party population:

> In Sydney things are very compartmentalized in terms of what groups people spend time with, and what groups they don't spend time with. ... The indicators are so apparent ... you could certainly tell someone who was a regular, say, underground warehouse dance party person.

Seventy-five per cent (n = 23) of the respondents had a structured developmental concept of 'the gay adult identity' similar to the life-stages of Kohlberg's (1969) social developmental theory. The fashion-oriented group was representative of the 'naively egoistic' stage of their gay social development, as described by Respondent 25:

> They're young, vibrant and they're happy, and they find it comfortable for the moment to conform to ... that pretentious fashion scene.

Some of the private gay organizers had recognized the potential market outside the gay subculture, according to many of the respondents. Respondent 13 said:

> They are trying to target different heterosexual populations now ... to enable them to make that profit.

Many of the respondents ventilated their indignation about the infiltration of these outsiders into their parties by devaluing the rave dance party institution's symbols (including their norms, values and behaviour). As described by Respondent 2:

> The rave we went to was very straight and we stood out because we weren't wearing clothes of the scene ... they wear loose baggy asexual clothes whereas the parties we go to [the] clothing is sexual ... like it tends to accentuate the best features of the person ... like the body.

Perhaps, these differences represented the 'support-posts' or reinforcements of the boundaries that defined the social identity of these opposing groups. One of the negative impacts of these inter-group dynamics was that groups usually became highly competitive and this often culminated in aggressive conflicts, as observed by Sherif *et al.* (1961). They also found that in-group cohesion and group identity were positively reinforced by these inter-group conflicts or external threats. The gay community social institutions (including Mardi Gras) reflected the gay subculture's commitment to a unified front on the legitimation of the gay identity. This in-group solidarity may have been 'an equal and opposite reaction' to the traditional devaluation of their gay identity and the unprecedented threat to their group's survival with the presence of HIV infections among their community.

Dance parties reinforce gay subgroup identity

In accordance with Sorrell's and Kelley's (1984a, 1984b) model the gay dance party institution constituted a social system, with its shared norms, values, symbols, lifestyles and experiences.

Durkheim (1954) suggested that these norms and rules gave rise to a set of prescribed behaviours, ideologies and belief systems that positively reinforced the individual's group identity. Respondent 7 described some libertarian attitudes of the dance party identity and by extension his own:

> People who attend the party scene have similar ways of thinking: very open-minded, very accepting ... without questioning.

Respondent 16 suggested that group identification and interaction were important dimensions in the evolution of group cohesiveness:

> There's a sense of belonging ... a whole big group of people that are doing the same thing at the same time.

The dance parties afforded many of the party patrons an alternative libertarian or socially empathic institution where they could gather in large numbers with people from similar lifestyles and use a wide range of illegal substances with little or no intervention or danger. Shared behaviours, including communal use of illegal drugs, also consolidated the group's cohesiveness and identity. The dance party was a social unit and, according to Jaspers (1959), such social units relied on the efficacy of its symbols to communicate meaning within the group. The ritualized use of recreational drugs (one of their symbols) was imbued with significant meaning within the context of the dance party milieu. The drugs helped create sociopsychological boundaries between the harsh reality of their everyday life and this preferred multi-dimensional environment. As Respondent 13 described:

> It also separates, excludes people from the rest of the world ... it creates a safer atmosphere ... where you can relate to other people on whatever reality you like.

According to Wotherspoon (1991), many gay men gravitated to the inner-Sydney area to be with people who shared a similar lifestyle. Respondent 1 described this phenomenon within the context of the dance parties:

> The parties provide social networks and when you're new to the city with no friends ... Ecstasy and the party scene

filled a huge chasm and the people became my immediate family. They provided the nurturing and affection I needed. ... They invite you into their space.

Many of the respondents suggested that they needed to be with a group of friends when they used psychoactive substances at the dance parties. Perhaps, they needed to retain this familiar group from their everyday life to reduce the anxiety of being surrounded by thousands of strangers. Lazarus and Folkman (1984) suggested that social support systems (such as friendship networks and substitute family structure) helped people to cope with stressful, often alienating social situations. Many of the party patrons were accustomed to fashioning alternative psychological mechanisms to help them cope with their often alienated and homophobic everyday existence (Evans, 1988; Wotherspoon, 1991).

The social organization of subgroups

Friendship and social groups were generally closed social units with similar goals, norms, values and behaviour, as suggested by Baron and Byrne (1987). Respondent 1 described the social function of drugs in the development of dance party groups:

Friends are determined by their use of similar drugs ... Conversation is all around the use of drugs and the party scene.

Previous research demonstrated that these shared experiences and external threats increased the solidarity and cohesiveness of the group (Sherif et al., 1961). Some of the respondents suggested that their need to belong to a group often overwhelmed their personal autonomy and discriminative capacity, as discussed by Burnstein (1983). Respondent 5 described these powerful group dynamics:

I took Ecstasy because my friends took it, and I knew it would be fun to do. On one occasion I didn't really want to take LSD; we were all going out and my friends were taking it too.

According to Cohen (1971), there was a strong association between group cohesiveness, other sociopsychological resolutions and possible deviant behaviour, particularly if these behaviours represented the norms and values of the group, similar to the use of illegal substances among the party patrons. Respondent 5 described the sociopsychological benefits derived from this socially dissident behaviour:

> My friends and I go on adventures together using LSD . . . It's fun to do, and it is illegal.

Other psychotherapeutic benefits were derived from attending the dance parties according to the majority of the respondents. The sanctioned use of psychoactive substances combined with the 'drug-empathic' environment helped many of the party patrons escape their everyday situations. They provided an important medium for escaping the often overwhelmingly stressful realities of their lives, including homophobia and HIV/AIDS issues. A similar phenomenon accounted for the rave dance party patrons' behaviour in northern England, according to Newcombe (1991), whereby the raves provided the patrons with a more satisfying 'reality' than that of their everyday alienated lifestyles. Respondent 3 summarized the therapeutic function of the gay dance party institution for many of its patrons:

> All our friends are HIV positive or they are going through difficult times in their life. . . . [It] may look very bleak but this gives you something to look forward to. . . . It gives you new vision, new hope, new optimism . . . and it restores your strength in your future . . . So Sleaze Ball and Mardi Gras have been very important for the gay people.

Many of the party patrons' safe-sexual perceptions may have been distorted by their use of psychoactive substances and the transformed environment of the dance parties, according to many of the respondents. It is possible that their everyday perception and discriminative powers were masked by the use of context- and state-dependent stimuli (Flexser and Tulving, 1978) including music, lighting and drugs. Paradoxically, the escape from the distress of HIV/AIDS may by its form actually contribute to its spread.

Many of the gay party patrons may have gained additional satisfaction from performing an illegal (deviant) act whilst immersed in the culture that traditionally repressed them, as suggested by Evans (1988). Cohen (1971) noted that subcultural norms and values were often more stringent predictors of behaviour within the group than the wider culture's mandates.

Intuitively there seemed to us to be a positive correlation between increased risky behaviour (including sexual) and the size of the crowd, that is, the larger the dance party crowd the less personal responsibility people took.

The impact of transformed reality

The dance party institution was made up of various independent elements (including those mentioned above), and the relationship between them may be understood in terms of the function, the set and setting or environment served in the development, maintenance and well-being of the patrons and the organization. Many of the respondents suggested that these transformed realities often created and maintained boundaries which insulated them from the external threats (Fustel de Coulanges, 1956) in their everyday reality, as described by Respondent 25:

> Once you're inside and they play the music ... you get absorbed by the whole thing and you start basically leaving everyday life. ... People on the dance floor together are definitely forming a really strong bond for one night ... that's why we have dance parties so we can all be there and all be loving.

The effectiveness of this environmental transformation on consciousness or reality was reflected in Ringdal's (1991) findings in a gay New York discotheque, where many patrons felt as if 'homosexual' men had 'actually conquered the world' and were now the dominant power. Respondent 14 applauded this important social function but recognized its limitations, including the possible distortion of a person's perception or world view:

> It is an expression of our sexuality and our identity and a display of gay pride ... [but] people within the inner-city area of Sydney have become rather complacent about being gay and have perceived the tolerance of homosexuality within the community. ... It is very easy to perceive that

tolerance when you are living in a ghetto . . . if you go more than 5km beyond the CBD [Central Business District] there is variance in that level of tolerance and that level of tolerance continues to drop the further you move away from the inner-city region.

However, some of the party patrons were stretching these protective boundaries to encompass their sexual activities, according to Respondent 5, rather than using a more reliable prophylactic medium, such as a condom:

> They give more opportunity to be more outrageous . . . from the anonymity aspect . . . I went to Mardi Gras . . . [and] I spent the whole night having sex . . . down in the bogs. . . . Fifty per cent of the men I meet are prepared to have unsafe sex . . . I say 'fuck off! nothing unsafe, do it somewhere else'.

One of the primary functions of the organizers was the dissemination and reinforcement of the gay dance party subculture's norms and values (including the use of drugs and sexual behaviour), according to most respondents. Respondent 13 endorsed the organizers' motives and efficacy in providing a drug-empathic environment:

> The organizers aren't really manipulating the crowd, they are creating certain themes. . . . They decorate the parties to enhance the drugs . . . and it's like going into another world.

Organizer 1 validated these motives:

> There's a ritual in what they do. . . . The design of our dance certainly is . . . if you're on drugs it'll be great. . . . There should be sufficient stimuli in the way it's created.

Respondent 16 also acknowledged the important contribution the set and setting had on the transformation of patrons' consciousness or mood:

> They are very well orchestrated, DJs know exactly what the
> crowd like. . . . They take drugs themselves, so they're
> aware of what's happening. The lighting is also very much
> orchestrated to the mood of the crowd.

The standard setting at the parties included spectacular light shows using laser, vari-lights, strobes, black lights, an artificial smoke machine and loud frenetic music. According to Bogoras (1979), shamans (healers) in pre-literate societies used similar stimuli (such as drugs, drums, music, dance, coloured objects and smoke) to facilitate an altered state of consciousness among their initiates. Both the shaman and the dance party organizers recognized the importance of set and setting in creating a consciousness-changing environment (Ringdal, 1991).

Disinhibitory effects

The use of psychoactive substances and the large crowds allowed most of the sample to escape the undesirable or inhibiting elements of their everyday reality, including the homonegative attitudes of the dominant culture, HIV/AIDS-related issues and the social constraints of their personal and professional identities. Respondent 16 also described the emancipating effects of the drugs:

> The drugs provide . . . a sense of being able to think with
> total freedom, without society or reality saying you should
> do it this way.

Respondent 1 described the sexual and social disinhibitory effects of the drugs:

> The drugs cut away the socialization process . . . Ecstasy
> permits you to drop your social guards, enabling you to
> approach a total stranger in a loving and caring way.

Fromm (1976) suggested that people often feared freedom because they were accustomed to being controlled or ordered by the patriarchal dictates of the dominant culture. Most of the respondents used the drugs to help them overcome these repressive cultural mores.

Anonymous status

By contrast, other respondents attributed these disinhibiting effects to their anonymous status within the context of several thousand patrons. According to Respondent 2:

> The parties provide an atmosphere where people can be less inhibited, because of the anonymity.

Stall *et al.* (1986) cautioned drug users that there may be an association between these desirable disinhibitory effects and increased risky sexual behaviour. Stoner (1987) also found that people were more likely to engage in risky behaviour whilst in a crowd or group situation than on their own; he termed this phenomenon 'risky shift'. However, most of the respondents' data indicated that this anonymous status was reduced with regular dance party patronage. This status re-instatement was an artifact of the social process of conformity and familiarization, as described by Respondent 1:

> If you attend the dance parties regularly then the excitement is dulled ... it loses some of its thrill. You could no longer be disinhibited, because people knew you ... they may frown on your behaviour. You resumed your familiar socially restrained behaviour.

Most of the sample suggested that the large anonymous dance party environment allowed many patrons to experiment without the responsibility of a social identity. For example Respondent 8 said:

> You can experiment with new ideas, and risk being yourself and know it was safe no matter how you behaved. By experiencing this in a public setting, it added a new dimension ... allowing you to be disinhibited.

Douglas (1986) suggested that many people among high-risk groups reduced stress by the abdication of personal responsibility or individualism in favour of group identity. They chose to be anonymous in a group situation because it helped to reduce the accumulated stress from being constantly in control or subject to social control. This anonymity may have been an important psychological stress-reduction valve for many gay men who were constantly under personal and social pressures to conform stringently to safe-sexual guidelines.

Meaning of the parties

Berger and Luckmann (1975) argued that meaning and knowledge emerged out of, and were defined by, the relationship between human thought and the social context. The meaning attributed to the dance party was influenced by the individual respondent's subjective interpretation, personal experience and the group's definition of this reality. For example, Respondent 13 said:

> I go mainly because I go with groups of friends to enjoy being with those people ... and I really enjoy the life and the atmosphere.

Berger and Luckmann (1975) further argued that group solidarity and identity were dependent on a dialectical process between the members and their consensual perception of reality. They suggested that these group dynamics were reinforced by a continuous correspondence between the individual's meanings and the group or culture's meanings in this world. Group members generally develop this consensus of reality through shared experiences and knowledge. As described by Respondent 30 within the context of the dance parties:

> It was something very special ... it had a feeling of relative security ... because there'd be a common link with everybody there.

The majority of respondents (n = 27) suggested that the gay-oriented dance parties helped reinforce their gay identity, as described by Respondent 26:

> Mardi Gras is a celebration of gay pride and being gay, so that's why I'll always go to Mardi Gras and Sleaze Ball and other gay ones.

Respondent 30 suggested that the high public profile of Mardi Gras and Sleaze Ball, both inside and outside gay subculture, mirrored the gay subculture's enfranchised status:

> Sleaze and Mardi Gras are traditions which people feel are celebrations of our position in the community [and] we've gained enough acceptance to be able to do that ... and that certainly has a very strong group identity there. ... It's identifying with the broader community as well. ... We have a part to play in the broader community ... and broader community attitudes have been changing in Australia quite rapidly in the last ten years.

Not many of the respondents shared Respondent 30's optimistic prognosis of the dominant culture's reformed homonegativity. According to the data there was a growing number of gay-sensitive patrons attending the parties which may have helped dissipate inter-group aggression as these outsiders (heterosexuals) accumulated contradictory stereotypic information about gay dance party patrons. Further, the more frequently these patrons interact the more spurious the social boundaries become between these groups. Respondent 21 described some of these social dimensions:

> A lot of straight people go to Mardi Gras and Sleaze Ball. It is an expression of sexuality ... and identity ... it's going against all of society's values.

Many inner-city gay men had been traditionally exposed to some form of homophobic reaction within the wider culture (Wotherspoon, 1991) and the dance party institution may have represented a counter-cultural reaction to these repressive social conditions. According to Newcombe (1991), this 'process of social construction of "moral panics" about "folk devils" has been repeatedly set in motion against various "deviant" social groups for several decades' (p. 7).

Hanna (1987) also suggests that the dance has historically provided a vehicle for the dissipation of collective anxiety among groups of people who face life-threatening situations, such as natural disasters and diseases, similar to the HIV/AIDS crisis among the inner-city gay dance party population.

The celebration of gay lifestyles

The parties were gay social institutions where many gay men experienced and celebrated *en masse* the survival of themselves and their community during the HIV/AIDS pandemic. Respondent 4 discussed the positive reinforcement he and other men living with the HIV/AIDS virus derived from participating and observing these gay-oriented celebrations of life:

> They're not well and yet they're out there having a really good time. They might be fucked on Sunday, but they are able to do it.

Siegel (1986) suggested that a psychological state of well-being was an important co-factor in the maintenance and promotion of a healthier lifestyle for a person living with HIV/AIDS or related disorders. Respondent 4 described his positive emotional reaction to other HIV-positive party patrons who bravely normalized their lives by regularly patronizing the dance parties:

> When I see them and say Wow! I haven't seen them for ages ... and think, well they're still around, I become emotional. .... I really am pleased to see them and they're really pleased to see me.

Ironically, the dance parties offered many patrons living with the HIV/AIDS virus the opportunity to reject the larger society's pre-scriptions for a person dying from a 'deadly disease' and experience the significant meaning of the will to live, as Frankl (1984) also found among the survivors of the Nazi concentration camps.

Political forums

The dance parties provided the gay subculture with an important public forum for the discussion of specific social and political issues. Hanna (1989) also notes that dance has traditionally been an effective social institution and forum for the expression of political attitudes, belief systems and grievances of marginalized subcultures. Gay and Lesbian Mardi Gras has played a similar role in the communication of gay social and political injustices. Respondent 17 described a significant message being communicated by these social institutions, particularly Mardi Gras:

> Mardi Gras in particular is a real political statement of the community coming out.

Respondent 17 used the gay generic term 'coming out' to describe symbolically the gay subculture's social and political evolution, including the social legitimation of the gay identity. Ninety-five per cent (n = 28) of the respondents suggested that the gay dance party institution (including Mardi Gras and Sleaze Ball) was an extremely important component of their gay identity or lifestyle. Respondent 12's testimony revealed some of these cohesive elements:

> I view Sleaze Ball as uniting the gay community ... one big party that gay Sydney can go to ... Mardi Gras is the same thing but more of an international and interstate event. ... They are a real unification of the gay community and their friends.

These public demonstrations of solidarity also communicated the formidable dimensions (including the possible size, age distribution, diversity, unresolved socio-political issues, and potential power) of this traditionally repressed subculture, as Respondent 12 suggested:

> The parties demonstrate that we're a very powerful group ... because there's lots of us.

According to the respondents' data, this rapidly growing gay social institution provided demographic barometers or windows for the estimation of important complex social and political elements relevant to this previously 'closeted' subculture. Respondent 20 compared the fundamental tenets of the gay community parties and their privately owned counterparts:

> The whole purpose of ACT UP parties is to raise money. It's a political organization. ... Mardi Gras and Sleaze are political because they represent the gay community but there are others which are purely commercial.

ACT UP (AIDS Coalition to Unleash Power) is (in Australia) a predominantly gay organization committed to direct political action to end the HIV/AIDS crisis (Crimp and Rolston, 1990). Respondent 20 implied that both organizations were motivated by profit but he failed to make the distinction of how this profit was distributed. However, this point was clarified by Gailbraith (1991): 'the profits from these parties fund the Mardi Gras Festival and Parade' (p. 9). According to Respondent 6, the patronage of a gay social institution constituted concrete evidence of an individual's commitment to a gay political agenda:

> I think if you're gay and you're at a gay dance party you are expressing ... making a political statement.

The gay dance party institution (particularly Mardi Gras and Sleaze Ball) afforded the subculture with a platform for the transmission of iconoclastic messages that challenged the dominant culture's narrow prescriptions of a gay stereotype. Many of the respondents suggested that they often debunked these insulting stereotypic prescriptions by parodying them. Respondent 2 described some of the gay political and social elements being addressed in these public demonstrations:

> They are open expressions of sexuality ... boys kissing boys. ... If you suddenly brought someone from Woop-Woop with their pre-set ideas ... then their social and political ideas are being confronted. ... The whole intent is to break down barriers ... have straight people and gay and lesbian people accept each other.

Stephen (1985) suggests that a high concentration of social interaction often reduces prejudice and discrimination, while Sherif *et al.* (1961) indicates that inter-group competition often increases ambiguities, prejudice and hostilities between groups. Respondent 14 described the overwhelming effect the growing number of heterosexual party patrons had on the future proprietorship of these gay social institutions:

> The dance party scene started off within the gay community and gay people started bringing their straight friends and then straight friends. ... Gradually more straight people started coming along and then some of the dance parties became quite mixed and then some of them became straight ... and gay people specifically are starting to lose their gay identity including the last Sleaze Ball.

Siegel (1970) argued that marginal populations in urban areas often establish social boundaries to protect them from losing their social identity through the process of assimilation into the dominant culture. Respondent 30 described this social filtering phenomenon:

> The whole argument going on in the gay community at the moment ... is they've decided to limit the parties to ... gay people and their immediate friends.

According to Respondent 11, this segregated policy increased the odds of the gay subculture retaining ownership of their institutions:

> It is very important that the Gay and Lesbian community maintain control over the Mardi Gras, that's why I think that this move to restrict ticket sales to members is a good one. ... I am hoping that they would only sign up other people who are gay ... [otherwise] we could have a lot of heterosexuals join up in the Mardi Gras and get elected on the board and become president and take over.

Respondent 11 described the disturbing presence of these homophobic outsiders at one of their major subcultural events:

> Last Sleaze Ball there was a lot of heterosexuals there who weren't particularly sympathetic to the gay groups.

Many people from the gay community voiced their dissatisfaction in *The Gay Community's Newspaper: Sydney Star Observer* with a 'barrage of complaints about large levels of inappropriate [heterosexual] behaviour at Sleaze' ('Yobs Out!', 1991, p. 1). Some of the private gay organizers were also frustrated by their aborted attempts at providing integrated venues for heterosexual and gay patrons. According to Respondent 8 these organizers responded to these incongruities by reconstructing the closed social boundaries within the context of 'closeted' gay venues:

> They want to keep it a secret ... it's gone underground. ... They were willing to come out ... but couldn't so now they only have the people they want.

These segregated conditions may have increased some patrons' pride and commitment to a unified subcultural gay identity, as Sherif *et al.* (1961) demonstrated. Respondent 2 described the liberating effects of the growing social and political awareness (inside and outside the gay community) of the diversity and complexity of the inner-city gay subculture and its institutions:

> There's a certain freedom [with] enfranchisement to gay men politically – they're powerful now ... demanding respect and rights because they're big events ... and also there's a mixture of sexuality types. At the dance parties you see every kind of expression.

Most of the respondents agreed that it was important for the gay subculture to continue with its high public profile if they were to develop and maintain their political and social gains. Respondent 14 suggested that:

> It is still very important that the gay people maintain that sort of political motivation and then we can display our gay pride and we can do that in an event like the Mardi Gras.

According to all of the respondents the inner-city gay dance party institution evolved into an extremely important multi-dimensional social and political platform for the public communication of a diverse range of contentious (often unheard) gay community issues, as also noted by Duffin (1992). He suggests that 'Mardi Gras has come to symbolize our courage in the face of this epidemic and our determination to keep living and enjoying life while still fighting the health crisis in our midst. AIDS is a part of our community's culture now. The community initially responded by using Mardi Gras events as a vehicle for prevention education' (p. 70).

The function and meaning of post-party venues

The majority of respondents attended a diverse range of post-dance party gatherings known as 'recovery parties' (at the conclusion of the dance parties), where they socialized with other gay-sensitive party patrons. These recovery parties were organized within the established gay social institutions such as hotels, bars, nightclubs, saunas and private parties. Previous researchers suggested that these traditional gay venues provided patrons with a relatively safe environment to interact sexually and socially with other men (Bell and Weinberg, 1978; Read, 1980; Wotherspoon, 1991). According to Respondent 30 some gay men preferred to join the dance party revellers during the latter stages of these social 'marathons':

> I know people who don't go to the parties but go to the recovery parties.

Respondent 1 described some of the therapeutic effects of the recovery parties' more intimate environments after attending the large-scale dance parties:

> It's like going to the cricket game and going to the pub afterwards. . . . Everyone sits in groups . . . you're all coming off the drugs. . . . It's really a post-mortem.

According to Altman (1982), traditional gay social institutions often 'play the role performed for other groups by the family and the church' (pp. 18–19). These social units, involving family, friends and significant others are the principal agents of a person's subjective reality (Berger and Luckmann, 1975). This reality is maintained through the exchange of information and the greater proportion of meaning in this conversation is implicit not explicit. For example, the term 'recovery' had different meanings for different party patrons, as described by Respondent 6:

> They are called recovery to burn off drugs . . . [although] some people keep it going all night and all day . . . after taking more drugs.

These socially liberating mechanisms may have increased the risk of HIV infection among the recovery party patrons (Stall *et al.*, 1986). Respondent 2 described the increased dangers of impaired judgement following their taking of drugs and alcohol within the context

of the recovery parties, as echoed by Butt (1989) and Mirin *et al.*
(1988).

> People are more likely to have risky sex ... because you
> add more alcohol, more drugs so the loss of the control
> factor is even greater. ... Alcohol has a stronger effect in
> terms of loss of control than drugs.

Almost half of the respondents (n = 15) used alcohol at the recovery
parties as an anxiety suppressor or sexual stimulant (Brown *et al.*,
1980). This may have increased their risks of engaging in behaviour
leading to HIV infection (Butt, 1989; Stall *et al.*, 1986). According
to most of the respondents the recovery parties were popular 'cruising' venues for many party patrons. Respondent 26 suggested that
the recovery parties were ideal locations for sexual negotiations:

> I go to the recovery parties because there's ... a lot of
> cruising happening. There's usually sex in the toilets too. It
> is quite easy to find a partner there and have sex.

Bell and Weinberg (1978) defined 'cruising' as 'looking for a sexual
partner ... in a variety of settings which were known in the homosexual community. ... Chief among these settings was the gay bar'
(p. 236). Respondent 5 described other patterns of sexual negotiations within these gay social venues:

> I tend to go on to a recovery party. ... My ideal is to meet
> someone and then go home with them and have sex ... or I
> go to the sauna to clean up and have sex.

The saunas were popular post-party venues for many of the respondents, as described by Respondent 4:

> I mostly go with friends to the sauna. ... We'll talk and
> laugh about how the dance party's gone. ... A number of
> people do that.

According to Bell and Weinberg (1978), these gay saunas or bathhouses were principally used by male patrons for impersonal sexual
encounters with other men. The predictability and universality of
this phenomenon was reflected in Respondent 7's declaration:

> If I wanna have sex I'll go to a sauna ... where I know I'm going to get it. ... I've partied and to go to a recovery party for ... sex is pointless.

The distinction he made between these two important gay institutions outlined the sexual specificity of the sauna venue, as suggested by previous researchers (Bell and Weinberg, 1978; Read, 1980; Wotherspoon, 1991). Respondent 21 also confirmed the reliability of these venues for sexual liaisons:

> If I wanted to do sex and drugs that's where I'd go: to the sauna.

However, these context specific behaviours may increase the risk of HIV/AIDS infection among patrons. As confirmed by Respondent 26:

> A few of my friends ... [who] have been going to the sauna for years and ... have unsafe sex ... they don't even ask their partner if they're positive. ... They think 'well now I've got it and I can't get it again so why worry about a condom'.

Respondent 20 reinforced the sexual specificity and increased likelihood of risky sexual behaviour in these post-party venues:

> I often go to the sauna to find sex after a dance party ... and there's unsafe sex going on. I went to the sauna last Saturday night and had sex with two guys at once and that certainly was not safe sex ... and I'm positive.

According to the majority of respondents, the saunas were the most reliable post-party venues for sexual interactions. Perhaps, this was because they were one of the least sexually ambiguous among the diverse range of gay recovery party institutions. However, many of the respondents suggested that there was resistance to condom use by some sauna patrons. Respondent 26 provided an account of this recalcitrant attitude in these almost exclusively gay subpopulations:

There's people at the sauna who won't have safe sex. I've
been with guys who have walked out of the room and
refused to have safe sex. They were adamant about it.

The social diversities and dimensions of the post-party recovery parties were also reflected in Respondent 1's description of the
privately organized recovery parties:

I'll go to a private recovery party rather than a public one.
... For every official recovery party there's lots of people
having little private recoveries.

According to Respondent 7 these private parties were the least
sexually and socially ambiguous recovery party venues. He also
suggested that these intimate environments reduced risky behaviour
because they permitted the patron the opportunity to familiarize
himself with a potential sexual partner before negotiating safer
sexual conditions:

[A private party environment] is more worthwhile than a
pick up in a public place ... [because] you don't know
much about him. ... You eliminate the risks at a private
party.

The respondents' data indicated that they were more likely to be
successful in negotiating sexual interaction within the context of the
gay-oriented recovery parties (including bars, nightclubs, hotels,
saunas and private parties) than at the dance party venue. This may
have been due to the reduction of sexual ambiguities within these
traditional gay venues by contrast to the reported significant rise in
the number of heterosexual party patrons at inner-city gay parties
(Keeping the Gay, 1992). Perhaps, the traditional gay social institutions acted as filters (Hanna, 1987) or distillation mechanisms. They
progressively extracted ambiguous heterosexual components (dance
party patrons) leaving the social composition of the recovery parties
as almost exclusively gay. However, many of the respondents reported increased incidences of risky sexual behaviour within these more
homogenous social institutions, particularly the gay sauna venues.
Surprisingly, the private recovery parties with the highest concentration of gay representation were among the least risky post-party

venues, according to some of the respondents. Perhaps the informal and intimate environment of these private venues facilitated more open and honest rapport between the potential sexual partners. This familiarization process may have assisted some of the patrons in making less risk-laden judgements about potential sexual partners than their counterparts at other recovery party venues. These suggestions require further investigation in the light of previous research that demonstrated the increased likelihood of HIV infection among similar gay populations (Butt, 1989; Siegel, 1986; Stall *et al.*, 1986).

Conclusion

The findings of these analyses suggest that the inner-city dance party institution, including Mardi Gras, Sleaze Ball, the gay commercial enterprises and the recovery parties, mirror the diversity and complexity of the gay subcultural identity. They have traditionally provided a public forum for the registration and amplification of gay subcultural issues, such as the social and political legitimation of the gay identity and HIV/AIDS issues.

The effectiveness of these gay social institutions, particularly Mardi Gras, is reflected in its growing popularity (in Australia and overseas), and the recent political enfranchisement of the gay identity in New South Wales. Ironically, these successes attracted an increasing number of homonegative heterosexual party patrons who disrupted the previously cohesive ambience of the inner-city dance party milieu.

The Mardi Gras committee implemented a restricted 'members only' ticketing policy to help control any future disruptive or incongruent elements. They acknowledged that there 'is little Mardi Gras can do to keep these events lesbian and gay focused ... [and a] decision was made to restrict sales as a deliberate strategy to return the ownership of the parties to the gay and lesbian community which created them' (Keeping the Gay, 1992).

The respondents' data suggest that these social boundaries help insulate them from their everyday lifestyle, its often stark homonegative reality and the ongoing presence of the HIV/AIDS virus among their subculture. Many of the respondents were concerned about being seduced into a false sense of 'safety' within these transformed realities which may, paradoxically, increase their risk of HIV infection.

This chapter has described the function, structure and meaning of the dance parties. Chapter Five focuses on the attitudes and reported behaviour that emerged from the respondents' data and their relationship to the use of recreational drugs and sexual behaviour within the gay dance party institution.

Chapter five

Drug Use and Sex at Dance Parties

ALMOST every Saturday night in the inner-Sydney city area, several thousand young adults gather at a suitable venue, use recreational drugs and dance through the night (Safe and Sager, 1990). The taking of psychoactive substances for recreational purposes (including dancing and sexual interactions) is a socially sanctioned custom within these gay-oriented contexts, as previous research has found (Evans, 1988; Ringdal, 1991; Solowij *et al.*, 1992; Stall and Wiley, 1988) and is similar to the use of alcohol within the context of licensed social clubs and other venues.

Many of the psychoactive substances, including Ecstasy (3, 4-methylenedioxymethamphetamine [MDMA]), used by these party patrons (Solowij *et al.*, 1992) are commonly known as 'designer' drugs (Beck *et al.*, 1989). The term was originally coined by the Drug Enforcement Administration (DEA) in the USA to describe the chemical manipulation used by pharmacologists trying to change the 'neuro-consciousness' in an effort to circumvent the illegal status of the drugs they manufactured (Beck *et al.*, 1989; Newcombe, 1988; Stevens, 1988).

Since the early 1960s there has been an upsurge in the manufacture and recreational use of designer drugs, such as MDA (methylenedioxyamphetamine), LSD (lysergic acid diethylamide) and the most recent addition, MDMA or Ecstasy (Beck *et al.*, 1989; Newcombe, 1991; Stevens, 1988). Although Ecstasy appears to be a recent addition to the list of recreational drugs available on the inner-Sydney illegal drug market (Chesher, 1990), it was originally developed by Merck Chemicals (a German pharmaceutical company) in 1914 and subsequently used as an appetite suppressor and stimulant for the armed forces during the First World War (Beck *et al.*, 1989; Newcombe, 1988).

Solowij *et al.* (1992) suggest that MDMA has gained world-wide popularity as a recreational drug, peaking in Australia around 1989–90. They found that it was mainly used by dance party patrons and to a lesser extent as an adjunct to psychotherapy. Newcombe (1992) reports similar findings from the British dance party experience in north-west England where the 'use of *ecstasy*... has increased dramatically over the last five years, largely because of their popularity as "dance drugs" on the *rave* scene ... ' (p. 1). In support of these findings, Henry (1992) also suggests that it is used almost exclusively by ravers in Britain, whereas in the United States it tends to be taken in private settings or at parties.

Beck (1990) suggests that a considerable number of American psychiatrists, psychotherapists and researchers were staunch advocates of MDMA's psychotherapeutic value and considered there was minimal harm associated with its use if carefully monitored. These proponents argued that MDMA expedited the psychotherapeutic process, in particular the rapid development of open and honest rapport (Beck *et al.*, 1989; Peroutka, 1990). However, the DEA in the USA described MDMA as a potentially dangerous 'designer drug', citing increasing incidences of abuse outside its use in psychotherapy (Beck, 1990).

A series of legal and political conflicts ensued for many years between these two camps culminating in late 1986 with the scheduling of MDMA as a class 1 drug in the USA (Beck *et al.*, 1989). The British government adopted a similar restrictive policy to the manufacture, sale and possession of MDMA almost a decade earlier in 1977 (Abbott and Concar, 1992). The Australian authorities also prohibited the manufacture, importation, possession, sale and use of MDMA (Chesher, 1990). Ironically, these legal restrictions may have increased rather than decreased the use of MDMA in these three countries (Beck *et al.*, 1989; Newcombe, 1991; Solowij *et al.*, 1992).

Ecstasy's popularity among the inner-city gay dance party patrons may be partly due to its convenient packaging (in capsule or tablet form) which avoids some of the risks associated with intravenous administration, such as the risk of HIV infection from sharing needles, and being found in possession of illegal apparatus (Monaghan, 1989; Newcombe, 1988). Further, its latency period (up to one hour) may have allowed some party patrons to consume their Ecstasy prior to attending the parties (Beck *et al*., 1989; Lansing, 1992; Newcombe, 1992). These benefits also have decided disadvantages, such as corruption with other substances (sometimes toxic) by indiscriminate manufacturers or street dealers who wish to maximize their profits (Beck *et al*., 1989; Monaghan, 1989; Newcombe, 1988). Newcombe (1992) suggested that Ecstasy was often corrupted with a variety of other drugs. Beck *et al*. (1989) attribute this variability in quality and composition to the lack of stringent pharmaceutical controls imposed on legal drugs. They also argued that the quality and price of street drugs are mainly controlled by the economic determinants of supply and demand. Their supply or availability is often controlled by the drug enforcement authorities who raid local dealers, illegal laboratories and smugglers and seize drugs (Beck *et al*., 1989; Safe and Sager, 1990).

Previous research has demonstrated that different people reported a variety of effects from the same drug (Beck *et al*., 1989; Newcombe, 1988; Solowij *et al*., 1992). This inconsistency may also be explained in terms of biopsychosocial factors (Abbott and Concar, 1992), such as mood (Butt, 1989), personality, context, belief systems (Stall *et al*., 1986), experience, frequency of use (Solowij *et al*., 1992), dosage, poly-drug use (using more than one drug concurrently) (Chesher, 1990), rate of assimilation or health status. Stall *et al*. (1986) suggest that these dimensions may also exacerbate the effect of psychoactive substances during sexual activity and increase the risk of HIV infection.

Some patrons may use recreational drugs (such as Ecstasy) to help them cope with their sexual anxieties and fear of the presence of HIV/AIDS among their community. It is impossible to identify a single causal factor for the use of recreational drugs (Newcombe, 1992) and possible increased risky sexual behaviour (Stall *et al*.,

1986) because of the heterogeneity of human attitudes and behaviour in the inner-Sydney gay dance party population. Stall *et al.* (1986) suggested that a multifactorial model (incorporating a variety of biopsychosocial factors) may be a better predictor of risky sexual and drug-related behaviour following the use of recreational drugs. As a consequence, this research has endeavoured to cast a wide net to tap some of these possible underlying dynamics and trends, rather than focusing on the individual psychology of each respondent.

The combination of drugs and sexual activity within a social context is not a recent phenomenon, or confined to the gay community and the dance party scene; it is one of the most ancient forms of human celebration (Eliade, 1974b; Evans, 1988; Herdt, 1982). In some pre-literate societies young males and their initiators used psychoactive substances, danced through the night with a large group of people often to loud music or chanting, and participated in homoerotic ritualized sexual behaviour as a 'rite of passage' in preparation for manhood (Herdt, 1982). A similar tribal atmosphere appears to account for many of the patrons' attitudes and behaviours in the context of the dance party milieu. However, the major differences between these pre-literates and the dance party patrons was that the former's wider culture sanctioned, legitimated and enforced these rituals, and they were not at high risk of HIV infection (as far as we know).

The main aim of this phase of the study was to generate hypotheses, using Glaser and Strauss's qualitative Grounded Theory (1967) model, about the relationship between risky sexual behaviour and recreational drug use, within the social context of the gay dance party. The results reported in this chapter have been structured to furnish the reader with a broad and sequential overview of the relevant sociopsychological issues related to the behaviour of the respondents in this context.

The sources and availability of drugs

The distribution of illegal drugs often involved a complex system of people, including 'professional' dealers and friendship networks, as found by Newcombe (1992) in the British rave dance party milieu. Gold (1989) suggested that new drugs were often introduced and supplied via peer groups and other social systems. Most of the respondents indicated that this distribution network was a social norm within the inner-city gay dance party milieu. Respondent 11 described the normalcy of this behaviour at the dance party:

> We went to a party and another friend came over and had this drug I've never used before.

These drug networks ensured continuity of supply and information about the latest drugs and their effects (Beck *et al.*, 1989; Newcombe, 1991; Solowij *et al.*, 1992). Respondent 14 described one of these drug distribution networks:

> I know a boy from the North Shore who buys one hundred Ecstasies and sells them to his friends.

The youthful dealer's residential location implicitly conveyed his possible class, socio-economic background and educational opportunities. The North Shore residential address strongly suggested that his family had a middle or high social status and income (including successful tertiary educated professionals, executives of organizations and private entrepreneurs). Respondent 1 described the phoenix-like resilience of these illegal entrepreneurs:

> Drugs are readily available from the dealers. Some get busted but there are always new sources.

The market's resilience and its symbiotic dependency on the continued growth of the inner-city dance party milieu was reflected in Respondent 16's description:

> Ecstasy is always around. They bust a factory ... but it turns up at the last moment before parties.

A major difference between the illegal drug market and the legitimate consumer market was that each person who sold or purchased illegal drugs was compromised by the illegitimacy of their behaviour. This in turn ensured a high degree of inter-group cohesiveness, secrecy and protection for all those involved and makes policing by the relevant drug authorities an almost impossible task (Newcombe, 1991).

Patterns of drug use

The respondents' data suggested that Ecstasy, Speed, Marijuana, Alcohol and LSD were the most popular dance party drugs, as previous researchers found (Beck *et al.*, 1989; Newcombe, 1992). Solowij *et al.* (1992) also reported that 75 per cent of their sample resided in the city or inner-Sydney suburbs. They also found that the inner-city dance parties were the most popular venues for using Ecstasy for 72 per cent of their sample.

Cocaine

Cocaine was gaining popularity among inner-city recreational drug users, according to many of the respondents in this study. For example, Respondent 1 said:

> Cocaine is on the increase: many people are using it intranasally.

Administration route

The respondents' data indicated a conflict of opinion about the most popular route of amphetamine administration by dance party patrons. Some respondents suggested that only a minority of party patrons inject drugs, but Respondent 4 suggested that

> Shooting up amphetamines is becoming more prevalent, because people are looking for more.

Klee (1991a, 1991b) reported a similar increase in the injecting of drugs, among young drug users in Britain. The organizer also confirmed that there was evidence of some injecting drug use among party patrons:

> They do find needles at the parties on the floor, so people are using and they would mostly do it at parties.

Mirin *et al.* (1988) argued that peer pressure was often responsible for different patterns of drug use. Respondent 1 described some of the social dynamics underpinning this peer pressure, including competition and conformity:

They tried to out-do each other, by boasting about how many drugs they use and that they are really in control.

Further, he suggested that some party patrons were deluding themselves with this concept of control. In reality they were controlled and conditioned by the drug and their patterns of drug use:

> People who use drugs weekly become so influenced by the drug, by the time they are getting over it, it is the weekend and they are back in the cycle.

Respondent 7 described his 'tried and true' poly-drug formula for a successful dance party evening:

I prefer the combination of drugs for the effects. I . . . normally have half a gram of Speed, half a gram of Ecstasy and half a gram of MDA. I take all of these together in a 00-size capsule.

Stall *et al.* (1986) also suggested that a range of belief systems determined many individuals' choice of drugs and their subsequent behaviours. Many of the respondents used the drugs intentionally for particular desired effects, as Respondent 3 described:

What I want to achieve determines which drug I use.

Alcohol

Alcohol was considered a 'light-weight' drug by many of the respondents and was often used to quench their thirst or facilitate ingestion of other drugs, as described by Respondent 16:

> Alcohol is just a drink to wet your mouth with . . . after you've used Ecstasy.

Hando and Hall (1992) were concerned about the serious public health implications of this common practice of combining amphetamines with (often large amounts of) alcohol. They reported that over half of their sample consumed five or more standard units of alcohol whilst using amphetamines. Further, they argued that this 'may be particularly hazardous because the stimulant properties of amphetamine may give drinkers the false sense of their degree of intoxication, and may make them more likely to drive a car or ride a motorcycle when intoxicated' (pp. 21–22) or perhaps, participate in penetrative sex without using a condom, as suggested by Stall *et al.* (1986).

Marijuana

Marijuana was also considered a fairly innocuous substance, according to most of the respondents' data. Marin (1989) reported similar findings. Respondent 8's description reflected these attitudes:

> I smoke Marijuana every day, like I wouldn't come home from work and have a scotch and dry, I'd have a smoke.

According to Westermeyer *et al.* (1989), most recreational drug users believed that Marijuana was relatively safe because it was a 'natural' drug and not easily contaminated. The organizer endorsed these findings:

> Marijuana is far, far less dangerous than amphetamines and heroin. They are in a totally different category.

Perhaps some people's responses to a particular drug were already biased by an 'expectancy' effect that they formulated in accordance with their previous experiences or prior knowledge (from friends, literature or other sources). For example, the disinhibiting effect of alcohol on sexual behaviour has been shown to be a culturally determined expectancy effect (Butt, 1989; Hull and Bond, 1986; Käll, 1992; Stall *et al.*, 1986). Asch (1951) also suggests that people's attitudes and behaviour are influenced by powerful social pressures, including peer-group pressures to conform. This sociopsychological phenomenon may also help to account for some patrons' patterns of sexual and drug-related behaviour within the context of the dance party.

Reasons for drug use

The respondents' data indicated that two core properties partly described their psychological and physiological reasons for using psychoactive substances within the context of the inner-city gay dance parties. For example, many of the respondents used 'speed' to help them dance to frenetic loud music for many hours (six to eight hours), often without resting or sleeping. Respondent 3 described these beneficial physiological effects:

> Speed gives people the energy to stay on the dance floor all night.

All of the respondents had at some time intentionally used a psychoactive substance for its 'psychotherapeutic' effects within the context of the dance party milieu. Solowij *et al.* (1992) also found that Australian users often derived a secondary 'fortuitous' therapeutic effect from using Ecstasy, even though this was not the primary motive for its use. According to the previous literature, Ecstasy's positive mood-modulating properties, including a sense of well-being or euphoria, feelings of intimacy, sensuality and closeness to other people, were 'ideal' qualities for a successful social occasion (Beck *et al.*, 1989; Käll, 1992; Newcombe, 1988, 1992; Solowij *et al.*, 1992) such as the inner-city dance party celebrations. Respondent 9 described some of these psychophysiological enhancing attributes of Ecstasy:

> Ecstasy makes me feel very sensual, very touchy, nice physical feelings.

Most of the respondents suggested that the drugs and the dance party scene provided them with an escape or sanctuary from unrelenting homonegative attitudes and discrimination in their everyday lives. Respondent 8 summarized these sentiments:

> The parties and drugs help me escape from the alienation, loneliness and aggression experienced in a big city such as Sydney.

Many of the respondents' data suggested that they also used recreational drugs to help them discard their social masks or to be disinhibited within the social context of the dance party, which was in accord with previous findings (Beck *et al.*, 1989; Butt, 1989; Power, 1990; Stall *et al.*, 1989). Respondent 6 described these disinhibitory effects:

The drugs help people to be less reticent to say things and do things that you wouldn't normally do.

Psychoactive substances have also been used in many different settings, cultures and historical epochs (Helman, 1990; Herdt, 1982; Huxley, 1954/1974; Stevens, 1988; Zoja, 1989) to facilitate creative thoughts and actions (by individuals such as Byron, Coleridge, Dali, Freud, Huxley, Leary, Orwell and Shelley). Some of the respondents were impressed with the insightful and creative effects they derived from psychoactive substances (particularly Ecstasy), as described by Respondent 14:

> When I'm really smashed I get incredible ideas ... and inspirations. Something goes click and I get great ideas.

However, Respondent 13 suggested that these positive attributes rapidly decayed following regular use of Ecstasy:

> I used to love taking Ecstasy, because it was very mind expansive ... eventually it had the reverse effect. For example I went to a party without taking it, I realized I had missed heaps ... my mind had been narrowed down. I thought I was seeing more.

Solowij *et al.* (1992) also noted that 'there seems to be a point at which the unpleasant side effects increase to the extent where they outweigh the pleasurable effects' (p. 1170). Psychoactive substances have also been used cross-culturally to modulate the individual's or group's state of consciousness or mood (Butt, 1989; Eliade, 1956; Helman, 1990; Newcombe, 1992; Stevens, 1988; Zoja, 1989). Mirin *et al.* (1988) also found many people used consciousness-changing substances to manipulate or modulate their mood to suit the social context. Conversely, many of the respondents suggested that their choice of a particular drug was moderated by their existing mood. The use of illegal substances also added an exciting dimension to many of the respondents' dance party activities. Respondent 9 described this added incentive:

> Standing outside the normal society ... it's all a bit outside the law, so it adds a bit of excitement.

According to the organizer, some party patrons used the dance party to camouflage their 'overuse' or abuse of psychoactive substances:

> There's overuse in a section of the community, and they use the dance parties as a vehicle for it ... possibly an excuse.

The overuse of dance party drugs 'is part of the way of life for many young, relatively free, inner-city gay men and lesbians. Unfortunately, for many the end of the party means the start of a ... drug or alcohol problem' (Lansing, 1992, p. 8).

The unpredictable quality of illegal substances

The quality and effects of drugs purchased from street-dealers were often unpredictable and sometimes dangerous, according to most of the respondents' data. Chesher (1990) attributed this unreliability to the illegal status of MDMA and to the lack of quality control. This often meant that the person was never sure of its chemical composition: it could be anything from aspirin to amphetamine. Respondent 6 described a strategy he adopted for control when purchasing corrupted illegal drugs:

> The drugs are often bought from strangers. They are not always predictable, that's part of it being illegal ... there aren't any guarantees, you tend to build up a source you can trust.

Most of the respondents' data also indicated that the strength and quality of street-purchased drugs varied considerably, particularly if, like Ecstasy, they came in tablet, powder or capsule form, as Newcombe (1988) also noted. Respondent 9 described this lack of reliability:

> Ecstasy can vary according to how it comes ... in tablet form or capsule ... so you're never very sure of the strength or how it is going to affect you.

At the very least they may have no effect and at the other end of the continuum they may be lethal. Many people self-prescribed a variety of drugs to compensate for the unreliability of these effects (Day *et al.*, 1988). Respondent 8 resolved this unpredictability by dispensing his own chemical prescription or 'original-designer' drug:

> They are not constantly reliable ... so I prefer to take a combination, rather than rely on one drug.

Many of the respondents continued to purchase and use these illegal substances even though they were aware of the potential risks. Respondent 3 said:

> What makes me angry is coming along to the parties and paying all this money to some arse-hole, who produces this drug in his backyard. I don't know what he's putting in it.

Although these illegal substances (including MDMA) were widely used there has been little or no significant research of their negative effects on human subjects (Beck *et al.*, 1989; Chesher, 1990), let alone the possible biochemical interactive effects of poly-drug use as discussed in detail by Solowij *et al.* (1992). Most of the respondents continued to use these illegal substances even though they were often aware of the possible negative side effects.

Unpredictable behaviour

According to the previous literature, an individual's behaviour directly after taking recreational drugs was often unpredictable or unreliable (Beck, 1990; Beck *et al.*, 1989; Butt, 1989; Newcombe, 1992; Stall *et al.*, 1986). Leary (1968) found that the prior psychological mind-set of an individual emphasized the subsequent effects of the psychoactive substances. The respondents' data indicated an awareness of this phenomenon, as described by Respondent 3:

> You have to feel pretty good ... anything you take accentuates the mood.

However, over-use of recreational drugs has been found to impair judgement (Stall *et al.*, 1986), interfere with sleep and cause weight loss (Newcombe, 1992). It may produce other adverse psychological and physiological side-effects (Beck, 1990; Westermeyer *et al.*, 1989) such as panic reactions, paranoid thinking and depression (Newcombe, 1992) and may contribute to an increased risk of HIV infection (Stall *et al.*, 1986). Respondent 13's testimony to such life-threatening effects reinforced the validity of these previous findings:

> I put them [Ecstasies] in my mouth and swallowed them. I was taking more and more ... I was awake for three days and so was my lover. We were so depressed afterwards ... my lover tried to commit suicide, I thought he was dead. So I tried suicide as well.

Loss of control, consciousness, memory, judgement and discrimination were some of the most worrying cognitive impairments attributed to the use of psychoactive substances, in previous investigations (Beck *et al.*, 1989; Butt, 1989; Newcombe, 1992; Solowij *et al.*, 1992). These cognitive deficits may have significant public health implications for the increased risk of unsafe sexual behaviour (Bagnall *et al.*, 1990; Stall et al., 1986; Stall and Ostrow, 1989) for some patrons who use recreational drugs within the context of the inner-city dance parties.

Other dimensions such as dosage, body weight, health status, poly-drug use and the unknown composition of these street-purchased drugs may also have contributed to some respondents' distorted perception and behaviour (Hando and Hall, 1992).

The risks of experimenting with new drugs

Experimentation with new drugs was an extension of youthful risk-taking behaviour, according to most respondents. Abbott and Concar (1992) also noted that 'young people have always been society's great risk takers, as research on smoking habits testifies' (p. 30). Respondent 10 described this inherent characteristic among young adults:

> It's because everything's new and exciting ... that's what life is about when you're young.

These predilections to experimentation often led to risky behaviour, including the contravention of recommended routes of administration of a particular drug, and possible unsafe sexual behaviour, as described by Respondent 4:

> I had some Special K [Ketamine] the other day, it was the first time I had it. You're not supposed to blast [inject] it,

but I did. .... I can't explain it really, I know it was great, I can remember that. .... He put the syringe in and I'm sure we were into it before I slid off the needle.

Ketamine or Special K was a 'dissociative anaesthetic' (Newcombe, 1992) used mainly by veterinary surgeons. Most of the respondents' data demonstrated that they had also experimented with other untested psychoactive substances within the context of the dance party milieu. These findings warrant further investigation because of their public health implications and their possible association with more generalized experimentation, including risky sexual and drug-related behaviour.

The effects of continued drug use

Most of the sample's data suggested that there were consistent patterns of beliefs which reinforced their continued use of recreational drugs within the context of the dance parties, as Stall *et al.*, (1986) also found. According to Hanna (1987), these social institutions often provided marginal populations, such as the inner-city gay subculture, with socially defined boundaries.

Previous research also suggested that some people use drugs to help them cope or escape the alienation, depersonalization and constant exposure to a multitude of external stimuli (Brennan and Auslander, 1979; Lazarus and Folkman, 1984). This was described by Respondent 9 as follows:

It's a holiday when you are on drugs. It's definitely an escape because it removes all pressures, less tension.

Some of the respondents were impressed with the psychological development, including increased insight, heightened sensitivity and enlightenment, they derived from using Ecstasy, results similar to those reported by Solowij *et al.* (1992) in their recent Sydney investigation. Respondent 10 described the durability of these transformational effects:

Once you have had Ecstasy you are never the same again ... it's a loving drug and you want to be with people you know and trust.

However, this transformed cognition may have also impaired some respondents' judgement and thus increased their risk of HIV infection, as Stall *et al.* (1986) cautioned. Respondent 13 reinforced these predictions:

> Judgement is impaired while you are on drugs ... I've wanted to have sex without a condom.

According to the previous literature some people had difficulty recalling previously encoded information (learnt whilst sober) once they were intoxicated or in another 'state-dependent' condition (Eich, 1977; Jenkins, 1974; Overton, 1972). Eich defined this 'amnesic' condition as 'state-dependent learning', suggesting that a person could usually recall information more effectively when in the same cognitive condition irrespective of whether they were sober or intoxicated during the encoding phase. Respondent 2 described this impaired cognitive process following the use of party drugs:

> Alter the mind with a chemical thing then the situation is different ... when they are in an 'out of it' state they make the wrong decision.

Between recreational drug users' perceptions (described as belief systems by Stall *et al.*, 1986), and the reality (actual effects) is the grey area which possibly accounts for memory loss, impaired judgement and the increased risk of HIV infection.

Drugs used to cope with stressful situations

Many respondents used recreational drugs to help them cope with stressful social situations and bolster their self-esteem, as found in previous research (Beck *et al.*, 1989; Gold, 1989; Newcombe, 1992; Stall *et al.*, 1986). Respondent 1 said:

> The drugs help me cope with a strange environment and lots of people. You don't feel lonely, inadequate, ugly or insecure when you're on Ecstasy at the dance parties.

Respondent 9 suggested that stress was the major causal factor for the continued use of recreational drugs:

If you weren't under some sort of stress, or you didn't feel some stress, or you didn't need to escape, I don't think you would take a drug. ... It makes you forget the stress, pressure and tension about the drama of life.

Respondent 8 used the drugs within social contexts to boost his self-esteem:

I feel more confident in a group situation when I use drugs.

Zinberg (1984) also noted that some people intentionally used drugs to bolster their low self-esteem or as a disinhibitor within social contexts.

Drugs used as social and sexual disinhibitors

Marin (1989) suggested that drugs often liberated the users from social conformity. Respondent 11 described these disinhibitory effects:

It takes away all the social inhibiting factors forgetting about the inner-city guard.

Many of the respondents indicated that they were free to drop their social masks within the context of the dance parties following their use of psychoactive substances, as described by Respondent 7:

The drugs allow you to be totally uninhibited, sometimes [I] just talk to anyone.

Respondent 11 described these metamorphic effects of Ecstasy:

Ecstasy has helped me enormously. I feel open more now than before. I've always been shy. When I use drugs I feel my real self coming out, whereas I'm not normally.

Most of the respondents reported they had experienced positive therapeutic effects (including personality transformations), from using psychoactive substances at the dance parties. These socially desirable transformations often increased the respondents' opportunities for rewarding sexual and social interactions at the inner-city dance parties.

Drugs used for aphrodisiac effects

Stall *et al.* (1986) suggested that some people may have used drugs as a sexual stimulant or aphrodisiac. Similarly many of the respondents used different recreational drugs for their aphrodisiac and disinhibitory characteristics, as described by Respondents 1 and 2 respectively:

> Ecstasy had an aphrodisiacal quality. . . . To be touched was incredible . . . you feel alive to every sense.

> Drugs help you have really good fun, wilder sex, less inhibited. If you're with someone you know, you have wilder sex on drugs.

It is important to establish through future research how generalized these intentions and behaviours (particularly relating to sexual behaviours) are in a more representative population of recreational drug-using party patrons. The efficacy of future safe sexual intervention programmes may be determined by the researcher's ability to re-appropriate or re-frame sensitively the subcultural norms and values of the dance party subculture instead of adopting the critical attitudes of the legitimate legal and social system.

The negative effects of drug overuse on cognitive functions

Some of the respondents' data described an accumulative negative reaction to the frequent use of recreational drugs, usually after only weeks or months (depending on the quantity used during this period). Stall and Ostrow (1989) also found that many people reported numerous negative side-effects from overuse of psychoactive substances. Respondent 1 described this accumulative process:

> The side-effects accumulate after regular use over and above ten occasions. . . . All drugs have a pay back . . . you get totally depressed. . . . Ecstasy claims its victims one way or another.

Other respondents complained of impaired cognition, including judgement, blackouts, depression and some memory loss during these intoxicated phases. Respondent 3 noted that his:

> Judgement is impaired while on drugs . . . I didn't actually blackout I just lost my memory.

Respondent 13 described a similar amnesic reaction following his overuse of drugs within the context of the major annual gay dance party celebration:

> I blew it very badly at the Mardi Gras, when I took two Ecstasies, two trips, and dope . . . lost it badly. I don't know what happened for three hours.

Day *et al.* (1988) warned that once alcohol was introduced into these poly-drug 'cocktails' the user increased their likelihood of impaired judgement and possible risky sexual and drug-related behaviour. Respondent 13 supported these findings:

> Alcohol impairs my judgement more than drugs . . . it's a deadly combination for losing consciousness.

Some people used alcohol for its aphrodisiac qualities, to reduce their anxiety or to bolster their low self-esteem in sexual situations (Brown *et al.*, 1980; Butt, 1989; Stall *et al.*, 1986). Paradoxically, Stall *et al.* suggested that there may be a strong association between these liberating or disinhibiting drug induced effects and increased risk of HIV infection. Respondent 15's description was a poignant example of these deadly predictions:

> I've blacked out many times on drugs. . . . I've been raped many times while I'm off my face. . . . That's very common, more common than it is not, I find.

Perhaps his normalization of this behaviour indicated his sense of powerlessness to change these potentially life-threatening patterns of risky sexual behaviour or he had an unresolved death wish. Butt (1989) also found that some people intentionally used psychoactive substances to help them abdicate responsibility for engaging in unsafe sexual behaviour. Most of the respondents' data indicated that they had experienced risky sexual behaviour at some stage whilst intoxicated on psychoactive substances, as supported by previous research among similar samples (Beck *et al.*, 1989; Butt,

1989; McCusker *et al.*, 1990; Newcombe, 1992; Solowij *et al.*, 1992).

Detrimental effects of drug overuse

Many of the respondents were concerned about the detrimental effects of the drugs on their health and lifestyles, particularly those who were unable to control or moderate their use, as Catania *et al.* (1984) also found. Respondent 5 was aware of the serious consequences of overusing drugs:

> I'm very aware of the negative effects of the drugs on my health ... I consider I'll die of lung cancer one day from smoking Marijuana.

This incongruity between attitude and behaviour may represent the central point of focus for future education, intervention and prevention of HIV risk because it generates an important research question: have previous HIV/AIDS-related educational programmes effectively targeted and changed dance party patrons' risky sexual behaviour *whilst* they are under the influence of intoxicating substances?

The respondents appeared to have no difficulty in recalling the significance of safe sexual and drug-related educational messages during their interviews while sober. But most of their reported sexual behaviour whilst intoxicated at the dance parties was not always congruent with this knowledge (Delaney *et al.*, 1989). Respondent 1 described an accumulative loss of cognition following the frequent use of psychoactive substances, as also noted by previous researchers (Beck *et al.*, 1989; Newcombe, 1992; Solowij *et al.*, 1992):

> There is a residual loss of memory over a couple of days when using over a lengthy period, such as a few months.

There appeared to be a type of cognitive short-circuit between some respondents' previously encoded safe sexual information and their ability to retain or recall the significance of these messages when in another cognitive state within the dance party milieu. Although several researchers (Siegel, 1986; Stall *et al.*, 1986; Stall and Ostrow, 1989) have previously discussed this phenomenon, there appeared to be little or no association drawn between risky sexual and drug-related behaviour and possible 'state-dependent learning' impairment from the use of psychoactive substances within a specific context, such as the inner-city gay dance party milieu.

Risks when HIV seronegative

An HIV seronegative diagnosis did not ensure future safe sexual practices, according to many of the respondents' data. This revelation in itself was not surprising, but when an individual celebrated the clinical affirmation of his negative HIV status by performing risky sexual behaviour in conjunction with the use of psychoactive substances, surprise might be replaced by serious concern. Respondent 16 described how this incongruency may have increased some individuals' risk of HIV infection:

> It's strange because you are so elated that you virtually go out and celebrate by having sex ... it wasn't necessarily safe sex.

He also suggested that this euphoric reaction dangerously distorted his perception of reality by over-ruling his capacity to discriminate in sexual situations:

> I just couldn't wait to go to the dance party, be with friends and have sex. It should have been, 'I'm going to the party and I'll have safe sex'.

One psychological explanation for these potentially life-threatening reactions may have been that they were 'seduced' or self-deluded into believing for a variety of reasons (including a recent negative HIV test result) that they had 'Special' or 'Magical' immunity to HIV infection, similar to those conditions discussed by Frazer (1976). This phenomenon is not unique to gay men who use recreational drugs; similar dynamics appear to explain some people's continued use of tobacco following medical advice of its ill effects on health.

Risks when HIV seropositive

Respondent 4 suggested that some HIV seropositive people had adopted a 'carpe diem' or 'live for the moment' attitude toward risky sexual activities at the dance parties:

> People with AIDS are willing to take risks ... after all, they've got the worst thing of all, so why bother? A lot of positive people say I might not be here for long, and there's things I haven't tried and want to try it ... and they do.

According to Nohl (1971), similar reactions were prevalent during the times of deadly plagues that claimed the lives of hundreds of thousands of people in Europe from the twelfth to the eighteenth century. Some of the respondents suggested that some HIV positive dance party patrons had also adopted a similar philosophy toward their sexual behaviour in the back-rooms at the dance parties. As Respondent 3 observed:

> There's some people in these settings who are HIV-positive and just don't care what happens.

Humphreys (1970) also noted that some men preferred to use public toilet facilities for sexual interactions to limit their interpersonal responsibilities, commitments to, and identification with, gay sexual behaviour. Further, an individual was more likely to take greater risks when in a group situation because of their anonymous status than when on their own, as Zimbardo (1970) found. Urgent research is needed to establish the validity and generalizability of these reported risky sexual behaviours among party patrons. If these predictions are supported then there is an immediate need to implement appropriate harm-reduction programmes focused on safer sexual behaviours.

Reaction to an HIV/AIDS seropositive diagnosis

According to most of the respondents the psychological issues related to life and death were amplified for a person recently diagnosed HIV-positive. As Reanney (1991) poignantly noted 'one only has to watch the face of a man who has just been told he is seropositive for AIDS to see how the mere suggestion of death shakes the pillars of life. Foreknowledge of imminent death invades the most personal part of us, threatening the sanctum of our very identity, the self, with extinction' (p. 1). A person who was diagnosed HIV seropositive may suddenly feel overwhelmed by the immediate compression or contraction of their life, and react in an unpredictable manner, including experiencing a sense of urgency to live life (no matter how brief) to its fullest.

The dance party institution may have afforded some patrons a sanctuary away from the stark reality of their own or significant others' HIV-positive status. Death tends to be less fearful and 'real' the further removed it is from a person's everyday reality, according to Laing (1978). Conversely, it becomes more meaningful and stressful the closer it concerns oneself (Sivacek and Crano, 1982). We only have to recall the qualitatively different reaction we have to the death of a stranger to that of a familiar or significant other. As Respondent 3 said:

> Another close friend who always attends the parties with us has just been diagnosed as AIDS positive. It's made us think what is this mystery disease? . . . that really scared us.

This collective fear of the HIV/AIDS virus and the homo-negative attitude of their everyday milieu helped consolidate or unify the inner-city gay subculture, similar to the group dynamics observed by Sherif *et al.* (1961). Respondent 4 encouraged HIV-positive party patrons to take a pragmatic approach to overcome their fears:

> What they need to do, is what I do, get out there, go to the dance parties and see for themselves that we're not all dead. Even if we've got it we're havin' a good time.

The dance party institution and its social functions serve a similar role to many of the dominant culture's social institutions, such as the church, synagogue or mosque, whereby members of both groups frequently attend a specific venue and perform formal ceremonies to help transform or escape their everyday realities and their group's common enemy.

Paradoxically, these institutionalized reactions to death (and its unrelenting presence) were also celebrations of life and the survival of the inner-city gay dance party subculture, as previously observed among people facing life-threatening crises (Douglas, 1986; Eliade, 1957; Helman, 1990; Kamath, 1978; Reanney, 1991).

The data also indicated that many of the party patrons were performing a multitude of roles including mourner, actor and observer (Jones and Nisbett, 1971) within the context of the dance party and the HIV/AIDS pandemic.

The contribution of age and experience to unsafe sexual behaviour

Most of the respondents considered youth and inexperience synonymous with risky sexual behaviour following the use of dance party drugs. Most of the older respondents (over thirty years) suggested that younger party patrons were responsible for the continued risky sexual behaviour. Conversely, many of the younger respondents (early to mid-twenties) implied that older gay men were responsible for the current HIV/AIDS crisis and they continued to be the high-risk group for the transmission of the virus. Respondent 8 (who was forty years old and a veteran of the dance party scene) suggested that inexperience was the prime determinant of risky sexual behaviour at the parties:

> The inexperienced are more likely to be in danger,
> especially in this day and age ... what with AIDS and
> everything.

Young inexperienced party patrons were at increased risk of unsafe sexual behaviour with other men because they did not self-identify as gay men or with the risk of HIV infection, according to Respondent 9:

> The lack of safe sex in the toilets, at the dance parties ...
> particularly if they were young and aren't actually in the
> gay scene. They don't have the same level of understanding
> of the dangers of risky sex.

According to Respondent 16 some novice party patrons' discriminative capacity was over-ridden by their need for experimentation and sexual gratification:

For those who are discovering their sexuality for the first time ... it doesn't really matter what happens, it's all wonderful. AIDS is just in the back of their minds ... especially since it's all anonymous. ... They are taken over by the passion, and it's hard to think of safe sex.

Most of the respondents' data indicated that there were three predisposing conditions for unsafe sexual behaviour among dance party patrons: age, lack of experience, and not identifying as gay. These findings warrant further investigation as they may be important predictors of risky sexual behaviours among the inner-city gay dance party population.

The eroticizing effects of set and setting

The set and setting of the dance party milieu were important co-factors in the overall effectiveness of the drug-induced consciousness and behaviour (including sexual behaviour), according to the majority of respondents. The term 'set' refers to the mind-set of the individual following the use of psychoactive substances, and 'setting' describes the social and physical contexts in which the drugs were used (Stevens, 1988). Respondent 5 described the sensual and sexually stimulating effects of the inner-city dance party set and setting:

Getting on the dance floor with other people, releasing energy, a kind of sexual energy, to try and maybe attract people.

However, Respondent 16 warned about the possible risk of these eroticizing altered states of cognition:

The drug does tend to heighten sex ... you put yourself in an environment, where just about anything can happen, and your life can depend on it, that's part of the party scene.

This ritualized dance phenomenon may be found throughout recorded history and in many belief systems, including the Judeo-Christian tradition according to Eliade (1957), Evans (1988),

Hanna (1987), Helman (1990), Newcombe (1992) and Zoja (1989). These researchers and many others (Huxley, 1954; Leary, 1968; Zinberg, 1984) agree that the intensity of this altered state of consciousness is contingent on set and setting. Leary also stressed the importance of establishing a controlled and congruent set and setting to offset any possible negative side-effects from the drugs. Stall *et al.* (1986) suggested that the social context (including its norms, values and beliefs) often influenced the effects of the drug and the person's subsequent sexual behaviour.

Venues for sexual behaviour

Many gay dance party organizations provided their patrons with in-house sexual (semi-private) venues, according to most of the respondents. This sexual consideration was an extension of an established gay tradition within the social contexts of gay bars, nightclubs (Bell and Weinberg, 1978; Read, 1980), gyms and saunas (Wotherspoon, 1991). Respondent 3 was concerned about some party patrons' loss of safer-sexual discrimination within these back-room sexual venues at the dance parties:

> Drugs have an incredible influence on some people. You see evidence of this at the dance parties in the toilets ... some people get really carried away and I don't think they know what they're doing, totally out of control.

The risk of HIV infection within these back-room sexual venues at the dance parties may have been compounded by four important impairing conditions: an erotic environment, the over-use of consciousness changing substances, the loud background party music and the lack of conveniently placed condom machines or facilities within this context, as described by Respondent 16:

> In the toilet scene people don't have condoms, it's one great euphoria. You're off your face on drugs so you are definitely not thinking of ... safe sexuality ... it is very much a hard sex line. ... There's people who do and they talk about it as the greatest aspect of the party scene.

Respondent 4's testimony supported previous findings of the increased possibility of unsafe sexual behaviour within the context of these anonymous sexual venues:

When I go to the dance parties, I do the 'bogs'. I love it . . . really sleazy, that's full on sex, that's en masse sex. People getting into it like there's no tomorrow and that's not safe . . . they get into this frame of mind that it won't happen to me. Just this one time won't hurt, and I see that, I see people in there who I know are positive fucking someone or being fucked.

According to Respondent 10 the anonymity within the dance party milieu also provided many of the patrons with a unique opportunity to disengage from an everyday life fraught with danger and burdensome responsibility:

The dance parties are more anonymous, they are not so much a part of the scene. . . . It's another way of meeting people . . . and they can have sex there in really dark rooms. . . . I've not been in them when they've been in full swing but from what I have heard they are pitch black and basically anonymous. . . . You can have the most fun . . . and leave totally anonymous.

The respondents' data also indicated that the anonymous atmosphere of the back-room sexual venues attracted patronage by some men who have sex with other men but do not self-identify as a gay person. Perhaps some of these 'straight' patrons believed that they were magically protected by their lack of a gay sexual identity against the AIDS virus or somehow their identity 'tricked' the virus (see Chapter Eight). These attitudes may also indicate that they were unprepared, ignorant or did not identify with their personal risk of HIV infection following unprotected anal intercourse with other men (Bennett *et al.*, 1989). The gay activist's slogan 'Silence = Death' appeared to encapsulate these party patrons' dangerous behaviour. Respondent 1 was concerned about the public health ramifications of these 'straight' interlopers' irresponsible attitudes and behaviours toward themselves, other men, the gay subculture and the wider community:

The party venues offer a crossover effect for spreading AIDS, whereby some of the straight guys want to experiment and have a gay encounter, and then later have straight sex with their girlfriends.

Most of the respondents provided personal accounts of risky sexual behaviour following the use of psychoactive substances, such as described by Respondent 2:

> I know people who always practise safer sex, and come up positive ... that must have been the night I got really out of it.

And Respondent 15 said also:

> I think that I'm more likely to take risky sex when I'm out of it ... People actually would not think of condoms when they are out of it ... not at all.

Similarly, Swanson and Kinsbourne (1979) found that the use of drugs usually impaired the person's discriminative capacity. Butt (1989) warned about poly-drug use (including use of alcohol) and increased risky sexual behaviour. Respondent 2's testimony supported these research findings:

> One Sleaze Ball I took the normal amount of drugs, but I drank an enormous amount ... I remember getting home ... I woke up to him penetrating me, and it wasn't just happening either. I was out of it and he wasn't wearing a condom, the other person was taking the risks.

According to Mirin *et al.* (1988), the combination of drugs and alcohol may be a fatal recipe for losing awareness or consciousness and then engaging in risky sexual activity, as described by Respondent 13:

> The last time I had unsafe sex I was drunk. Alcohol impairs my judgement more than drugs ... It's such a deadly combination for losing consciousness.

Westermeyer *et al.* (1989) noted that the use of a specific drug (such as alcohol) for its idiosyncratic effect increased the risk of unsafe sexual behaviour. Respondent 1 ranked party drugs in accordance with their potential for risky sexual behaviour.

> MDA is possibly a dangerous drug for risky sex: you're so raunchy. The drug that is potentially the most dangerous for unsafe sex is LSD ... it has no detrimental effects on sex [such as erectile dysfunction].

Respondent 3 described a risky sexual incident where the partners played a sexual form of 'Russian roulette', following their use of psychoactive substances:

> I had a friend who was going out with a person who was antibody positive, they both took something and spent the whole night doing everything without a condom. I asked him why? He said ... 'we had no condoms and I thought well why not.' It's pretty frightening that drugs would relax him to such a degree.

Some respondents may have biased their data in accordance with a more 'socially desirable' response during the interview sessions (particularly towards items relating to sexual behaviour). They may have wanted to provide the 'right' answers or respond to a question because they did not wish to appear ignorant (Crowne and Liverant, 1963). Respondent 4 (who worked in a clinic) described the inherent dangers of biased self-reports:

> A lot of people bullshit about using condoms and their sexual behaviour, in general. I see a lot of people and I'll say 'have you had unsafe sex since your last visit?' And they say 'no'. Yet I've seen them fucking other people at the Hordern or in the steam baths. I think: don't bullshit me, I've seen you and you've seen me.

The organizer's responsibility for providing safer-sexual venues

In summary, the organizer suggested that organizers had a responsibility to acknowledge (instead of denying) the reality of possible risky sexual behaviour within the context of their organizations, co-operate with future safer-sex intervention programmes and maintain a supply of condoms within the context of the sexual venues at the dance parties.

> [I] think the idea of making condoms and safe sex available in the toilets of parties is most appropriate, and should be available in the toilets anyway.

He denied any responsibility for the use of psychoactive substances at his dance parties:

> We didn't encourage the use of drugs and sex.

According to most of the sample, the combination of these eroticizing effects and the over-use of drugs was a potentially deadly formula for increased risky sexual behaviour. The validity of these data on the common use of drugs at dance parties is graphically illustrated (Figure 1) by the pre-Sleaze Ball cartoon 'Living with Adam' in *The Sydney Star Observer*, the main free gay newspaper. The use of Ecstasy ('E's') and other amphetamines, and darkened toilets as a venue for sex, are sufficiently widely known about and accepted to be the subject of a cartoon.

The lack of conveniently located condom-dispensing machines, the common use of psychoactive substances and the sexually eroticizing environment of the dance party milieu (particularly in the toilet or back-room sexual venues at the party) may be the three main determinants of increased risky sexual behaviour within these contexts. Respondent 4 supported these predictions:

> Lack of condoms at the parties are really irresponsible. Because if the person you want to have sex with is out of it and you're out of it people forget ... I know myself. I don't care any rate, I'm positive.

The interviewer endeavoured to control for these respondent biases by continuously reassuring them that there were no correct answers and their interpretation of the dance party reality was as valid, reliable and valuable as other respondents' data. In summary, the most consistent reasons provided by the respondents for unsafe sexual behaviour at the dance parties were the lack of condoms and lubricant, and loss of control or discrimination following over-use of recreational drugs.

Figure 5.1: reprinted by permission of Jeff Allan

Recommendations for a non-judgemental intervention model

The organizer recommended a non-judgemental collaborative approach between the researcher, other organizers and himself for a future safer-sexual intervention programme within the context of the dance parties:

> Instead of coming down heavy, and making a huge drama [which] would be counterproductive, people need to see for themselves the dangers of drugs. Education is a major part of that ... they've always lumped together ... saying that they're all dangerous. ... We have to be responsible ... see where it's coming from, where it's going, and what we can do to alter it.

Organizer 1's commitment was an important contribution to future safer drug and sexual educational intervention programmes within these contexts.

Conclusion

There is a serious discrepancy between most of the sample's knowledge about safer sexual and drug-related guidelines and their reported behaviour following drug use within the context of the dance party institution. Many of the respondents were concerned about the potentially life-threatening ramifications of these discrepancies and their inability to modify them.

Dorn and South (1990) suggest that most of the previous intervention programmes have failed effectively to modify risky sexual and drug-related behaviour. Perhaps, the problem has been that the safer-sexual and drug-related information was only retrieved when the respondents were sober, and had little or no meaning once their cognition was altered by the drugs within another context (Eich, 1977; Eich *et al.*, 1975; Flexser and Tulving, 1978; Smith, 1979). Respondent 2 attributes this gap between knowledge and action to the use or over-use of psychoactive substances within the context of the dance party milieu. He said:

> Combining sex and drugs alters the way you think. If
> you're straight then most people go to great lengths to have
> safe sex.

Many previous studies suggest that the efficacy of information
retrieval from the memory was conditional on the mind-set or
cognitive state of the person during the encoding or learning phase
of this information, albeit intoxicated or sober (Eich, 1977; Overton, 1972; Swanson and Kinsbourne, 1979). Higher retention is
reported by subjects in these studies, who are intoxicated at the time
of encoding information, rather than when sober at the time of
retrieval. Houston (1986) also suggests that the 'situation, or context, in which we learn something is very important when it comes to
remembering ... Similar effects can be obtained with chemical
states' (p. 294). This psychological phenomenon is termed 'state-
and-context-dependent learning' (Eich, 1977; Overton, 1972;
Swanson and Kinsbourne, 1979). Some of these cognitive impairments are illustrated in Figure 2 by a pre-party cartoon 'Living with
Adam' in *The Sydney Star Observer*.

The efficacy of any future safe sexual and drug-educational
programme may depend on several important factors, including the
mental set or receptiveness of the target population, the suitability of
the context in which these messages are encoded or learnt (Jenkins,
1974) and the sensitivity and appropriateness of the cues or symbolic language used to recall this previously encoded information
(see Chapter Seven). According to previous research the process of
the human memory is also dependent on the grammar, form, style,
shape, colour and verbal context in which the information is learnt
(Smith *et al.*, 1978; Stanovich and West, 1983).

These intervention programmes could be introduced to the
population at different stages of their intoxication phase (within the
context of the dance party setting) to evaluate the most efficacious
point for the learning, retention and recall of the safe sexual and
drug-related information. This may be the critical period where they
are more likely to appreciate cognitively the significance of their
possible risky behaviour. One of the most appropriate periods of
intervention may be after the party patrons are intoxicated but

Figure 5.1: reprinted by permission of Jeff Allan

before they have started to engage in sexual activities, either at the dance parties or at the post-party venues.

This study suggests an important area warranting further investigation as a way of reducing the risk of disseminating the AIDS virus among party patrons following their use of recreational drugs. The proposed co-operation by the dance party organizers would be an invaluable asset for the successful implementation and evaluation of such intervention programmes. This is an important considera- tion with the recent dismantling of the large-scale private dance parties at the Hordern Pavilion and the rapid growth of smaller, less accessible underground dance party venues.

The findings also represent a rich source of data, from which a number of hypotheses may be generated for future investigations. Some respondents reported varying degrees of cognitive impairment that may have been due to unknown biochemical effects, poor quality drugs (Newcombe, 1988) or poly-drug use (Solowij *et al.*, 1992). There has been almost no significant research on the pharma- cological and toxicological effects of MDMA (or many other illegal drugs) on human subjects because of its illegal status in Australia and internationally (Beck *et al.*, 1989; Chesher, 1990; Newcombe, 1992). Chesher pointed out that 'there have been little experimental data, both toxicological and therapeutic, for the activity, efficacy or safety of MDMA' (p. 76).

In summary, the findings discussed in this chapter and pre- vious chapters regarding the incongruity between the respondents' knowledge of safer sexual guidelines and their reported risky behav- iour, led to further investigations into the attitudes and belief systems that appear to sustain this risky behaviour. Chapter Six examines the possible impact these attitudes and belief systems have on the respondents' use of, or experimentation with, a 'new' drug, known as Ice (d-methamphetamine hydrochloride) and its possible implications for increased risk of HIV/AIDS infection within the context of the inner-city gay dance parties.

Chapter six

Sex on Ice

DURING the course of this investigation a 'new' drug, 'Ice' (d-Methamphetamine hydrochloride [HDI]), enjoyed brief popularity as a recreational drug among the inner-Sydney gay dance party patrons, according to several sources. These sources included data from a previous study, anecdotal evidence and the popular media (*Rolling Stone* and *The Herald Magazine*). The literature suggested that the use or over-use of Ice had reached 'epidemic' proportion in the USA (particularly in Hawaii and on the West Coast) and Japan, among similar marginalized subpopulations to the inner-city gay dance party patrons. The studies found that its overwhelming popularity was mainly due to its highly valued psychophysiological characteristics; these included increased self-esteem, awareness and control, along with feelings of euphoria, hyperstimulation and transformed reality. The durability of these effects over time (from eight to sixteen hours) added to the drug's appeal.

Some researchers suggested that Ice was the most hyperstimulating of the amphetamine analogues on central nervous system activity (DEA, 1989; Miller and Tomas, 1989). Ice can be administered orally or by injection, snorting, or smoking. Smoking was the most popular route of administration in these studies, because it accelerated the process of assimilation (approximately seven seconds) and reduced the risk of HIV infection via needle sharing.

However, these positive attributes were precursors of increased risky behaviour that included: overuse, 'bingeing', cognitive impairment, disassociative reality, lifestyle problems, impulsiveness, paranoia, loss of control and hyper-sexual stimulation (DEA, 1989; Miller and Tomas, 1989; US Department of Health and Human Services, 1991). These findings alerted the researchers to the potential risk of a similar phenomenon occurring in the dance party subpopulation and the possible increased risk of unprotected anal intercourse following its use. Perhaps its rapid decline in popularity among party patrons was due to its negative reputation in the popular press.

This sample population was primarily chosen because of the members' reported common use of recreational drugs (Lansing, 1992; Solowij, 1992), including Ice (and the centrality and significance of the HIV/AIDS pandemic among the gay subpopulation). The verbatim extracts used in this chapter are derived from the transcripts of the 10 respondents. As previously, they represent their construct of reality or truth relating to the sociopsychological dimensions of the inner-city gay dance party milieu and are not necessarily 'the truth', a difference discussed by Berger and Luckmann (1975).

Sources of Ice

Although most respondents complained about the scarcity of Ice, none appeared to have difficulty in procuring it. Respondents 7 and 4 were inner-city dealers who purchased their supplies of Ice from two different sources. Respondent 7 acquired his product from local manufacturers:

> I know they are making it here ... I happen to know one of the people who is making it.

Respondent 4 claimed Ice was imported:

> It's imported stuff, but from what I heard, I don't think it's difficult to make.

Respondent 7 believed the limited availability of Ice was a deliberate 'market control' policy by the manufacturers:

> The manufacturers are trying to control the amount of Ice, they don't want to produce heaps and heaps of it, and

flood Sydney with it, because they are very professional people. They are the only people making it in the Eastern Suburbs.

Respondent 7 endeavoured to legitimize the manufacturers' status and the illicit drug market by defining their role as 'professionals' (which in turn upgraded his occupational status by association). The majority of respondents used Ice initially because of the limited supply of other drugs, such as Ecstasy. It is possible that manufacturers were intentionally controlling the supply of other recreational drugs to create an artificial demand for this new drug. Respondent 4 confirmed this market phenomenon:

> We basically couldn't get anything else, and this thing came up ... because that was the thing at the time. There was nothing else around, no one was taking anything, no one was buying Ecstasy.

Some of the respondents suggested that the recreational drug market was subject to market trends similar to fashion, music and clothing. For example, some patrons experimented with new drugs because they were bored with the 'old drug', including Ecstasy. Respondent 5 predicted that Ice would become extremely popular because of this phenomenon:

> I think it has enormous potential to be used among the gay community ... a lot of people are getting tired of Ecstasy.

Many of the respondents were concerned about the quality and toxicity of street-purchased drugs which lacked the stringent controls of legally produced pharmaceuticals. These illegal substances, particularly those in powder, capsule or crystal form, were often corrupted by indiscriminate manufacturers and dealers, as previous researchers also found (Chesher, 1990; Newcombe, 1988). Respondent 4 described this procedure:

> It wouldn't be difficult to cut, definitely not. ... They cut it with basic ammonia like when you cut Speed you have to watch what you cut it with.

Most respondents suggested that they used Ice initially because of its availability, novelty and desirable effects, although they were also aware of its possible contamination, due to a number of powerful illegal market dynamics, including profit-driven motives. Inside information, such as where it was manufactured and by whom, appears to be a way of measuring quality control.

Characteristics of the Ice-using subpopulation

According to the respondents' data, Ice attracted a fairly homogeneous population of professional users among the inner-city recreational drug-using subculture. However, Respondent 4 warned of the possible dependency problems among this population:

> The professional people, who use recreational drugs, are more likely to get addicted to such drugs as Ice. . . . It's not just the deviants . . . like me, who are using drugs. But now you've got people who are respectable people . . . who have come into contact with Ecstasy, and Speed, and Ice. . . . It's becoming more socially acceptable.

Respondent 7 provided a contradictory report about the socio-economic background of people who used Ice, for on the one hand:

> It's not a drug for everybody. . . . The reason the professional elite crowd use it in preference to Coke is that the Cocaine here is rubbish.

And on the other hand, it is used by

> . . . bums on the dole, who are around the Cross, to the fashionable people of the Eastern Suburbs. . . . I have a friend who is a doctor, who really got into the dance parties and drugs.

Respondent 1 believed that the price was a major determinant of who used Ice:

> It would even appeal to the low income people as well . . . because of its price, because you don't need very much.

The economic viability of Ice appeared to be a guarantee of its widespread use and continued success among a wide range of users, including the inner-city gay dance party patrons.

Social networks and the use of Ice

Ginzburg *et al.* (1985) suggested that unique social groups were often organized around the use of a particular drug, partly because of the illegal nature of these activities. The respondents' data suggested that some party patrons derived positive reinforcement from their identification with the dance party group and their use of Ice. According to Respondent 6, for example:

> It has helped develop a unique social structure. Most people are prepared to share Ice more than other drugs because it is so cheap. So it has helped social interaction among small groups.

Previous findings also indicated ritualized sharing reinforced group identity and cohesiveness among drug using populations (Buffum, 1988; DEA, 1989; Ginzburg *et al.*, 1985; Newcombe, 1988). Festinger and Carlsmith (1959) showed that the need to conform to peer pressure and belong to a group often determined behaviour, even if this behaviour was incongruent with an individual member's beliefs. Respondent 1 described an example of the powerful group dynamics:

> My flatmate one weekend had it ... and I became very moral ... and then I thought if they think it's okay then alright ... I said can you get me some. Then another friend decided they'd have some and so on, and so on, you know how it is. People will bend to peer-group pressure, as boring as it is ... and then it became a larger group of people who tried it.

Respondent 1's initial and subsequent reaction was similar to patterns of attitudes and behaviour found in a sample of Ice users in the USA (Miller and Tomas, 1989). These drug-using subcultures (including the dance party population) usually developed a unique set of ethical codes or norms and values that determined members' attitudes, behaviour and identity. The group's security, solidarity or cohesiveness was often dependent on the majority of its members' adherence to these prescriptions (Zoja, 1989). The use of Ice and prohibited substances acted as powerful bonding agents among this traditionally 'deviant' group of gay party patrons.

Reasons for use

Several properties emerged from the respondents' data to describe their motives for using Ice and other party drugs and their subsequent risky sexual behaviour. Cho (1990) attributed these behaviours to the idiosyncratic biochemical characteristics of Ice. Most of the respondents used Ice and other recreational drugs intentionally to transform their mood, as Butt (1989) also found. Respondent 1 described the mood-modulating effects of Ice:

> Ice turns your mood around into a better mood. I take it because I want to take the drug and experience the drug ... because I need a lift.

Raymond (1988a, 1988b) suggested that the effects of a particular drug often determined its use in particular social situations. Respondent 7 described the effects after he used Ice:

> Physically I feel very calm, I feel very relaxed, no tension at all.

Some of the respondents used Ice to escape their everyday reality, similar to the use of the drug 'Soma' in Aldous Huxley's *Brave New World* (1986 ed.). Some of the respondents' beliefs were grounded in existential ideologies, as Solowij *et al.* (1992) also found. Respondent 8 described some of these esoteric effects:

> The effects were really profound ... it opened up a new consciousness.

Respondent 6 suggested that some of the ritualized behaviours associated with the use of Ice reinforced its use among party patrons:

> I think one of the big attractions [of] Ice is the ritual practices.

Many of these ritualized practices among the dance party patrons developed in reaction to the HIV/AIDS crisis and lack of a medical cure for this deadly disease, as found among other cultures confronted with similar life-threatening situations (Helman, 1990; Zoja, 1989). This fearful situation was exacerbated by increased homonegative attitudes since the outbreak of the HIV/AIDS pandemic in Western gay subcultures. The high concentration of HIV/AIDS cases among these subcultures helped legitimize homonegativity, according to Davenport-Hines (1990). Raymond (1988a) suggested that a person's belief system also influenced their drug-induced experiences in social and sexual situations. The efficacy of this phenomenon was widely recognized among behavioural scientists and termed the 'placebo effect'. Some of the respondents' data may have been biased by their prior knowledge or expectancy of the effect of Ice, as has been found previously in the USA (DEA, 1989). Information about Ice preceded its arrival among the inner-city gay dance party patrons via popular tabloids and the local media (*Rolling Stone* and *The Herald Magazine*). Respondent 6 described this 'placebo' phenomenon:

> Even though the drug hasn't taken effect, you're instantly in that good mood ... you're almost part of it already ... because you've done it before or because you know what's coming.

Some of the respondents' reactions to Ice were negatively biased by prior knowledge of its effects, as Raymond (1988b) also found among recreational drug users. Respondent 1 described his reaction to a recent media report:

> I read the article in the *Rolling Stone* about all the side-effects, where people who become addicted to it ... started to take it at work ... and I thought: this is really bad.

Perhaps, this negative reporting of Ice influenced the local manufacturers' marketing policy, as described by Respondent 7:

> The manufacturers are keen to have people stop calling it Ice. I mean it's called Methamphetamine ... they just want people to call it good Speed. They're very uptight about it being called Ice.

Respondent 8 was puzzled by the negative attitudes toward Ice, given its positive attributes:

> Not only do you get the best of all three drugs – Cocaine, Speed and Ecstasy – but you get the price of Ice. This will make Ice a very popular drug, if it loses its stigma ... it's so strong, so cheap, and so new. It's interesting it's not cool to use Ice. It's such a fun drug, but everyone goes it's OH! ... SO! ... BAD! for you.

Control

The respondents unanimously agreed that Ice afforded them greater 'control' over their behaviour than other drugs. This concept of control was a powerful motivation for the continued use of Ice, particularly among a group of individuals who have not traditionally been free (either politically or socially) to express in a public setting their gay-oriented lifestyle. Respondent 6 described these beneficial effects:

> You're in more control than when you're on other drugs.
> Ice gives me the confidence I need.

Miller and Tomas (1989) reported similar findings among Ice users in the USA. They suggested that these initial beneficial effects were generally overwhelmed by negative effects after regular use. Most of the respondents self-prescribed other psychoactive substances (poly-drug use) to control these possible undesirable effects, as Solowij *et al.* (1992) also found among a similar sample of recreational drug users. Respondent 4 described his serendipitous discovery of this phenomenon:

> We'd been drinking and we decided to smoke this stuff, and almost instantly the effect of the alcohol isn't there any more. I haven't had that with any drug. If you use it with any other drugs, it seems to increase that.

According to Miller and Tomas (1989), similar poly-drug use was practised by Ice users in the USA to help control the accumulative negative effects of this drug. According to Bradley (1978), individuals who were preoccupied with the concept of control generally emphasized the positive attributes of these social dynamics. Goffman (1974) argued that this need for control was often present among stigmatized groups, such as the inner-city gay dance party patrons. This fear of being out of control was also exacerbated by their possible increased risk of HIV infection and the unwanted attention from the drug-enforcement authorities.

Loss of Control

The controlling effects of Ice were its most desirable attribute, according to the respondents. Paradoxically, they also revealed that they were deeply concerned about their lack of control after frequent use of Ice, as Miller and Tomas (1989) also found. Respondent 3 discontinued using Ice because of this phenomenon:

> The word to describe it was 'volatile' ... it's extremely, extremely potent. ... It just went on and on, and on. ... The amount I used would have been on a fingertip ... I lost control, that is, it took me for a ride and just wouldn't let me go. ... You have no control, and going in top gear the whole time ... I just couldn't believe how strong it was and that just turned me right off it.

Many of the respondents suggested that they had difficulty recalling their behaviour (to varying degrees) whilst intoxicated on Ice. These episodic memory impairments ranged from perceptual distortion to total blackouts for up to eight hours, as described by Respondent 3:

> At the Sleaze Ball I would have said all the time I was in control of what I was doing ... but ... I couldn't actually remember. I thought I was in control ... but I couldn't account for eight hours of what happened. What did I do?

What did Respondent 3 do? His concern and Respondent 4's personal testimony supported previous research findings among similar drug-using samples (Butt, 1989; Mirin *et al.*, 1988; Stall *et al.*, 1986). As Respondent 4 poignantly said:

> One of the biggest risks for contracting AIDS is being out of it on drugs and having sex. That's how I got it.

Respondent 9 shared similar concern about these cognitive impairments and possible risky sexual behaviour following his use of Ice:

> You definitely get blackout periods, like when you're on alcohol, like that period I lost four hours. I thought: shit what have I done? . . . that was my concern because I'm HIV-positive. I think I'd neck myself if I gave it to someone.

Siegel (1986) also found the longer a person remained in an intoxicated state the less likely they were to recall safe-sexual information learnt whilst sober. Respondent 4 described this phenomenon:

> The more you're feeling the effects of the drugs, that's when the dangers are for unsafe sex . . . because you're removed from everyday reality.

There appeared to be an association between the duration of the respondents' intoxication phase on Ice (or other psychoactive substances), impaired recall of their behaviour and increased risky sexual behaviour. Recent research on 'state-dependent' cognition following the subjects' use of consciousness-changing substances provides credibility to this theory (Haaga, 1989; Lowe, 1988).

Disinhibiting Effects

Many of the respondents used Ice and other psychoactive substances intentionally, to disinhibit them in various social and sexual situations, as Solowij *et al.* (1992) also found among a similar population of dance party patrons. Respondent 7 described this psychotherapeutic transformation:

> It makes you feel so open . . . it helped the gay community, and not just the gay community, a lot of my straight friends benefited from it as well.

The drugs helped transform some respondents' inhibiting personality traits, as Respondent 6 described:

> I'm pretty shy and quiet, and I don't have much confidence at all . . . and the drugs have helped me overcome it.

The drugs were often used to help party patrons forget worries such as the homonegative reality of their everyday lives and HIV/AIDS-related issues. Ironically, this 'amnesic' effect also reduced or removed the significance of the dangers of unprotected anal intercourse, as Stall *et al.* (1986) also warned. Respondent 9 described this transformational process:

> You could do things and not worry about it, I suppose you could be irresponsible.

Such a statement is concerning, given his HIV-positive status, his previous disclosure of cognitive impairment and the reported association between use of drugs and the high incidence of risky sexual activity (Butt, 1989; Stall *et al.*, 1986). Most respondents believed they were less socially and sexually inhibited following the use of recreational drugs at the dance parties. Respondent 10 described this shift in social realities:

> You're not so aware of social morality ... you tend to ignore the things you wouldn't normally ignore, and the guards you would normally put up. You're less inhibited.

Some of the respondents continued to use Ice and other psychoactive substances because of their disinhibiting characteristics, even though they were seriously concerned about their impaired judgement, loss of control and the possible deadly consequence. Perhaps, these incongruities reflected the dire need for some patrons to escape the stark reality of their everyday lives, including the HIV/AIDS crisis. Paradoxically, these highly valued attributes also contributed to many of the respondents' discontinued use of Ice.

Ecstasy versus Ice

Ecstasy (MDMA), by contrast to Ice, did not share the same degree of 'bad' publicity prior to its arrival. It was considered by many experts as the ideal drug for systemic therapy (particularly couples) because it facilitated empathy, insight, and open and honest rapport (Beck *et al.*, 1989; Chesher, 1990; Solowij *et al.*, 1992; Stevens, 1988). Respondent 5 compared the two drugs in terms of their emotive-effects:

Ice is not a highly emotional sort of thing, you don't feel any of that emotional stuff you feel on Ecstasy.

It also provided them with a more intense, sustained and economical drug-induced experience than Ecstasy, as Respondent 8 described:

Ice offers people the best characteristics of Ecstasy, Cocaine and Speed, combined with the price. Ice will definitely end up being a very popular drug.

Respondent 6 suggested that Ice was a more appropriate drug than Ecstasy for the dance party scene because of its hyperstimulating effects.

You're in control when you're on Ice, whereas on Ecstasy sometimes you can't communicate, or all you want to do is dance, or your eyes are rolling and you're sometimes out of control.

It also induced a more sophisticated consciousnesss for seasoned drug-using patrons, according to the respondents. As Respondent 6 described:

We used to be all terribly big Ecstasy users, but it shifted to Ice ... a younger group are experimenting with it now, drugs do the rounds.

Many of the respondents considered Ice the ideal successor to Ecstasy because of its powerful and enduring effects, as previous research also found among similar Ice-using samples (DEA, 1989; Miller and Tomas, 1989). One of the main advantages of using Ice, according to the respondents, was its versatility in various lifestyle settings.

Ice used in a variety of venues and social situations

Ice was a multi-purpose drug that could be used in a range of social, occupational and sexual situations, according to the respondents. Respondent 6 described the versatility of Ice:

> I used it with friends socially, at nightclubs, or during the day, or at a party.

However, Stall *et al.* (1986) cautioned drug users of the increased risk of unsafe sexual behaviour, particularly within a 'drug-empathic context', such as the dance party milieu. Most of the respondents' data suggested that Ice increased their energy, self-esteem, competence and productivity in a wide range of occupational and recreational activities. Respondent 5 described some of these benefits:

> You get confidence and feel really great ... you can go to work on it with a really clear head, and you just get so much done, it's extraordinary.

According to the data these beliefs became conditioned over time and were incorporated into the dance party patrons' norms and values, similar to research findings among other recreational drug-using samples (Beck *et al.*, 1989; Cho, 1990; Solowij *et al.*, 1992). Respondent 6 was impressed with the mood-modulating effects of Ice:

> It always puts me in an instantly good mood and Ice gives me the confidence I need.

Respondent 9 suggested that these chameleon characteristics were also transformed by external stimuli:

> The environment would have a lot to do with it, that is, if you're in a party environment well you'll party, and if you're in a work environment then you'll work really well ... it's an adaptable drug.

The sanctioned use of drugs at the dance parties permitted many novice patrons to experiment with these consciousness-changing substances. According to Respondent 7:

> A lot of professional people got into drugs through the dance parties.

Respondent 3's initial reaction to Ice supported this suggestion:

> I had a fantastic time. It was a great party ... and the
> whole thing carried on into the next day ... and it was like
> wow! I'd tried this fantastic new drug.

Some of the respondents used Ice to escape their everyday reality,
similar to the use of the drug 'soma' in Huxley's *Brave New World*.
Respondent 9 described this phenomenon:

> I came back from holidays where I had ... the largest
> amount of drugs I've ever had ... and I blasted [injected] it
> ... I don't know why I did it.

Potential for dependence

However, Respondent 4 suggested that many of the drug's
highly prized attributes may reinforce the users' dependence on Ice.
He said:

> The danger is that these people can work and hold down a
> responsible job on Ice, unlike Ecstasy or other recreational
> drugs.

The majority of respondents also reported an overwhelming
need to have sex every time they used Ice. Respondent 8 described
this compulsive-obsessive phenomenon:

> Unlike Ecstasy every time you use Ice you have to wank,
> you have to fuck ... every time you use it, even just a tiny
> bit.

One of the major and most concerning differences between Ice and
Ecstasy, reported by respondents in regards to increased risks of
HIV infection, was the degree of hypersexuality they experienced at
the same time as impaired judgement. On the one hand they suggested that Ice increased their ability to focus on a task and be in
control, and yet on the other they often reported that they were
sexually out of control when they used the drug. The perceived
'advantages' often increased some people's dependence on Ice, as the
DEA report (1989) also found in the USA. Respondent 1 was
concerned about this risk of dependency:

I think it's addictive because you can use it in a normal situation ... then I started to see people I knew using it all the time, and it was pretty ugly ... one person in particular who is a dealer.

The term 'addiction', as used by most respondents, did not necessarily relate to a medical concept, but to the overwhelming need to consume all available Ice in one episode. This phenomenon is termed 'episodic dependence' within the context of this work. Respondent 9 described this phenomenon:

> They get confused, between Crack and Ice. I think people conceive it as Crack, because it is really moreish like Crack ... I honestly think it would be on the same level.

Most of the respondents were concerned about this 'episodic dependence', as described by Respondent 3:

> I see how addictive it could become, because it can be very moreish ... to maintain that high it would be very easy just to turn around and say I'll have some more.

Drug authorities in the USA warned Ice users of its 'addictive' qualities, although this term may constitute a culturally-predisposed US stance (Peele, 1987). Respondent 10 supported this interpretation:

> I think when you're on it, it's addictive in a sense ... you continue to take as much as you've got.

Respondent 9 adamantly reinforced the concept of 'episodic dependency':

> OH! YES! YES! YES! ... you could become addicted if you could get your hands on it all the time ... because it just feels so fabulous.

Ratner (1988) also found that some people became so focused on the use of drugs that they neglected other issues in their lives. Respondent 4 described this intrusive phenomenon:

> You think about the drug a lot ... it dominates your thoughts.

As mentioned, similar patterns of compulsive ideations were also reported among Ice-using populations in the USA (DEA, 1989; Miller and Tomas, 1989). Most of the respondents also suggested that the frequent use of Ice manifested a compulsive pattern of behaviour, as described by Respondent 4:

> If someone put the stuff in front of me now there would be no hesitation to using the stuff. There's the psychological dependence first, and then the physical dependence comes after you've used the stuff for a while.

Most of the respondents used other drugs to control the undesirable effects of Ice. This pharmacological control was often used at the conclusion of the dance party evening to counteract or manipulate their intoxicated condition. Respondent 1 described this procedure:

> I just take something to put you to sleep and you wake up the next day and you're feeling fine.

Respondent 2 justified this behaviour in terms of a gay tradition:

> You knock it on the head with a couple of schooners of beer. That seems to be the local gay practice.

Some of the respondents were aware of the self-delusory nature of this 'sober state', as Respondent 4 described:

> When you've wanted to bring yourself down you've taken Hammer [Heroin] and stuff, and so you're bent.

The respondents were unanimously concerned about their possible over-use or 'episodic dependency' on Ice and their increased risky sexual behaviour. However, they suggested that its limited supply created an inbuilt control mechanism.

Potential for increased risky sexual behaviour

The respondents' data support the hypothesis of Stall *et al.* (1986) that many people used drugs to enhance their sexual performance (as an aphrodisiac), to liberate them from inhibiting personality traits and to disinhibit them sexually. Respondent 4, for example, described the disinhibiting effects of recreational drugs within the context of the sexual venues (the toilets or 'bogs') at the dance parties:

> Many gay men went along 'specially to do the bogs . . .
> there was no inhibitions and everybody dropped their
> reserves.

Stall *et al.* (1986) also suggested 'that the association between risky sexual behaviour and drug . . . use . . . are artifacts deriving from underlying personality needs, which demand the concurrent use of intoxicating substances' (p. 368). Respondent 7 supported these findings:

> I'm really shy and I don't come across the way I want to,
> especially if I'm in a pick-up situation or anything like that.
> I simply go to pieces if I'm not on anything.

The sanctioned use of psychoactive substances and sexual activity contributed to some party patrons' increased risky sexual behaviour, according to Respondent 4:

> If you've smoked enough Ice . . . and you're feeling the
> effects that's where the dangers are for unsafe sex. Because
> you are removed from your everyday reality.

Most respondents praised the powerful aphrodisiac effects of Ice, including hypersexual stamina, enduring penile erection and multiple orgasms, as described by Respondent 1:

> You can sustain an erection. Everything takes a quantum
> leap . . . you can fuck for hours and that makes you want to
> use it more.

Chaisson *et al.* (1987) found a strong association between hypersexuality (repetitive, prolonged sexual behaviour whilst using psychoactive substances) and increased risk of HIV infection. Respondent 8 applauded Ice's enduring aphrodisiacal qualities:

> It's a beautiful drug for sex . . . I was really, really horny . . .
> I managed to do it three times and I would have liked to do
> it another thirty. I ejaculated six times . . . in about six

hours. It's a true aphrodisiac. There is no way I could naturally do that.

These hypersexual characteristics often potentiated many of the respondents' risky sexual behaviours, according to the sobering description of Respondent 8:

If you had a lot of it you'd be an insatiable, sex-crazy, manic beast that dribbled and fucked anything, which is a real worry . . . safe-sex wise, because you have to have sex.

Mirin *et al.* (1988) argued that many people abdicated responsibility for, or control over, their risky sexual behaviour by blaming the drugs. Respondent 4 suggested that the dance party context reinforced sexual behaviour among party patrons:

It's the ethos. I've paralleled the parties to the saunas, real meat markets, that is 'I like you let's fuck'.

Respondent 9 described a risky sexual scenario following the use of Ice:

If you were using Ice with other drugs . . . and you had a crowd of fifteen homosexual men I'd wonder how many would actually use a condom, or even think about it . . . because of the sense of urgency. They wouldn't even think about using a condom and I think it would interfere with your judgement to the point of, just fuck me.

Some of the respondents' data indicated that they were dissatisfied with the quality of these sexual encounters, although they were driven to act on this need for sexual gratification. Chaisson *et al.* (1987) also found similar 'compulsive-obsessive' sexual reactions following the use of psychoactive substances in their drug-using subpopulation. Respondent 1's description of this phenomenon was almost a text-book account of obsessive-compulsive behaviour, as defined in the *Diagnostic and Statistical Manual of Mental Disorders* (American Psychiatric Association).

The reason you keep having more sex is you are looking for something . . . It gives you a false impression of satisfaction through an orgasm ... although you are having an orgasm it's an illusion in a way.

Respondent 9 also complained about these apparent obsessive-compulsive characteristics when using Ice:

> You do have a sense of urgency ... you're not satisfied sexually after you have sex ... I don't find sex on amphetamines all that overly satisfying at the time.

Respondent 4 was concerned about the association between the availability of Ice and possible increased risk of HIV infection:

> If you could get [Ice] more easily and frequently, that would be much more worrying in relationship to unsafe sex and AIDS.

Most of the respondents were concerned about this compulsive-obsessive need for sexual gratification whilst intoxicated on Ice. Respondent 9 also described how this need overwhelmed or excluded the concept of safer-sexual guidelines and survival:

> You don't think to use a condom, because you have feelings of urgency ... like you've got to do it NOW!

Respondent 4's testimony supported previous findings in regard to increased risk of HIV infection following the use of psychoactive substances:

> I got into a drug spiral, and I got really bad ... and it was like drugs and sex go together. That's what I was in it for, and I'd lost a lot of the reasoning in that period of time. Especially if you've got one partner instigating unsafe sex, and the other partner is a lot more likely to go along with it. ... Basically that's how I caught AIDS in the first place ... I hadn't played it unsafe until then.

Respondent 9 also graphically described a possibly deadly sexual scenario:

> Well if you have got a hard on and you are out of it, and someone is there willing to fuck you'd just do it, you'd do it ... and that was my concern because I'm HIV-positive.

Respondent 4 described the instant aphrodisiac effects of Ice:

> We blasted the stuff and we were practically fucking each
> other before you even think about it. . . . If you're out to it
> at that stage where he's practically in you anyway you're
> not going to worry at that point in time. You're pushing
> risks aside and you're saying I'll worry about that later . . .
> You're really living for that moment.

Some of the HIV-seropositive respondents consciously used Ice and
other party drugs as a statement of control over the virus that was
threatening to terminate their lives prematurely. Paradoxically, the
urgent need for sexual gratification often overwhelmed the significance of, or control over, safer-sexual behaviour, as described by
Respondent 4:

> To get a condom would be a hassle, and even if it's only a
> matter of going outside and asking for another condom,
> some people still wouldn't do it . . . . because that's still two
> minutes out of your life . . . that you could've got another
> fuck. Are you going to stop and slip a condom on?

However, he appeared to be concerned about the consequences of
his risky sexual behaviours:

> From my own experience now that I'm HIV . . . if I fuck
> someone unsafe now I can give him this deadly disease. I
> sort of suffer a guilt complex when I don't comply.

His next question and statement appeared to be a form of self-
justification for his behaviours:

> The question is after we are ten years down the track with
> the AIDS virus among the gay community . . . are gay men
> becoming blasé about it? I've gone to the sauna a number
> of times and the number of men that are quite prepared to
> have unsafe sex . . . and they're not immensely worried.

The statements of Respondent 4 were not unique; some of the other
respondents also shared these risk-laden behaviours, following their
use of Ice and other psychoactive substances within the dance party
context. These findings warranted further investigation because of

their serious ramifications within the reality of the HIV/AIDS pandemic and the inner-city dance party milieu.

It was difficult to determine through these interviews and limited cross-sectional data, if the underlying determinant of this risky sexual behaviour was the drug or the respondents' inherent personality traits which were potentiated by the drug. However, these respondents did not describe such extreme behaviour when using Ecstasy. Or it may have been in some instances, a multifactorial phenomenon, as Stall *et al.* (1986) suggested, whereby 'the relationship between drug and alcohol use during high-risk sex [was the] result of a complex web of determinants' (p. 369).

Conclusion

The concept of *control* was the most saturated core category to emerge from the respondents' data and the major incentive for continuing to use Ice. It enabled them to increase their confidence, self-esteem, concentration or focus, awareness, sensory modalities, disinhibitions, sexual prowess, duration of penile erection, number of orgasms and paradoxically their risk of HIV infection. These findings are similar to previous research findings among similar gay drug-using samples (Miller and Tomas, 1989; Quadland and Shattls, 1987; Stall *et al.*, 1986).

Helman (1990) notes that individuals who are at risk of contracting or transmitting a life-threatening disease often demonstrate an overwhelming preoccupation with self-control. In addition, Goffman (1963) argues that stigmatized individuals often over-emphasize the need for self-control because being out of control may attract unwanted attention that increases and justifies their alienated or marginalized status. Previous researchers reported a similar phenomenon whereby 'AIDS was equated with homosexual behaviour and was used to justify antigay discrimination and hostility' (Herek and Glunt, 1988, p. 888). Ironically, these increased homonegative reactions also force some gay men to seek asylum within the context of their own social institutions (such as the dance parties) and to use psychoactive substances which may increase their risk of HIV infection (Stall *et al.*, 1986).

The data indicate that gay men derive positive reinforcement or affirmation of their identity within a predominantly gay recreational drug-using milieu. However, the threat of HIV infection may involve an area central to a gay person's identity and possibly inhibit their spontaneous sexual expression. They may be no longer able to exercise control over their sexual expression without extreme caution, as losing control may result in risky sexual behaviour, as Quadland and Shattls (1987) also found in their drug-using subpopulation. However, Ice seems to let them do this and not remember it.

Paradoxically, the use of Ice as a form of control often results in the person being out of control, whereby the same mechanism that permits them to control their social and sexual lives may also impair their cognition or judgement, including access to safer-sexual guidelines which were previously encoded whilst sober. This suggestion assumes greater significance when considered in the light of Respondent 4's testimony, in which he says:

> One of the biggest risks for contracting AIDS is being out of it on drugs and having sex ... that's how I got it.

Most of the respondents' data suggest an overwhelming need for sexual gratification with little or no regard for safe sexual practices following their use of Ice. This phenomenon is summarized by Respondent 8:

> Every time you use Ice you have ... to fuck.

Ice appears to act as a kind of psychological 'Philosopher's Stone', in which the social and individual's awareness is transmuted into believing they are disinhibited and free. Like the Philosopher's stone, it may also provide a sense of immortality in terms of forgetting about the HIV/AIDS pandemic and, unfortunately, the personal risk of infection or transmission.

However, this loss of control over cognition and sexual behaviour, and the consequent increased risk of HIV infection, appears to account for Ice's rapid disappearance from the gay dance party patrons' list of recreational drugs. The data suggest that Ecstasy has once again established its supremacy over Ice because of its more easily controllable and manageable effects on conscious-ness. This self-monitoring of drug use indicates the importance of this concept of control for many of the party patrons. Any inter-vention measure should take into consideration the reinstatement of a person's sense of control, irrespective of whether they are sober or intoxicated, by educating them to remain 'aware, awake' and 'focused' on the inherent dangers of practising unsafe sex, in both states of cognition. According to previous research the target pop-ulation needs to be educated in both state-dependent conditions so that they may recall previously encoded safe sexual information (Eich, 1977; Overton, 1972). They found no significant difference between these two treatment conditions or groups' ability to recall information as long as they were in the same state-dependent condition as when it was encoded. Some dance party patrons may perform unsafe sexual behaviour whilst intoxicated because they are unable to recall the dangers they were familiar with when sober. Previous intervention techniques appear not to have taken this well-documented phenomenon into consideration when targeting a population who use psychoactive substances. To accommodate this phenomenon intervention models should endeavour to reach and educate the target population in both the sober and intoxicated states.

The findings in this chapter and several previous chapters indicate the need for further investigation into the possible sig-nificance of ritualized behaviour, including the use of consciousness-changing drugs within the context of dance parties and the HIV/AIDS pandemic. The emerging data from this qual-itative pilot study is extensively examined and discussed in Chapter Seven in light of possible dance party rituals, ideologies, attitudes and belief systems that may reinforce increased risky sexual behav-iour at the dance parties.

Chapter seven

The Evolution of Ritualized Behaviour and Belief Systems among Gay Dance Party Patrons and their Relationship to Risky Sexual Behaviour

Only in dancing do I know how to utter the parable of the highest things.

Friedrich Nietzsche: 'The grave song' (1896)

They dance, that keeps them busy ... and then the dance mimes secretly, often without their knowing, the refusal they cannot utter [to death].

Jean-Paul Sartre: *Les Damdes de la Terre* (1961)

RITUALIZED behaviour, according to Zoja (1989), including dance and the use of psychoactive substances, often emerges among a subculture in crisis, such as in the inner-Sydney gay community in the HIV/AIDS crisis. According to previous research this behaviour has occurred throughout history and across cultures among groups of people who faced similar life-threatening situations (Eliade, 1974b; Evans, 1988; Mackay, 1991; Tuchman, 1978; Zoja, 1989).

Daniel Defoe, who wrote *A Journal of the Plague Year* (1722) during the time of plague, described the widespread prophylactic use of drugs among the plague-swept population of Europe (from the twelfth century on). He commented that many people 'keep their spirits high and hot with cordials and wine and such things, even physicians used them [as an] anti-pestilential pill' (p. 75). Nohl (1971) noted that large numbers of people during this same period also performed dance rituals (such as 'choreomania' and the Dance of Death) as an antidote or prophylactic for unremitting plagues. Choreomania or dance mania, according to Nohl, 'swept the earth [during the times of plague] ... people began to dance and rush about ... and while dancing fell to the ground ... By this they believed that they could cure themselves of illness' (p. 145). Other people coped with the threat of death by maximizing each moment of their lives. This phenomenon known as 'carpe diem' or 'seize the day' (Koenigsberger, 1991), was immortalized in seventeenth-century literature by poets such as John Donne and Andrew Marvell, who wrote during one of the great plagues (Zoja, 1989). A similar phenomenon may also be occurring among the inner-city gay subculture where some people may wish to live for the present without consideration for the consequences.

Albert Camus (1947) also notes that some people (during the time of plague), engaged in abandoned behaviour in an effort to cope with the overwhelming realities of their imminent death. He said 'once these people realized their instant peril, they gave their thoughts to pleasure. And all the hideous fears which stamp their faces in the daytime are transformed in the fiery, dusty nightfall into a sort of hectic exaltation, an unkempt freedom fevering their blood' (p. 102). According to Nohl (1971): 'they engaged without shame in their dances, both sexes as if possessed, in churches and in houses. ... Psychologically all these *danses macabres*, dances of death ... as well as choreomania ... represent a more or less violent reaction of the enormous mass of sentiments which had accumulated in the deeply impressed minds of individuals during the time of the Black Plague' (p. 149). These dances and others represented a sociopsychological reaction and resolution to a collective anxiety among a group of people at high risk of a deadly disease (Tuchman, 1978), in many ways a similar situation to that of the inner-city dance party patrons.

One of the major contributory factors to the evolution of rites and the social institutions during times of plagues, Nohl suggests, was the communities' loss of confidence in the establishments' (medical, church and state) powers to control or cure these deadly diseases. Similarly, many gay men may also share a sense of frustration and disillusionment with the current medico-scientific establishment's inability to provide a satisfactory prophylactic or cure for HIV, as argued by Evans (1988).

The dance party institution subsequently developed into an important multi-dimensional social institution for many inner-city gay men (Wotherspoon, 1991). This social institution appears to be continuously evolving in accordance with dynamic and complex local and international influences (political, economic and cultural).

According to Hanna (1987), dance has traditionally provided individuals and communities in crisis with an adaptive (and often instant) psychological coping mechanism. The dance parties may help attenuate some patrons' stress from living in an often alienating, homonegative environment (Evans, 1988: Wotherspoon, 1991) which is compounded by HIV/AIDS-related issues (Reanney, 1991). Hanna also notes that dance often provides marginal subgroups with stability, identity reinforcement and a forum for integration. They are able to perform 'traditional' dances and experience a sense of belonging. According to Graves and Graves (1974), these social institutions afford marginalized groups with an 'isolating mechanism' or reduced social boundaries where they can escape the hostilities and ambiguities in the wider culture. A similar phenomenon appears to have contributed to the evolution of the inner-city gay dance party institution.

Hirabayaski *et al.* (1972) suggest that many urban North American Indians revitalized tribal rituals to help them cope with the often alienating environment of urban lifestyles. Since the early

1950s mass-cult movements have developed among these tribes in response to their growing social and political demands for the reinstatement of traditional American Indian rituals, such as the 'new initiatory' ritual of the Peyote cult (Eliade, 1977). Zoja (1989) reports that many of these 'millenarian' (see below) movements sanctioned the ritualized use of consciousness-altering drugs, such as Mescaline (crystalline alkaloid -3,4,5, Trimethyphenylethyl-amine) contained in the Peyote cactus shoots. Cohn (1970) describes millenarianism as a salvation belief system in which the initiate or the group avoid extermination (or assimilation) through the redemptive powers of a supernatural force (such as the Christian interpretation of the resurrection of the righteous following the second visitation of Christ). The Sioux Indians performed the Ghost Dance ritual in 1890, to summon the divine intervention of a Messiah who had similar redemptive powers to Christ, as an adaptive response to the impending destruction of their culture. The recognition of cultural genocide 'grew among the despairing Indians, [and] a great religious revival appeared among them' (p. 242), according to Wellman (1958). They attempted to re-empower themselves through the restoration of traditional dance rituals and the reinforcement of their subcultural identities, according to Mooney (1965). There appears to be a parallel phenomenon occurring within the context of the inner-city gay dance parties, where some patrons may be endeavouring to re-establish structure in their lives following the chaos wrought by the HIV/AIDS pandemic and their on-going battle for social legitimation. Both HIV/AIDS and the homonegative attitudes the pandemic has released threaten the gay subculture at several levels.

Howard (1976) argues that group dancing is an important self-identifying symbol that communicates group membership (to self and others). Many of the patrons may derive affirmation of their gay identity within the context of the dance parties, which in turn may reinforce their self-esteem (Hanna, 1988). Mitchell (1956) suggests that social institutions similar to the dance parties act as social filters for a marginal population who are daily immersed in a potentially confusing heterogeneous population. The increased homogeneity of the dance party population may help to reduce ambiguities for some gay men who are seeking sexual partners within this context. This phenomenon, whereby members of a subculture attempt to establish a positive self-image through social interaction with individuals who share similar lifestyles and belief systems, is known as 'defensive structuring' (Siegel, 1970). As a social process it may help nullify the negative effects of the dominant culture's denigration of their gay identity and provide an adaptive social apparatus for coping with personal and group issues related to HIV/AIDS.

It has been suggested that our scientific, technologically oriented culture is impoverished when it comes to providing social coping mechanisms for people in crisis, particularly crises which involve death and sex (Davenport-Hines, 1990; Douglas, 1991; Evans, 1988; Reanney, 1991). Homosexuality and death shared something in common prior to the current HIV pandemic: they were two of the major categories in a taxonomy of social taboos in many western cultures (Helman, 1990). According to Zoja (1989), 'death has been perceived as the great repressed theme of our century, comparable to the sex taboo of the last century' (p. 58). These repressive sexual prohibitions were only recently partly redressed for gay men in New South Wales in 1984, with the decriminalization of homosexuality (Wotherspoon, 1991). Similarly, death is rarely discussed or observed in most contemporary western societies; for someone of an advanced age, death is generally expected to take place in a medically supervised institution (Helman, 1990). There is a deficiency of appropriate institutions, traditions or rituals within contemporary culture to help the people cope with premature death (Kübler-Ross, 1975), let alone the number of losses to date and the projected mortality rates from HIV/AIDS (Reanney, 1991).

These deficiencies were particularly poignant for many gay men at the onset of the HIV/AIDS crisis because there were even fewer social institutions or traditional customs available to them. Three main factors contributed to this lack of social support systems or institutions for the inner-city gay community at this time. Firstly, gay men had not had sufficient time to establish appropriate social institutions since their legal 'coming out' or enfranchisement. Secondly, there was a lot of confusion about the scale and diversity of HIV-related issues among their community, and thirdly, many of the traditional religious groups were unsympathetic toward gay men's lifestyles (Evans, 1988; Reanney, 1991). An inner-Sydney Uniting Church minister, Fred Nile (of the radical right Festival of Light), epitomized these attitudes with his unrelenting homonegative propaganda, which has escalated since the onset of the HIV/AIDS crisis and since the social and political profile of the gay subculture has increased.

The large-scale dance parties were one of the only institutions where gay men could derive reliable information about the size and diversity of their community. This was particularly pertinent in the early days of the HIV/AIDS epidemic with the paucity of reliable scientific information (demographic, biographic, statistical, ethnographic or medical) about their population. Vital information about reported cases of HIV, risk factors, possible prophylactics or cures and life-expectancy following positive diagnosis, was almost nonexistent. This already fearful situation, according to Davenport-Hines (1990), was fuelled by the mass media's sensationalizing of local and overseas HIV/AIDS-related issues. It also contributed to an increase in homonegative reactions from the wider culture toward gay men.

Although the gay community responded immediately to the HIV/AIDS crisis by mobilizing personnel and emergency organizations, they were probably not catering for all the needs of the gay subculture. Moreover, some gay men, for a variety of reasons, may not have utilized these resources to help them cope with their reactions to, and experiences of, the HIV pandemic. These social deficits may also have contributed to the emergence, evolution and reported proliferation of the inner-city gay dance parties (Safe and Sager, 1990).

One of the aims of this descriptive and qualitative research was to investigate the possibility of ritualized responses to the HIV/ AIDS pandemic among the inner-city gay dance party patrons, and to examine other factors that illustrated the development of this social institution.

In this pilot study, the quotes that follow are verbatim extracts from the transcripts of thirty-two respondents and three organizers. They are expressions of the respondents' individual social constructions (perceptions) of the inner-city gay dance party reality, as noted in previous chapters. Some of the findings in this chapter are similar to data reported in previous chapters. They were included intentionally to illustrate and support the consistency of these attitudes and belief systems across the six investigations and their reported relationship to increased risky sexual behaviour among the sixty respondents and the three organizers (in all).

The significance of the dance party institution to gay subculture

The proliferation of gay dance parties may also reflect the changing social and psychological needs of this subculture in crisis with the constant threat of HIV infection. Respondent 14 confirmed the therapeutic benefits derived from attending the dance parties:

> I take enough recreational drugs to enhance my escape from reality. . . . There are things within reality which do depress me . . . concern about AIDS and my friends who are HIV-positive is bringing me down. . . . The dance parties lift you out . . . and take you away from those worries . . . it's just the music and the people.

Many people in crisis, according to Fanon (1977), develop life-reinforcing celebrations often involving the use of consciousness-transforming media such as music, dance and intoxicants. The party scene also evolved out of a need for some people to celebrate and participate in institutionalized social celebrations, rituals and festivals, according to Organizer 1:

> [There was] an underlying need for these parties, especially the big ones . . . in our society to celebrate. . . . It certainly has a ritual base to it.

Helman (1990) suggested that 'rituals are a feature of all human societies, large and small. They are an important part of the way that any social group celebrates, maintains and renews the world in which they live and the way they deal with dangers that threaten that world' (p. 192). Such important social stabilizing mechanisms (as well as their symbolic significance) have all but disappeared from contemporary western culture, Reanney (1991) argues. According to Organizer 2 the parties were designed to redress such deficiencies with their re-introduction of ancient Greek rituals:

> [We] decided to restart the Bacchanalia rituals ... Over two thousand years later the Bacchanalia has been revived and revamped ... utilizing sophisticated modern music and space-age lighting and special effects.

The Dionysian tradition appeared to be an appropriate belief system for the promotion and legitimization of many inner-city party patrons' recreational activities. As Organizer 3 suggested:

> They are important rituals of our times [and are] dances to Dionysus ... Bacchus the god of ecstasy ... divine intoxication, sensuality, dancing and theatre.

Respondent 24 was a Dionysian enthusiast who challenged the efficacy of the organizers' replication of the Bacchanalian rites:

> The party ... organized by the Bacchanalia ... was [a] perfect opportunity for the Dionysian rite ... But I wondered how many people there had even heard of Bacchanalia let alone know what it meant ... I wish we could get enough people together to actually do a proper one ... really go for it ... orgiastic, a real go.

According to Loudon (1966), the evolution of social institutions reflected the social conditions of the individuals or group participating in the rituals. Respondent 25 described the lifestyle-reinforcing ideology behind the rituals performed within the context of the dance parties:

> The parties are celebrations of life. ... It's a community and the dance part[ies] originated out of gay scenes ... a group of people who are constantly oppressed through no fault of their own ... and they are rejected constantly. The dance party brings all these people together ... and not have any restrictions upon them.

The dance party institution also provided many gay men with a social safety valve where they could ventilate their accumulated anxiety and aggression from living in a society that had traditionally devalued their lifestyle (Herek, 1984). Respondent 28 described this adaptive psychological function:

> It allows you to express yourself and allows you to release any built up aggression.

According to Respondent 20, some party patrons coped with these unrelenting homonegative stresses and HIV/AIDS-issues by self-prescribing high doses of consciousness-altering psychoactive substances:

> I have close friends who have taken unbelievable quantities of drugs at these parties ... partly because of their fear of AIDS ... [but] mainly it's the fear of living as a gay person and having to deal with the anger ... constantly hurled at gay people. ... There's a whole kind of 'dis-ease' about it.

According to Helman (1990), stress-related diseases are a by-product of a person's inability to resolve life-crises, such as chronic illness or bereavement. Further, he suggested that 'stress can also be viewed as a causal factor in disease or a contributory one – by reducing the individual's "resistance" to disease processes, such as viral infections' (p. 251). It is possible that some party patrons may have contributed to the progression of HIV/AIDS-related disorders through accumulated stress from living in a predominantly homo-negative environment and experiencing the concrete reality of HIV adversities in their community (Siegel, 1986).

The taxonomy of dance party rituals

The respondents' and the organizers' data indicated that there was a diverse range of rituals performed by the gay dance party patrons. Helman (1990) suggested that rituals occurred in a variety of sacred and secular settings and performed many different func-tions. Anthropologists have categorized these public rituals into three typologies: (1) calendrical rituals celebrating changes in the cosmic cycle, (2) rituals of social transition ('rites of passage') that are related to individual life-issues, and (3) rituals of misfortune which are usually performed during times of unexpected crisis (Helman, 1990). The last two overlapping classes of rituals were reflected in the data and will be analyzed in this section.

Many rituals of social transition and misfortune have developed among the inner-city gay dance party community in response to both growing concern about HIV-related issues and increased homonegativity expressed by the wider culture since the crisis (Davenport-Hines, 1990), according to most of the respondents and organizers.

Rites of social transformation

Since the early 1980s most inner-city gay men were becoming acutely aware of the unprecedented crisis (related to their sexuality and survival) and the social transformation of their subculture with the growing numbers of AIDS cases (the cause not identified until the discovery of HIV in 1983).

In a subculture as complex and diverse as the inner-city gay community there were few institutional characteristics that individual members had in common other than their self-identified sexual orientation and bars/discos, prior to the arrival of HIV/AIDS and the legal legitimation of homosexuality. The large-scale dance party milieu transformed many gay men's recreational lifestyles so that they could 'come out' and socialize with a wider range of gay men. Respondent 10 described the role the dance parties played in this social transformation or rite of passage:

> From hiding away in little bars to a community in Sydney who is leading the society towards sexual liberation . . . and the dance [parties] helped bring people out, letting them express pure spontaneity.

These social institutions also provided a higher public profile for the introduction of social and sexual reforms for the gay subculture. Respondent 2 suggested that size was one of the main advantages the dance parties had over previous gay social venues.

It can be argued that the dance party institution has provided many gay men with an adaptive social and psychological coping mechanism. This social institution may have also been a subcultural gateway or entrance for some men to cross the social boundaries which in turn reinforced or initiated their gay identity. In Leach's (1976) view most ritual occasions in any society are concerned with this social transformation, enabling individuals to cross social boundaries from one social status to another.

Rites of initiation

According to Zoja (1989), initiation rites are based on the fundamental themes of life and death and usually involve the use of consciousness-transforming media, such as dance, sex, drugs, music and external stimuli.

The dance party institution provided many patrons with a context where they could experience a reality transformation which removed them from the everyday experience of death among their community. Respondent 3 described the metamorphic effects of the dance:

> When they dance ... it's exquisite to see someone move out of their created image ... to just be spontaneous to the music ... they're another personality, they become very sexual.

According to Perls (1969), such a personality transformation or gestalt can facilitate an integration of the person's fragmented life-experiences through the process of self-actualization. Dance was often used metaphorically to signify an initiate's changed status and integration of his identity (Hanna, 1987). Respondent 3 suggested that the dance parties were accurate symbolic representations of his identity transformation and integration:

> I lived two different lifestyles ... one straight, one gay. It moved towards being predominantly gay and those parties have been an expression of that ... it's been a real freedom thing ... it's amazing, it was a revelation.

Respondent 17 described the social transformational role of the dance parties whereby many gay men were initiated into the gay community:

> The parties emerged out of the gay community ... when they started out they were smaller ... it was gay people

wanting to have something bigger and better and get more people to come out.

Rites of passage among many cultures traditionally involve the legitimation of a person's adult identity, which in turn often means that they have access to a sexual partner and the use of psychotropic substances (Frazer, 1976; Hamilton, 1969; Malinowski, 1927; Nilsson, 1957). These transformation rituals celebrate the person's changed status and perception from the fantasy world of the child to the 'real' world of the adult (Eliade, 1957). Respondent 31 described a similar phenomenon among young gay party patrons:

> The dance parties are very empowering for the younger people; they show ... that there is a lot of people like you around [and] this can help the people coming out.

The respondents suggested that many gay men sought validation of their identity within the context of the dance parties because of the dominant culture's rigid opposition to their radical transformations of social prescriptions related to sex, death and drugs. Maslow (1970) similarly argues that the first two elements belong to the most important classes of basic needs or well-being for the evolution and survival of the species. Many gay men have been continuously reminded of the need for self-control in one of the most important areas of their lives: their sexuality. For many of the respondents it was like walking a tight-rope, particularly if they had used psychoactive substances that removed them from their everyday responsibilities and awareness of safe-sex guidelines. Respondent 18 described this phenomenon:

> In the gay scene ... everybody knows everybody ... so everybody stays in control. ... AIDS and all the things you can catch is part of it. ... Being out of control means you don't know what you're doing ... not even caring. ...
> There's just that fine line ... to the point where being over that fine line means putting your life at risk.

Organizer 2 suggested that his parties were symbolic representations of ancient transformation media for the initiation of his party patrons:

It's all to do with sexuality and all the energy needed for
dedication and initiation ... this became the mascot of
Bacchanalia ... it emphasizes things like sex and drugs.

Evans (1988) suggested that this ideology was the essence of the
Dionysian tradition with its affirmation of the 'whole self' through
the enactment of ecstatic ritual. The dance parties afforded patrons
a novel vehicle for the transformation of their everyday consciousness and reinforcement of their identity through the use of similar
mind-altering media. The god Pan was celebrated as the creator of
music and dance rituals. He 'was a very sexual Greek god, often
having sex with both men and women. ... His Roman counterpart
was called "Penetrator" (or more accurately translated, "Fucker"
...)' (Evans, 1988, p. 120). Many of the patrons' world view was
transformed by the introduction of the dance parties, according to
the organizers and respondents. According to Eliade (1974), the
significance and durability of this reality was dependent on the
construction of meaningful institutionalized rituals. However,
Respondent 25 was concerned about the dissociative effects of these
transformed realities:

> You see it as the world of bondage. Everything us gays are
> trying to get away from by taking the mystique out of sex
> and they're putting it back in there ... They want their
> fantasies to come real. ... There's too much emphasis on
> the maleness of the good old Greek gods. The gods with
> the huge dick; it's all dick-orientated.

Most of the respondents' data suggested that these ritualized celebrations restated on a regular basis the values and principles of the
gay dance party institution and how its members should act within
this context. This process reaffirmed many of the patrons' and
organizers' transformed status and collective world-view which in
turn enabled them to transcend the boundaries of their everyday
reality and the uncompromising presence of HIV-related issues. The
parties also provided a 'gateway' or initiation route for some
patrons into the gay subculture and often a new or revitalized
identity. The dance, music, drugs and sex were all important elements of ritualized behaviour.

Moreover, Eliade (1974) argued that there were very few opportunities in contemporary western societies for a person to participate in a genuine initiatory ritual. These few exceptions were generally confined, as noted by Hanna (1987) to the innovative or creative institutions of urban marginal groups, similar to the inner-city dance party subculture.

Rites of passage

In traditional and modern cultures an individual generally achieved a state of awareness and identity through social interaction with people who shared a similar world view (Berger and Luckmann, 1975). This rite of passage was similar to the initiatory ceremony of bar mitzvah which celebrates the Jewish community's legitimation of the thirteen-year-old male's adult status. These rituals reduce ambiguities for all members of the group by making a societal statement of the initiate's changed status and relationship within the community. Respondent 13 described a similar rite of passage in becoming a member of the inner-city gay dance party community:

> When I first started going to the dance parties . . . I wasn't used to them. I felt that everyone was more in than I was . . . I was a stranger . . . but the more I go to them the more I feel relaxed and I start dancing with other people and smiling at everyone and having a good time.

Organizer 2 confirmed this by suggesting that his parties provided a forum and structure for this rite of passage into the gay community:

> We are trying to identify and help the gay community to come of age in their struggle in the community and for the first time start to look at itself.

Respondent 20 was sceptical of some dance party organizers' entrepreneurial motivations and their proclaimed gay social conscience:

> I know people who have gone into dance party in commercial enterprises and a number of these people have

made quite a few political pretensions such as how they are doing a great service to the gay community and I know that personally to be pure bullshit, bullshit!

Most of the respondents were aware of the self-serving interests of some organizers but they suggested that the benefits outweighed many of the negative aspects. One important element of regularly attending the parties was their newly acquired social identity as a member of a significant gay subgroup. Berger and Luckmann (1975) suggested that such rites of initiation communicated a shared symbolic universe that ordered and legitimated the lives of its members within a particular social context or reality.

Moreover, within these contexts even the most trivial incidences become imbued with profound significance. According to Van Gennep (1960), there were three stages in these rites of passage: separation, transition and incorporation. The inner-city dance parties provided the social vehicle for the enactment of social transformation (separation from their everyday reality) for a prescribed period of time (transition) and re-integration (or incorporation) back into the wider social order.

Healing and regeneration rites

Helman (1990) suggests that 'healing rituals are also rituals of social transition whereby an "ill person" is transformed into a "healthy person" ' (p. 203). Organizer 2 described how one of his patrons experienced a significant healing transformation:

> He had AIDS for several years. He hadn't gotten really sick ... he reached a part where life lost all meaning for him ... that's very dangerous if you've got AIDS. In a way it was having a rebirth experience ... he experienced himself in the future and like in a way he'd never experienced it ... he got new hope, new vision and since then his t-cells have gone up.

Traditionally, healing and regeneration rites have been enacted by many different cultures for the reinstatement of health and homogeneity of the group (Frazer, 1976). Ill-health among communities constantly reminds individuals of their vulnerability to death, and healing rituals help dissipate accumulated anxiety. Organizer 2 described the healing and regenerative effects of the Bacchanalian rituals for an HIV-seropositive patron:

> He is HIV-positive and his experiences with Bacchanalia and LSD ... transformed him; he is actually healthier and fitter than ever ... his t-cells have gone up and he's like healthy.

According to Hamilton (1969), one of the implicit beliefs of the Bacchanalian tradition was the life-regenerating powers of the god Dionysus (who, as Evans (1988) says, was also known as the Lord of Dance and the Giver of Ecstasy). His followers were healed, transformed and energized from participating in ritualized activities, such as dance, music, orgiastic sex and intoxicants. The inner-city dance party institution provided some men with a similar sociopsychological medium that helped legitimate their identity and insulate them from their everyday reality of a homophobic world. As described by Respondent 20:

> It is like being able to say to all the homophobes, to everyone, 'fuck you' for five or six hours ... and I'll do all the things that society says are not right ... I'm going to get myself so out of it I won't know where I am, I am going to fuck myself stupid and if I want to have unsafe sex I'll have unsafe sex ... and I'll make out with someone on the dance floor ... I'll show you how deviant I can be ... the whole truth is that we're harmless.

These iconoclastic attitudes and behaviours may have increased the risks of HIV infections among party patrons. Respondent 24 described the beneficial healing effects of participating (consciously or unconsciously) in celebrations of gay identity in a semi-public setting:

> It's a celebration of our own sexuality and allowing it to be expressed freely in an unhibited [sic] way ... when people say they are celebrating they are not always sure themselves ... It's a cathartic experience ... it's very healthy that we are in a situation where we acknowledge those instinctive roots and give them some kind of credence.

These attitudes and behaviours were consistent with historical records (during the time of plagues that swept Europe from the twelfth to the eighteenth century) where 'nuns in the convents also, neglecting their rules, abandon themselves to carnal lust, and deem that by voluptuousness and excess they will prolong their lives ... The most reliable medicine, they maintained was to drink excessively and to have a good time ... with song and merriment, satisfying ... every desire' (Nohl, 1971, p 127). Respondent 31 described a similar phenomenon of 'carpe diem' among many HIV-seropositive people he had encountered:

> I've noticed [HIV-positive] people don't tend to talk about
> the future. Well my group certainly don't do a lot of
> talking about the future ... there's a lot to living very much
> for the moment and short-term planning.

Martos (1981) argued that the health of the individual or the group was one of the prime objectives of humanity. Healing rituals often emerged in cultures where the social institution responsible for the health of its members had failed to provide satisfactory protection or cure from a deadly disease (Eliade, 1957; Nohl, 1971) such as was the case in the inner-city gay community.

Death and rebirth rituals

The dance parties also helped grieving people to find the meaning of death within their culture by assisting them in coming to a deeper understanding of that meaning (Reanney, 1991), according to the respondents and organizers. Organizer 3 described the regenerative effects of the dance parties:

> Your life may look very bleak to you but this gives you
> something to look forward to. You go there and it gives
> you a new vision, a new optimism, a new hope. You can
> see the clear light again and it restores your strength in
> your future.

The dance party milieu helped many patrons cope with their losses and accept that life in the gay community continued after the death of some members and confirmed that being gay was still a 'positive' identity and not the cause of HIV/AIDS. According to Respondent

28 his HIV-seronegative status symbolized the importance of this phenomenon for many of his gay friends, particularly those who were HIV-positive:

> I've got close friends who are positive and they know my status and they're very keen to see me stay that way. . . .
> Each time I have a negative result they are very happy and supportive.

Kübler-Ross (1975) argued that 'the dying stage of our life can be experienced as the most profound growth event of our total life's experience' (p. 149). Respondent 27 described a similar philosophical approach to his HIV-seropositive status:

> What being HIV-positive does to a person psychologically is . . . it makes you take your life seriously and not waste time . . . and you face up to your own mortality and realizing that we're all mortal anyway . . . in a way that most people don't, especially at my age. . . . It really puts the onus on you to get what you want out of your life. Because time's running out and there's no time not to.

These rituals provided a standardized structure for the reconciliation of life-threatening ambiguities following the recent death of a significant other (Helman, 1990). Many of the patrons' fundamental existences were being undermined by the number and proximity of premature deaths among their community, as described by Respondent 26:

> I'm negative but eighty per cent of my friends are HIV just from where I work. . . . A few of [them] . . . continue to have unsafe sex . . . but not all of them. . . . There's no reason for them to pass it on but they think: well now I've got it and I can't get it again so why worry about a condom?

A person's death was mourned at two different levels of existence: the biological death of the organism and the individual's social death which marked the end of their social identity (Hertz, 1960). As described by Respondent 4:

I went out on the Saturday night ... after we buried [him] ... because I had to do that. ... There were lots of ghosts [and] there were a lot of people still around who were there when my other friends were around on the dance floor.

Organizer 2 suggested that they incorporated ancient Greek symbols into their dance party themes to promote a sense of well-being and survival among their party patrons. For example, one of their parties, Hyperborea was modelled on the mythological immortal land of the ancient Greeks:

Hyperborea is actually the golden land of the Greeks where one could never grow old.

Hamilton (1969) described Hyperborea as a timeless ancient region located in Northern Greece. It was 'the abode of the blessed dead ... [where] sickness and deathly old age had no part' (p. 68). This optimistic concept represented the antithesis of many patrons' everyday reality where death played a central theme (directly or indirectly) for many years, with the presence of the HIV/AIDS pandemic in their community. The respondents suggested that parties provided them with an adaptive coping mechanism that helped them find new meaning through the discovery of a shared future and the survival of the gay identity.

Rituals of misfortune

Rituals of misfortune usually evolved during periods of unexpected crises such as natural or human disasters, or plagues (Douglas, 1991; Nohl, 1971). According to Helman (1990), rituals provided a standardized mode of communicating and controlling the unknown in situations of unexpected or unrelenting misfortunes. It was a way of reducing the ambiguities and anxieties for the individual and the group by providing a structure out of uncertainty or chaos (Reanney, 1991). These rituals operated at two levels: (1) they solved a specific problem for members of the group, and (2) they served a latent function of re-establishing order, as Loudon (1966) argued. Respondent 31 used the incorporeal term 'spooky' to describe the angst of being surrounded by unrelenting misfortune among one's own community:

> It feels pretty spooky to be a gay man without HIV, there's a lot of adjustment going on. . . . My boyfriend and I are both negative and just about all our close friends are positive, the majority of them, and you feel a bit isolated.

The fear of death was the most existentially threatening factor in an individual's life, according to Reanney (1991). It assaulted the most central part of their existence, menacing the foundations of their identity: the self. Respondent 7 suggested that death-related anxiety was often so intensely unbearable that many people intentionally used drugs to remove themselves from the source of their stress or everyday reality:

> Even my friends who know exactly what to take sometimes feel like getting absolutely bombed out at the dance parties . . . because someone has just died.

Individuals often need to take part in ritualized behaviour to reduce the intolerable stress of facing the reality of death (Helman, 1990; Reanney, 1991). Most gay men have been subjected to the reality of HIV/AIDS-associated stresses, including death of significant others, for over a decade. Organizer 2 described the universality and gravity of these HIV/AIDS-related losses:

> All of us have got someone who we have lost to AIDS or are dying of AIDS.

Dylan Thomas (1982) suggests to his father to fight death and

> Do not go gentle into that good night
> Rage, rage against the dying of the light.

The use of the term 'rage' is interesting: according to the *Concise Oxford Dictionary: Fifth Edition*, it is a 'rapturous feeling, a state of frenzy, to move wildly or turbulently'. It is also a common colloquial term used to describe disinhibited social activities, such as dancing and the use of psychoactive substances, similar to behaviour at the dance parties. Dance parties are sometimes known as 'rages', and going to a dance party as 'raging'.

According to some of the respondents, the dance party institution served the function of a wake or venue where some patrons could reflect on their own HIV status or mourn the loss of a significant other. Zoja (1989) noted that most people preferred to share life-threatening ordeals with people who empathized with their predicament, rather than confront such a profound experience on their own. In most contemporary Western cultures the reality of death is censored (Reannèy, 1991) by being relegated to an almost invisible status behind the dehumanizing doors of institutions, such as sanatoria, hospitals and funeral parlours.

The inner-city gay dance party institution appears to have served an additional function as a social support system or 'family of choice', similar to the traditional role of the family, church or state (Kamath, 1978), for some patrons who were endeavouring to reconcile themselves with their HIV/AIDS-related losses.

Sacred time and space

The organizers suggested that the parties afforded the patrons a safe and sacred place outside 'real' time and space, with its stark reality of the HIV/AIDS pandemic and widespread homo-negativism. The term 'sacred' is used to describe the contrast between the respondents' descriptions of their everyday reality (profane), and the sacred environment of the dance party milieu, as suggested by Eliade (1977). *The Concise Oxford Dictionary: Fifth Edition* defines 'sacred' as an element 'appropriated to a person or purpose; made holy by religious association, associated with religious symbolism, e.g., concert, music'. Tillich (1952) argues that any object, place or event is sacred where there is an agreed perception in a transcendent reality (other-worldly). According to Organizer 3 some of these sacred elements were incorporated into his dance parties:

> We are trying to create a peak experience ... it means that
> people on the dance floor or on the seats could forget
> where they are and transcend their everyday reality ...
> overcome your inhibitions and forget where you are in time
> and space.

Many of the patrons endeavoured to escape their everyday space and time by taking consciousness-changing substances within an already created or controlled environment at the dance party.

Loudon (1966) suggests that the rituals performed by a group usually reveal the state of affairs or social conditions of the participants. Respondent 25 described this social phenomenon:

> At the parties you're free of the everyday worries ... you
> don't have to think about being a gay person on the street,
> you always have to think about it no matter where you are,
> even Oxford Street. ... You can't really display emotions
> ... whereas at the dance party you can walk up to anyone,
> there's just no boundaries ... and that's what I like the
> most about the dance parties ... that escapism, that
> intimacy ... it's very Utopian.

Eliade (1977) suggested that these ritualized behaviours represented symbolically the eternal quality of time and space and each time they were re-enacted the initiate or group re-established a connection with these eternal dimensions. Ringdal (1991) described a similar phenomenon in a gay New York discotheque during the 1980s, where patrons 'felt tempted to believe that homosexuals actually conquered the world' (p. 67). Organizer 2 described this transformation of temporal time and space within the context of their parties:

> Bacchanalia is also unique in bringing together, for ten
> hours of celebration, a wide variety of people, breaking
> down the barriers between them, and providing them with
> a night of spectacle and ritual that would make the ancient
> Greeks proud.

Ringdal (1991) described this transformation of profane time into the infinite where 'time did not exist, only space – the limitless, space of the universe ... [where patrons felt] invulnerable, immortal, destined to live for ever' (p. 72). Respondent 25 described the emancipating effects of this transformed reality:

> They are no longer deviants ... once you are inside that
> hall you are not inside society any more ... you're in a
> place that's totally of its own ... it's an idealistic
> environment.

One of the major risks consistently reported by the organizers and the respondents was being removed from everyday reality and the awareness of safer-sexual guidelines. As described by Respondent 29:

> It's a celebration of freedom, your own self ... and a group of like-minded people and it becomes a group celebration. It's ritualistic in a way too ... Initially they pulled the community together and [they] celebrate sexuality ... and freedom. ... Sometimes, though, this is an excuse for another drug binge ... [and] sex ... and afterwards they say 'I had unsafe sex with him ... what am I gonna do?' It's too unreal a world you live in when you use drugs.

According to the organizers, the dance party venues were charged with significant meaning derived from the sacred elements of the various rituals, such as rites of passage, sacred food, intoxicants and healing, funeral and ordination rites.

The dance party organizers' and the disc jockeys' roles (Ringdal, 1991) conformed with Martos's (1981) description of the criteria for Catholic ordination rites, whereby all these roles required a similar strong commitment of service and endorsement of their respective institution's norms and values. According to Eliade (1974), these ritualized patterns of behaviour permitted a person the opportunity in contemporary Western society to enter into a sacred reality or religious dimension of human existence.

Sacred actions

Most belief systems, according to Eliade (1977), have similar symbolic elements of a sacred reality, such as venues, objects, persons and actions. Martos (1981) argues that sacred action often involves the performance of relevant rituals which in turn reinforce the person's identity and commitment to the group's norms and values. The actions and objects used in these venues are imbued with new meanings and significances which are usually only relevant within that time and space (Eliade, 1977). Leach (1976) notes that rituals involve the use of standardized symbols, such as objects, actions, clothing, gestures or music. Respondent 6 described the transformational effects of the dance party symbols:

You get in there and you're dancing to the beat for hours and hours on end ... Whether you're on drugs or not ... it's a cathartic experience.

This consciousness transformation or 'autointoxication' was often due to external and internal stimuli, such as engaging in frenzied dancing, listening to specific types of music, audience encouragement or the use of psychoactive substances (Hanna, 1989). Respondent 5 described these autointoxicating effects:

Music has power and the rhythm has incredible power. It really gets the body moving and it's very sexual and it's very energetic.

According to Cartwright and Zander (1968), the group's survival usually depended on members' adherence to its social prescriptions, in this case, the use of drugs and sexual behaviour within the context of the dance party milieu. Paradoxically, these behaviours were likely to increase the risks of HIV infection among patrons. Berger and Luckmann (1975) argued that these shared norms and values were essential for the definition of the group's construction of reality, whereby, ritualized actions restated and reinforced on a regular basis this collective view of the world. Organizer 3 described the cohesive effects of these sacred actions among party patrons:

We played 'Infinity': everyone turned and faced the laser ... (it was a quasi-religious ceremony), they all went into a state of delirium and raised both hands. I was quite stunned, you know, it was very spontaneous.

Respondent 29 described the personality-transforming effects of these dance party rituals on some patrons:

I've seen people who can hardly communicate ... very shy, very withdrawn, afraid because they think they're not very good, but you can move them into the dance area and they blossom. ... Over a period of time you watch them changing, it's unbelievable ... more confident.

The respondents' data indicated that some patrons attributed sacred significance to specific actions (such as the use of drugs), within the context of the parties. Paradoxically, according to Stall *et al.* (1986) these life-affirming actions may have increased their risk of HIV infection.

Sacred persons

Some of the respondents and all the organizers suggested that the disc jockeys (DJs), organizers and drug dealers held positions of power (to varying degrees) within the dance party milieu similar to the role of a religious leader (Newcombe, 1992). Organizer 1 described his influential role within the dance party community:

> I believe I can actually make a difference to what people say because I influence people through what I create and produce.

The organizers' leadership was also dependent on their legitimized roles as custodians of the dance party institution and its prescriptions or norms and values. Organizer 2 suggested that they had been successful in transforming and elevating the social identities of the dance party patrons:

> We got people and they were changed ... they all didn't go out and buy a crystal or tarot cards but they did get self-improvement.

Bateson (1972) argued that the 'myth' of power is a very powerful myth and probably most people in this world more or less believe in it. The universality of this belief system becomes to that extent self-validating, as described by Respondent 4:

> The DJs and the organizers are considered cultural heroes.

Ringdal (1991) suggested that a similar phenomenon was occurring within the New York gay discotheques where the DJs and organizers were revered by the patrons. They held a status analogous to the 'high priest' in religious orders with Messianic qualities. They were similar to the phoenix that mythologically was constantly under an obligation to renew itself. The organizers and DJs were similarly committed to creating a new and novel environment; but they were also 'responsible' for the salvation of the members of their congregation. The importance of their divine status was encapsulated, according to Ringdal (1991) in the lyrics of a popular piece of music:

'last night a DJ saved my life' (p. 68). Nohl (1971) described similar situations among musicians during the Black Plague who played music 'till they were quite exhausted ... [rather than] allow the patients to relapse in the midst of the health-restoring dance' (p. 148). Some of the dance party patrons according to Respondent 10 had also sanctified the role of their musicians within the dance party milieu:

> Some people do like the DJs ... they put them on a pedestal.

According to Respondent 14, the survival of the private dance party industry was mainly dependent on the charismatic attraction of the DJs:

> It is important for dance party organizers to target a particular crowd by the DJs that they are using because people ... know the music that a particular DJ plays.

Ringdal suggested that the DJs were also responsible for the transformation and modulation of patrons' moods and the subsequent success of their sexual liaisons. They were charismatic leaders, who provided important services to their community, similar to their counterparts from the Sydney gay dance milieu. As described by Respondent 13:

> The DJs have a big pull. ... If they've got a good name they're a draw card. Some have a powerful effect on the people going to that party.

According to Weber (1947), a charismatic person was 'set apart from ordinary men and treated as [if] endowed with ... specifically exceptional powers and qualities' (p. 358). The roles, services and actions of the dance party organizers, DJs and drug dealers were similar to those of a charismatic leader. These social responsibilities separated the institutional leaders from the ordinary members of the dance party establishment. Ringdal (1991) suggested that these boundaries prohibited patrons from socializing with the DJs: 'it was simply out of the question to talk to the DJ, so people tried to attract their attention through their dancing ... they would be the ones the conductor heeded most' (p. 68). Respondent

3 described a similar phenomenon within the context of the dance parties:

> X ... from the Bacchanalian party ... had his finger on the music. He watched the dance floor and they look for people they know and watch movements in the dance.

Parsons (1949) also suggested that a charismatic leader is 'outside the realm of everyday routine and the profane sphere. It is "extraordinary" as opposed to the "everyday", "sacred" in contrast to the profane' (p. 658). Further, the DJs', organizers' and dealers' authorities were legitimized by their commercial roles as organizers and directors. Respondent 18 described his significant commercial role at the dance parties:

> I was a well-known figure but very low key, I didn't go onto the street ... I go [to the dance parties] for business ... I was one of the biggest Ecstasy dealers in town.

The drug dealers, according to Respondent 8 (who also claimed to be one of Sydney's biggest Ecstasy dealers) were also significant persons for the dance party patrons. They were responsible for the dispensing of consciousness-changing substances, caretaking and healing where necessary, a role similar to that of a shaman or some contemporary medical practitioners. He described one of his intervention methods:

> If there's something wrong ... with the drug or with them ... it can usually be overcome with a hug to release that bit of tension ... I say to them 'look love, go to the toilet and sit down ... because you must be relaxed. ... ' They shouldn't take lots on your own. ... I saw people come down off drugs pretty badly ... they'd be crying and I'd say 'come on over, or do you want me to come over?'. They'd come round by talking to you [then] they're fine.

Respondent 25 respectfully acknowledged the drug dealers' role within the dance party subculture:

> They're actually doing a service to society ... drugs are just the ultimate.

Moreover, he suggested that his perception of drug dealers was transformed through his association with them:

> Drug dealers are just ordinary people. ... There is a mystique about them ... but as I meet more of them I realize that they've the guts to go out and do it ... I admire them more these days. ... It's been a real big turn-around in my perception from when I was younger. ... You're told what to think, you're being socialized.

Weber (1963) pointed to the function of the sacred in social control, with its reinforcement of the institution's norms and values by virtue of the leaders' socially legitimized authority. The organizers' ideological commitments may also have been influenced by economic factors, such as the viability, expansion and continuing success of the dance party industry.

Weber argued that belief systems were often shaped by economic forces and under certain conditions the reverse occurred. Moreover, Weber's social action theory suggested that human behaviour was determined by an individual's world view and the meanings they derived from their subsequent actions. These dimensions often governed the individual's attitudes and behaviour within a wide range of social contexts, such as the dance party institution.

From this perspective the organizers', DJs' and drug dealers' social roles served an important function by reinforcing inter-group cohesion and solidarity, which in turn ensured the continuance and smooth running of both the social system and their commercial enterprises. The organizers suggested that their role was the most influential within the dance party institution, however, most of the respondents saw the role of DJ as carrying the greatest status. The drug dealers' role was also significant because they provided an essential infra-structural service to the dance party milieu, being the conduits for one of the basic tenets (drugs) on which the social system of the dance party institution was established and maintained. For the efficacy of future intervention programmes, it is important to analyze the significance of these three roles (DJs, organizers and dealers) within the social structure of the dance party institutions, both as 'sacred persons' and influencers of opinions, norms and behaviours. Forsyth (1983) pointed out that group members were more successful in changing attitudes and behaviours than were outsiders, because of their shared reality, norms and values and the social pressures of conformity to these dimensions.

Rituals and drug-use reactions to life-threatening crises

Intoxicants have been used traditionally by individuals and groups to help them cope with an intolerable (or incurable) situation (Evans, 1988; Tiger, 1971; Zoja, 1989). A similar phenomenon may partly account for the widespread use of psychoactive substances among the dance party patrons (Safe and Sager, 1990) who were also members of a subculture in crisis.

The 'designer drug' Ecstasy was considered by the organizers as the ideal dance party drug. Newcombe (1991) pointed out that Ecstasy was also the prototypical drug of the dance party or rave scene in north-west England. Perhaps it was originally named Ecstasy to signify to the user the idiosyncratic ecstatic effects of the drug. *The Concise Oxford Dictionary: Fifth Edition* gives the Greek root of the word 'ecstasy' as 'ekstasis', designating it an 'exalted state of feeling, rapture (esp. of delight) ... put (person) out of (his senses)'. We have already noted the connection between Bacchanalian rituals and the status of Bacchus as the God of Ecstasy. Organizer 2 claimed that his organization was chiefly responsible for the introduction of the recreational drug Ecstasy to the dance party patrons:

> We were more responsible than anyone else in the city to introduce Ecstasy to a large number of young people ...
> The parties started a whole new culture of Ecstasy-taking young people.

His apparent pride in this achievement reflected some of the differences between the dance party organizer's attitude toward the use of Ecstasy and other psychoactive substances and the dominant culture's mandate deeming them illegal substances. He also suggested that Ecstasy was an integral component in the transformation of party patrons' consciousness:

> The parties were actually designed for people to take Ecstasy, for people to reach another level of awareness.

This phenomenon is similar to the Roman Catholic sacrament of the Eucharist where the bread and wine is transubstantiated (changing one substance, or consciousness for another) into the body and blood of Christ, becoming a symbolic representation of the Divine (Martos, 1981). Through this, the individual was also transformed. The efficacy of this transformational process in the dance party depended on the adept's commitment to, and immersion in, this other reality. Respondent 25 described the transforming effects of the dance party milieu:

> You get absorbed by the whole thing and you start
> basically leaving everyday life.

Steiner (1977) argued that the initiate's consciousness was transmuted by the physical ritual act of absorption of sacred symbols (such as food, beverages and intoxicants). Martos (1981) states that the Eucharist ritual symbolized the transformation of realities from the profane to the sacred where Christ was actually present. However, Respondent 14 was concerned about the precarious quality of this ecstatic consciousness:

> There's a fine line between losing, it's like it's not there at
> all. You've lost it and you don't know where reality is
> starting and ending. . . . It happened to me . . . I lost my
> sexual control . . . and I'm [HIV-] positive.

These descriptions were similar to the reported effects of the drug Ecstasy, according to Newcombe (1988) and the respondents discussed in Chapter 6. According to Weber (1963), the novice in the rites of initiation or rebirth usually experienced similar ecstatic states following his transformation into manhood. The social reality and physical boundaries were transformed in these ecstatic states of consciousness often by the ritual use of intoxicating drugs or 'music and dance . . . sexuality; or by the combination of all three' (Weber, 1963, p. 157). Organizer 2 described a similar social reality at their dance parties:

> At some of our parties including the Hordern . . . we could
> have honestly said that 75 per cent of our crowd was on
> Ecstasy . . . [where] they can experience ecstatic moments.

According to McKirnan and Peterson (1989), gay men in Western cultures have traditionally used psychoactive substances in a variety of settings to ameliorate the psychosocial stresses of everyday life in a predominantly homonegative society. Respondent 14 said:

> When I do go to the dance parties and use drugs ... it's an escape from reality.

Drug use and ritualized behaviour were traditionally part of pre-existing gay social environments (such as bars, nightclubs and other social institutions) that promoted the use of psychoactive substances among their clientele (Stall and Wiley, 1988) prior to the inception of the inner-Sydney gay dance party institution (Wotherspoon, 1991). Organizer 2 suggested that their dance parties were sacred initiation venues for a large number of party patrons through the symbolic and organic use of Ecstasy. He described a sympathetic magical association (Frazer, 1976) between the use of the drug Ecstasy and the efficacy of the initiation ritual into the Bacchanalian tradition. Frazer noted that the 'Principles of Magic [were] ... found to resolve themselves into two: first, that like produces like, or that an effect resembles its cause' (p. 14). Organizer 2 described the magical transformational effects of his dance party organization:

> It was a conscious attempt to initiate as large a number of people as possible ... as the golden generation. ... By introducing the people to Ecstasy we felt it all came together ... of course Dionysius is the god of ecstasy.

Evans (1988) suggested that this was not a new phenomenon among gay men: he also encountered a group of gay men in the United States who were modern day adepts of the Dionysian tradition. He said 'I came to the conclusion that an old agrarian underground religion long existed in Europe and that it had a traditional place in the rites of lesbian[s] and gay men' (p. 185). Organizer 3 suggested that they had succeeded in transforming the patrons' everyday consciousness through authentic replication of these Dionysian traditions:

> Dionysius was trying to create an ecstatic environment and so are we. . . . The drug Ecstasy is one factor . . . we are effecting a change of consciousness.

According to Hanna (1987), there was a greater interest among urban residents in innovative environments, such as in the institution of the dance party. They were also traditionally more critical and reactionary against social injustices (than non-urban residents), often demonstrating their dissatisfaction by engaging in counter-cultural behaviour (such as dance, music, art, theatre, demonstrations, parades and using intoxicants). Organizer 1 appeared to be confused or cautious in his statements about the use of drugs at his parties. His responses may also have been biased by the legal implications of the reported use of recreational drugs at the dance parties. On the one hand:

> If you're on drugs it'll be great. . . . For a lot of people the added catalyst is recreational drugs.

Followed by this ambiguous statement:

> It's definitely not designed for drugs. Sometimes it might look like that way but . . . the people who design for [my parties] have used recreational drugs and they may be subliminally affected.

However, Respondent 18 had a vested interest in the use of drugs at the dance parties and suggested that they were an integral part of this milieu:

> The last three or four years I've been selling drugs . . . a lot of drugs there . . . a lot! . . . I had to because of financial reasons.

Organizer 1's statement suggested that he was either naive or not very involved in the design of his parties or he was censoring his comments in accordance with the wider culture's norms and values in relation to drugs and gay sexual behaviour. He may have biased the data in accordance with what he believed were the researchers' attitudes to these social behaviours.

The 'unorthodox' ideologies postulated by the organizers and respondents may have reflected the social, political and psychological needs of many inner-city gay men. Camus (1947) argued that such innovative social institutions were to be expected in response to life-threatening diseases when he said that 'religion in a time of plague could not be the religion of every day' (p. 183). However, Stall *et al.* (1986) cautioned that these belief systems, combined with the use of psychoactive substances, were also likely to be predictors of risky sexual and drug-related behaviour.

Ritualized sexual behaviour

Organizer 2 indicated that the gay community had a responsibility to sacramentalize the use of drugs and sex by performing ancient rites:

> I believe the gay way to God is through the use of sex and drugs . . . sex magic. . . . We had to revive Bacchanalia to help redress a balance which two thousand years of Christianity had caused.

These ritualized symbols (sex and drugs) have been used traditionally by many different cultures as vehicles of liberation (or rebirth) from the bondage of the dominant culture's repressive taboos, often related to sex and death (Douglas, 1991; Garber, 1992). Organizer 2 was committed to liberating his party patrons from the repressive Judeo-Christian conditioning that inhibited their sexual and personal freedom:

> They were loving their bodies, they were losing all inhibitions about their anuses, their cocks . . . they were breaking down all those barriers about shame and guilt and dirt. . . . We attribute this to the dance parties and Ecstasy.

It was not made clear by the organizer whether the patrons consciously or unconsciously participated in these cultural transformations. Respondent 17 testified to the efficacy of Organizer 2's liberating Bacchanalian model and the ritualized use of drugs within this context:

I think that there is for a start less sexual inhibition. People feel more sexually overt and comfortable and these parties may be the only times some people will only take drugs ... they don't take them otherwise.

However, there was considerable concern expressed among the respondents about the increased risks of HIV transmission following their adherence to some of the dance party prescriptions. As Respondent 29 described:

Drugs consume you ... you really don't know what you're doing ... you know you can have sex! You're rampant sexually at that stage, MDA heightens it like Ice ... multiple orgasms you can go for about six hours ... it's lethal, absolutely lethal ... it's one to watch out for in relationship to unsafe sex.

Organizer 2 suggested that the safe-sex educational programmes had been incredibly successful in eliminating risky sexual behaviour among the inner-city gay community:

Since this AIDS thing has come along people are really into promoting safe sex ... they did succeed ... now 99.9 per cent of the people that you come across in a sexual encounter want to use a condom.

Most of the respondents and the literature (Paul *et al.*, 1993) did not fully concur with Organizer 3's appraisal of the effectiveness of safe-sexual campaigns. Respondent 29 suggested that some of the party patrons abdicated responsibility for their sexual behaviour by consciously or unconsciously masking their recall of safer-sexual guidelines:

The young ones are going to go through a lot of problems ... 'specially with their sexuality because promiscuity is still a BIG thing in the gay community. ... The next day it's forgotten about shutting it away ... so you're not responsible for your actions. ... This attitude cultivates unsafe sex.

Previous researchers have demonstrated that some of these patrons may have had difficulty recalling previously encoded information (Eich *et al.*, 1975; Flexser and Tulving, 1978) because their memory was impaired by their chemical and contextual states (as previously noted). 'Memory seems to be dependent on the state, or situation, that existed during the original learning [phase]' (Houston, 1986, p. 294).

The significance of sexual venues

All of the respondents suggested that specific contexts (such as toilets or shower blocks) for sexual activities were allocated by the organizers. Respondent 31, one of the organizers of the gay community dance parties, confirmed this phenomenon:

> If you don't provide for sexual behaviour they'll usually make it, they'll just congregate in the darkest most appropriate area.

Respondent 2 described the eroticizing effects of these *en masse* sexual scenes at the dance parties:

> There's a lot of raunchy sex going on and it's very erotic ... I went into the showers in the last dance party to have a look ... and it was so dark ... I had a fun grope with somebody: it felt wonderful.

However, these anonymous erotic environments may also lead to increased risks of HIV transmission (as previously noted). The loss of individuality within these unlit venues potentiated some patrons' diminished personal responsibility for their safe-sexual behaviour, according to the respondents. Respondent 1 summarized this phenomenon:

> In the toilets at the dance parties a lot of them are off their faces and when you're in that state you're vulnerable ... you're not clear headed ... all your barriers are down. ... You could end up having unsafe sex ... in this moving mass of flesh.

Stall *et al.* (1986) also suggested that there was a strong association between the use of recreational drugs and increased risky behaviour within contexts that sanctioned these behaviours, such as the gay inner-city dance parties. According to Respondent 31, some of the party patrons needed to be protected by the organizers from their drug-induced diminished responsibility:

> I always call them the Romper Roomers. They get so excited they overdose or they mix drug[s] and alcohol, they get caught up in the moment and then all of a sudden they find themselves in a dangerous situation like having unsafe sex or black out ... and we do everything we can to protect them.

'Romper Room' was the title of a popular and long-running national television programme for pre-school children. This patronizing term appeared to reflect Respondent 31's frustrated attempts, in his role as organizer, to modify some party patrons' recalcitrant risky behaviour. Respondent 17 was also incensed by the irresponsible sexual behaviour of patrons in the backrooms at the dance parties and the homonegative consequences for the inner-city gay community if this behaviour became public information. He was particularly concerned about providing ammunition for the Reverend Fred Nile, one of the prime antagonists of the Sydney gay subculture:

> Those people in the back rooms are taking too big a risk for the whole community. ... If it becomes common knowledge to the people out there ... it gives an argument for people like Fred Nile ... like people who are ... on drugs [are] not going to be safe therefore you know more people are going to be infected and they are just taking a bigger risk to the community overall.

Some of the organizers' statements may also have been biased by their concern about adverse publicity related to sexual and drug behaviour at the dance parties, and the serious ramifications this information may have on the future of the dance party industry. This concern may be reflected in Organizer 1's denial of sexual behaviour at his parties:

> I didn't see any sex ... but there could have been honestly.

On the other hand he may have been genuinely unaware of the reported sexual activities at the parties. However, what was confusing was his eyewitness account of 'rampant sexuality' at the Mardi Gras Ball some years previously:

> They used to knock the lights out in the toilets and you'd go down there and it'd be like whoo! whoo! In the old days at the showground when they used to be held there ... around '83 ... I went out looking for somebody ... and there were people doing it everywhere in the stables. Not just one but groups of people. It looked like a Fellini movie.

The contrast he projected between his commercial parties and the gay community dance parties (including Mardi Gras and Sleaze Ball) served two functions: (1) it shifted the responsibility of this behaviour onto others and (2) it distanced the behaviour by providing an incident that occurred years ago, in 1983. He supported his argument by claiming that risk-taking behaviour had been modified by the presence of HIV/AIDS among the gay community and had coincided with the inception of his parties in late 1983:

> The gay community have become very responsible ... I see Mardi Gras and Sleaze Ball as a major breeding ground for AIDS, and yet you don't see that any more at the Mardi Gras.

However, Respondent 31 was not as optimistic as Organizer 1 about the transformation of patrons' risky behaviour within the context of the Mardi Gras and Sleaze Ball:

> We had to try and get the safe-sex message across [but] we had problems with keeping the lights on in the toilets and keeping people out of dangerous areas. ... They'll do anything. We go through amazing lengths to try and protect them.

Organizer 1's ambiguous statement was confusing given his earlier denial of drug use and sexual behaviour at the parties:

> Personally I can have sex on anything ... I can remember having sex at a party on magic mushrooms, but not having it, and thinking I was having it.

Organizer 2 gave a similar account with a comment about a sexual encounter he had at a dance party:

> Being absolutely honest, there was a party where a friend of mine wanted a sexual encounter with me ... we were incredibly out of it and messy and we just couldn't find any condoms.

The three private organizers provided ambiguous data about sexual behaviours within the context of their dance parties by contrast to many respondents' concerns (including Respondent 31 who was one of the gay community dance party organizers) about the possibility of increased risky sexual behaviour following the use of psychoactive substances. Organizer 1 appeared to provide the most socially desirable data with his consistent denial of sexual behaviour at his parties. Whereas, Organizers 2 and 3 suggested that they promoted sexual and drug-related behaviour among their party patrons, but were '99.9 per cent' confident that they practised safer-sexual behaviour. However, most of the respondents, including the organizers, acknowledged the aphrodisiac effects of some party drugs.

Conclusion

It would seem that the evolution of the gay dance party milieu as a significant gay social institution that included ritualized behaviour was necessary for more reasons than just the need to unite in the face of legal opposition, as Wotherspoon (1991) also concludes. These social institutions developed in conjunction with, and in reaction to, opposing political and social elements which co-existed in the mid-1980s. For the first time gay men were experiencing political, social and sexual enfranchisement which paradoxically was overshadowed by the threat of contracting a potentially fatal disease (HIV/AIDS) and the recurrence of anti-homosexual sentiments associated with this (Davenport-Hines, 1990).

A culture in crisis often develops rites or social structures in an effort to re-empower itself, particularly when the established paradigm fails to contain or subjugate the life-threatening crisis, such as the current medico-scientific paradigm and the HIV/AIDS pandemic. The dance party milieu is a social structure where gay men may derive positive reinforcement of their identity, meet potential partners and ventilate their accumulated stress and anxiety over HIV/AIDS-related issues. The pervasiveness of this anxiety in cultures or subcultures facing plague conditions or the threat of death similar to the inner-city gay community was summarized by a character in Camus's (1947) novel *The Plague*, who said: 'this here blasted disease – even them as haven't got it can't think of anything else' (p. 97). Zoja (1989) suggests that the greater the loss of control among a subculture in crisis (such as the increased risk of HIV infection among party patrons) the higher the drug consumption. Although the drugs the party patrons use (such as Ecstasy) are relatively new compounds, the optimism they endow is ancient. The consumption of intoxicants is perennial and universal for the transformation of perception and emotion, particularly among a culture facing a life-threatening crisis (Camus, 1947; Eliade, 1977; Evans, 1988).

Quadland and Shattls (1987) suggested that the need for control was often the major incentive for using psychoactive substances. Paradoxically, this collective response may lead to loss of judgement, cognitive impairment (Eich, 1977) and a reduction in control (while retaining the feeling of being in control): a potential formula for problems among a population at risk of HIV infection (Butt, 1989). Yet some patrons, according to the data, were relying on flawed symbols, including attitudes, belief systems and ritualized behaviour as a prophylactic against HIV infection.

Chapter Eight investigates the fragility and strengths of the inner-city gay dance party argot, or communication symbols, and their possible relationship to an increased risk of HIV/AIDS infection among this sample.

Chapter eight

Dance Party Argot and Symbols in the Context of the HIV/AIDS Pandemic

Love wouldn't be blind if braille weren't so much damned fun.

Armistead Maupin, *Maybe the Moon* (1992)

'MAN'S unique position is based on the dominance of symbols in his life' (von Bertalanffy, 1965, p. 27). Hacker (1965) also suggested that 'symbols can and do serve a survival function. They, may in fact, [sic] constitute the essence of man's survival technique . . . the essence of a symbol is the simultaneous unifying organization of heterogeneous elements' (p. 78). A symbol stands for something else (Royce, 1965); it is a metaphor that is historically framed by the socio-political forces in a particular culture, or subculture (Leach, 1976); and its primary function is to carry 'short-hand' information (Sless, 1986). The main focus of this investigation is to 'decipher', translate or interpret the meaning of the inner-city gay dance party patrons' symbolic language and its possible relevance to increased risky sexual behaviour.

The applicability, durability and significance of these symbols (including the gay dance party institution) are embedded in the historical, sociological and psychological dimensions that forged and framed their meaning. As short-hand communication symbols or argot they serve a number of significant functions for some party patrons: they provide a convenient method for the evaluation of, and negotiations with, a potential sexual partner. They also imply that both parties are aware of their embedded meaning. The efficacy of future safer-sexual intervention programmes may be determined by the fragility or durability of this 'hidden-language' (including dance party context, clothes, body, drugs, etc.) and the researcher's ability to decipher, deconstruct (Foucault, 1976) and reframe (Culler, 1988) it in terms of safer-sexual messages. Leach (1976) argues that 'we must know a lot about the cultural context, the setting of the stage, before we can even begin to decode the message' (p. 77) and similarly communicate with the members of that culture. Hawkes (1965) also argues that the full significance of any symbol cannot be perceived in isolation: it must be interpreted as a part of an integrated social context.

The social context of the inner-city gay subculture including the lack of social legitimation of the gay identity, the prevalence of HIV/AIDS-related deaths and other gay issues may influence (to varying degrees) the lives of many dance party patrons including their beliefs, behaviours, perceptions and use of communication symbols (including dress, body image and drugs). The terms 'identity', 'image' and 'stereotype' are used interchangeably or synonymously in this chapter. The perceptual masking effects of the external and internal stimuli (including thousands of intoxicated party patrons (Lansing, 1992)), continuous 'deafening' music and subdued stroboscopic illumination (Safe and Sager, 1990) may have also contributed to the emergence of non-verbal dance party symbols. The gay dance party argot may be used consciously or unconsciously by some party patrons to communicate sexual information (including a person's HIV serostatus) to a potential partner.

According to Goffman (1974), these non-verbal communication symbols, a covert language, often evolve among traditionally stigmatized groups, such as the inner-city gay subculture. The term 'stigma' is used in this book in accordance with Goffman's description of the 'deeply discrediting' attributes prescribed by the dominant culture to disqualify gay men from social legitimation. Many gay men were 'forced to form a secret system for interacting and for meeting people similar to themselves ... [and they] had to develop a private means of communication' (Goddard, 1992, p. 2) because of the risks of being discredited (Goffman), or worse incarcerated, for their sexual proclivities (Wotherspoon, 1991). A similar phenomenon may partly account for the development of a symbolic language among the gay party patrons.

The inner-city gay dance party subculture may provide many gay men with a homoempathic reality where they may safely use illicit psychoactive substances (Lansing, 1992), dance through the night (Safe and Sager, 1990) and negotiate sexual interactions with other men, by using a range of dance party communication symbols. Goodwin (1989) suggests that 'a subculture will develop an argot, a private method of communicating. ... [Moreover the] use of argot also serves as a means of mutual identification and helps foster subcultural cohesion' (p. XII). Berger and Luckmann (1975) suggest that symbolic language is determined by the reality of living and the insights that emerge from these experiences constantly transform the quality of existence and the meaning of these symbols. The reality of living for many inner-city gay dance party patrons may be undermined by their quality of existence, with its lack of social legitimation, and the stark reality of the growing number of HIV/AIDS-related deaths (including the constant reminder in obituaries in *The Gay Community's Newspaper: Sydney Star Observer*) among their subculture. Goddard (1992) comments on the prevalance and predominance of HIV/AIDS-related issues among the Australian gay subculture where it continues to be overwhelmingly 'a disease of gay men'.

'AIDS has become one more burden with which gay men must deal, one more source of stress making them turn to their subculture for support. Before getting that support ... they must be acculturated and learn the traditions of the gay world' (Goodwin, 1989, p. 85). The gay dance party institution may provide many gay men with a social support system where they may learn the norms, values, beliefs and reality of identifying as a gay man (coming to terms with their HIV serostatus, either positive or negative) during the most life-threatening period in gay history.

According to Goddard (1992), 'gay men who are ... HIV positive now need to learn the painful lessons of coming out for a second time' (p. 12). The dance party milieu may afford some of these HIV-seropositive gay men with the opportunity to come out in a socially supportive environment. Goodwin (1989) notes that 'AIDS is a great threat to gay men ... Rarely is anything as nearly universally anxiety provoking as AIDS has proved to be' (p. 82). The gay dance party institution is a unique multi-faceted social system (see Chapters Four, Five and Six) where gay dance party patrons, irrespective of their HIV status, may witness and celebrate the survival of themselves and their subculture.

'AIDS has brought new fears to the gay world. Not only do gay men fear disease and death; they also fear the rejection they face simply because AIDS is so closely associated in the public mind with homosexuality. The AIDS epidemic has caused some political set-backs for gay men and lesbians. It has made coming out more difficult than it has been for decades. In fact it has chased many gay men back into the closet' (Goodwin, 1989, pp. 80–1). Subcultures facing life-threatening crises tend to turn in on themselves (Zoja, 1989) or close their social boundaries (Hanna, 1987). They may develop new, or revive traditional rituals and mores to cope with their collective anxiety. As previously noted, these sociopsycho-logical reactions and resolutions to a life-threatening crisis have occurred across cultures and millennia (Eliade, 1956; Evans, 1988; Reanney, 1991).

Hanna (1987) suggests that groups or subcultures create identities and maintain their social boundaries by using symbols (including rituals, dance, music, intoxicants, body image and cloth-ing) already in existence or by producing new ones. Similarly, the inner-city gay dance party institution may afford many gay men with a social safety-valve where they can escape their everyday reality and dissipate their accumulated existential anxiety by using mind-altering drugs or dancing through the night to non-stop music with thousands of patrons in a similar state- and context-dependent condition. This alternative reality may serve an important socio-psychological function by offering some of these stigmatized party patrons a symbolic universe where their gay identity (including their

HIV serostatus) is authenticated or validated as a member of a significant subculture by contrast to their everyday lives.

The inner-city gay dance party institution appears to be a multi-faceted mnemonic with each facet corresponding to the norms, values, beliefs and behaviour of the gay party patrons. These facets may also determine the range of symbols used, the mode of communication, the meaning encoded and decoded, and the efficacy of such symbols to communicate meaning. The meaning may include vital information about the possible risk-status of subsequent sexual behaviour within the context of the dance party milieu. This information may assist the researcher in the development and implementation of future intervention programmes. Helman (1990) suggests that 'each symbol has a whole range of associations ... it tells them something about the values of their society. ... This [is] particularly important at times of danger or uncertainty – when people feel that their world is threatened by misfortune such as ... death ... or illness' (p. 194).

Rapoport (1965) suggests that symbols have played a significant role in the survival and development of humanity. The survival of some dance party patrons may also be determined by the efficacy of their communication symbols, particularly those used to determine the HIV serostatus of a potential sexual partner and the possible increased risk of HIV infection following the use of flawed or fragile sexual symbols. The main aim of this study was to investigate the range, form, mode, meaning, durability, or fragility of the respondents' communication symbols within the context of the dance parties and their relationship to possible increased risk of HIV/AIDS infection.

The following statements are verbatim quotations derived from the transcripts of the thirty-four respondents in this pilot investigation. They represent, as previously, the respondents' individual social construction of the inner-city dance party reality.

Drug-empathic set and setting

According to the respondents, their construction of reality or state-dependent cognition was transformed by their exposure to a variety of external and internal dance party symbols or stimuli, including continuous deafening music, elaborate subdued stroboscopic lighting shows and thousands of intoxicated party patrons.

The party patrons' cognitive processes may have also been impaired by their use of psychoactive substances, as Swanson and Kinsbourne (1979) found among a sample of amphetamine users. The respondents' data indicated that the external and internal stimuli, including music, subdued lighting and drugs, often masked their sensory modalities and communication channels (visual, auditory and verbal). Respondent 25 described the cognitive masking effects of some dance party symbols:

> In the dance party atmosphere it is sometimes difficult to make clear distinctions because the artificial stimuli . . . can blur your lines.

The combined interactive effects of these biopsychosocial dimensions may have confounded some party patrons' judgement about the deadly significance of the 'invisible' HIV/AIDS virus within the dance party context.

The meaning of dance party symbols

It was suggested by most of the respondents that the dance party milieu helped transform their homonegative reality by providing a symbolic 'homoempathic' universe. Respondent 3 described some of the social elements that underpinned the symbolic meaning of the dance party reality:

> The gay dance parties are to do with the pleasures of life, sex, drugs, partying, socializing with people regardless of their status (professional).

Leach (1976) noted that these forms of symbolic meaning were situationally specific and generally had little or no meaning outside a particular cultural milieu. The dance parties afforded the respondents a rare opportunity where their gay identity and lifestyle were positively reinforced and socially legitimized. Berger and Luckmann (1975) argued that a social identity emerges out of the dialectic between the individual and society. Respondent 30 described this dialectical phenomenon within the reality of the dance party milieu:

> It's a group identity ... a reinforcer of identity ... it's a large gathering of people at least of the same sexual persuasion.

Foucault (1976) noted that the dominant culture's repression of marginal groups was responsible for creating the stereotypic elements that defined a deviant identity. Paradoxically, this social oppression often provided the catalyst for reverse discourse culminating in social and political conflict. Respondent 20 suggested that some of the dance party symbols and their meanings were reappropriated homonegative symbols:

> The dance parties say ... you just come in here and we'll show you what deviants really are like ... it's a very gay thing. ... It's ... say[ing to] all the homophobics to everyone 'fuck you' for five or six hours ... and I'll do all the things that society says are not right ... I'm going to get myself so out of it I won't know where I am, I am going to fuck myself stupid and if I want to have unsafe sex I'll have unsafe sex ... and this is called 'deconstructive re-appropriation' which is the actual activist term ... where people call themselves 'queer' and you take the term of the enemy and reappropriate it and thereby deconstruct the symbol and make it yours.

Respondent 20's provocative statement appeared to reflect his accumulated and unresolved frustration of being an HIV-seropositive man and belonging to a traditionally stigmatized subculture. Sartre argued that 'we only become what we are by the radical and deep-seated refusal of that which others have made of us' (1977 edn, p. 15). A similar phenomenon may have unconsciously contributed to some inner-city gay dance party patrons' rebellious attitudes and risky sexual behaviour within the context of the dance party milieu.

Identity symbols

There was a wide range of dance party subgroup identity symbols, according to most of the respondents. Respondent 20 described the efficacy of these identity symbols in communicating information:

> The indicators are so apparent in Sydney you could certainly tell someone who was a regular say underground warehouse dance party person ... it's almost like a postcode. ... You can tell their sexual preferences too by their clothes, their bodies and their level of sophistication.

Respondent 15 supported the reliability and universality of these interpersonal dance party symbols:

> You can tell everything from their hair, makeup, how they walk, how they dance, who they talk to. ... Everything they do is an assessment of ... what sort of person they are.

These identity symbols were considered efficient media for the communication of subgroup membership within the context of the dance parties, according to some of the respondents.

Clothes

Clothing has traditionally been used as a short-hand symbol for the communication of social, political and economic information, including sexuality (Garber, 1992). Respondent 30 endorsed the contextual and historical specificity of clothing as symbols:

> Dance party clothes certainly do give a message. ... In the old days in the '70s there was this business of wearing a handkerchief which signaled your sexual preference. ... People don't do that any more.

Patton (1991) suggested that these communication symbols often become obsolete because 'people from certain subgroups become afraid to speak their native tongue when their "texts" – [such as] a red hanky ... [which they] thought private, suddenly come under ... scrutiny and become public, rendering the private language and symbols of the subculture vulnerable to ... readings by someone with greater social power' (p. 47). McDowell (1992) also maintained that sexual messages and clothing have traditionally been inextricably interwoven within specific locations. Respondent 2 described this sexual specificity of dance party clothing:

> There are sexual messages definitely. . . . Everyone tries to look their best in a very sexy sort of way . . . to attract sexual partners.

According to Respondent 13 some of these sexual symbols or argot were sufficiently transparent to be literally translated:

> Leather type of people are sending specific sexual messages about what they like sexually: S & M . . . with the predominance around their lunch around the groin.

Some of the respondents, however, considered clothing an unreliable transmitter of specific sexual information within the context of the dance party. Respondent 14 said

> It's difficult if not impossible to tell much about a person's sexual preference from their clothes.

Respondent 11 dismissed the concept of clothing as a reliable communication symbol:

> I don't think you can tell anything about a person from their clothes.

Respondent 20 also considered clothing a fragile or unreliable symbol:

> But sometimes clothes lie. . . . What they were wearing would be cosmetic compared to what they really were . . . it's hard to tell.

Respondent 25 suggested that the 'chameleon' characteristics of the dance party attire undermined its efficacy as a communication symbol:

> Clothing is not such a good guideline at the dance parties . . . you change yourself for that period of time . . . because you can blur the distinctions.

According to many of the respondents the growing number of similarly dressed male heterosexual party patrons had also eroded the reliability of the sexual information previously embedded in gay dance party clothing. McDowell (1992) suggested that clothing was no longer a reliable indicator of sexual identity because 'straight' men tend to emulate gay men in both behaviour and dress. Respondent 2 described this ambiguity at the dance parties:

> I don't think it's as clear cut as it used to be. .... Now you'll get straight boys who wear skimpy costumes. The gays set up a code of dress then the straight crowd followed it.

Most of the respondents used clothing to communicate sexual messages to a potential sexual partner, although they frequently questioned their efficacy. These ambiguities were concerning because some of the respondents suggested that they often determined their potential sexual partner and subsequent sexual behaviour in accordance with the information they derived from these fragile dance party symbols.

The face

The face was considered the most reliable mode of communication, particularly expressions around the eyes, according to the majority of respondents. It is 'the part of the body with which we perform the majority of our conscious interpersonal communications and which we are most skilled at "reading"' (Foster and McGrath, 1988, p. 54). Saint Augustine (1973, ed.) says that the face and eyes are universally used to communicate information and Cicero philosophized over 2000 years ago (55 BC) that the facial characteristics are the portrait of the mind and the eyes are its informers (Grant, 1979), or 'Imago animi vultus est, indices oculi' (Stevenson, 1967). Similarly, in 394 AD, St Jerome said 'Speculum mentis est facies et taciti oculi cordis fatentur arcana': the face is the mirror of the mind; and eyes, without speaking, confess the secrets of the heart (Collison and Collison, 1980). Most of the respondents considered the face and eyes reliable indicators of a person's character. Respondent 29 described this physiognomical interpretative process:

You're judged by your eyes and face ... you generally look at the eyes first.

Glover (1988) argues that 'we can read faces. ... We also interpret them. We can often tell what people are looking at, or even thinking about, and what their reaction or emotional state is' (pp. 71–2). Respondent 28 described some facial expressions that were used to communicate sexual information during the initial stages of inter-personal interactions:

> Sometimes you get the right look. ... You've got to catch someone's eyes and they catch yours ... then there's a bit more eye contact and one thing leads to another. ... You move closer together.

Ekman and Friesen (1975) also argued that facial expressions or characteristics (including the eyes) have been used universally as media of non-verbal communication. According to Magli (1990), the 'strongest meanings are to be found in the parts close to the eyes ... the forehead, the face ... all of man is in his face' (p. 93). Interest is intuited by pupil dilation, and drugs may have a significant impact on pupil dilation.

Body image

The body image (including its parts, shape, form, movements and fitness) was the most frequently used interpersonal sexual symbol, according to the respondents' data. Foster and McGrath (1988) argued that 'if we fail to understand how meanings for the body are constructed, then we shall remain strangers to ourselves' (p. 60). The human body communicates a wide range of information about an individual, including age, sex, self-regard, fitness and strength (Glover, 1988). Helman (1990) also noted that 'the human body has a *social* as well as a physical reality ... the shape, size and adornments of the body are ways of communicating information about its owner' (p. 12). Some of the respondents used their sculpted bodies as a mirror to reflect or communicate the type of person they preferred as a sexual partner. As described by Respondent 24:

> You can tell what sort of partner they would be ... that's the main reason most gay men work out ... [it] is the

desire to attract other desirable people ... and to look like them as much as possible. ... That's certainly why I did it.

Respondent 18 described the sexual specificity of some dance party symbols:

He was communicating sexual messages with his actual body movements.

Respondent 24 described some of the morphological characteristics he used to interpret information about other party patrons:

You can tell things ... by the look of their body or how they carry themselves. There's ... an attitude of walking ... they're emphasizing the body.

Gardner (1973) suggested that people used the human body as an instrument of symbolic communication because of its intimate familiarity and ontogenetic importance as a vehicle of communication. However, Respondent 20 described some of the limitations of using the human body as a communication symbol:

You can't really tell much from the way they look ... it's the new look, the masculine body, power.

Paradoxically, his data revealed that he imputed a significant subcultural meaning to the new gay dance party body symbol. Birdwhistell (1970) argued that the non-verbal (body) language was culturally determined behaviour which was communicated via form, movements and gestures. Respondent 4 described some of the social, political and psychological ideologies inherent in the recent trend among party patrons toward a healthy muscular body image:

All these muscles are saying we're healthy, we're strong ... and we're here to stay.

Helman (1990) also suggested that 'the human body is more than just a physical organism, fluctuating between health and illness. It is also the focus of a set of beliefs about its social and psychological significance, its structure and function' (p. 11). Many of the respondents attributed this recent emphasis on health, fitness and body-sculpting to the inner-city gay subculture's anxiety and fear of the HIV/AIDS pandemic and related issues. As described by Respondent 12:

> It was HIV and personal crises ... which moved gay men into more fitness and body building.

Respondent 27 also suggested that this new gay body symbol communicated a collective concern about the HIV/AIDS crisis:

> The new body-building drive is a reaction to the health crisis.

Respondent 31 suggested that many of the party patrons deliberately sculpted their body to shield 'magically' or insulate them from the detrimental effects of drug over-use and the HIV virus:

> This body fascism came out particularly after AIDS. ...
> They think the healthier body and looking after yourself
> will protect them from AIDS. ... It's bullshit because they
> ... take more drugs and because they look good they go
> out more ... and they're not healthier at all. ... It's
> paranoia about AIDS ... particularly in the last four years.

Many of the respondents were relying on this dangerously flawed symbol to evaluate the HIV serostatus of a potential sexual partner and whether or not they would have unprotected anal intercourse with him. Respondent 32 was concerned about the prevalence of these potentially life-threatening assumptions:

> A lot of these people are set in their ways. I suppose it is
> surprising how stupid they can be ... it's not as though
> their cocks glow purple in the dark when they get an
> erection if they are HIV-positive. ... It is not as though
> there are any signs. ... I admit I am guilty of thinking you
> are able to pick the person who's got HIV. ... There is no
> bell that rings in any way to say that you've just caught it.
> ... It is like a shadow, a silent thing that just passes
> through the back door and you don't pull your upfront
> conscious cognition, particular[ly] if you're on drugs.

Many of the respondents continued to use the body to interpret the HIV serostatus of a potential sexual partner even though they were aware of its fallaciousness, as described by Respondent 18:

> When you think of someone with AIDS it's the one who sticks out, bags under his eyes, blotches on the face ... the last stages before death ... more so than: they're an AIDS carrier and they look really healthy. ... Some people who are HIV-positive are going to the gym to disguise their condition ... and others to stay ahead of the disease. ... A lot of people would be deceived like that ... lots of people are still going on appearance.

Many of the respondents suggested that the lengthy asymptomatic phase of HIV infection, often lasting for many years, contributed to this life-threatening misinterpretation. As described by Respondent 24:

> If you look healthy [as though] there's nothing wrong with you, it's a deception ... a very big deception. ... We know with AIDS or HIV ... there's a long period involved. ... You can still be HIV and very healthy and you can still [body] build.

Similarly, some HIV-seropositive party patrons may have believed they had 'magically tricked' or transformed their HIV status by developing a healthy, muscular body. Respondent 17 appeared confident about using this schema to evaluate the HIV/AIDS serostatus of a person:

> It does say that a person is healthy and they don't have HIV. ... It's because you get so used to walking down the street and being able to pick someone that's HIV just by the look of them.

However, some of the respondents were extremely critical of gay men who intentionally disguised their seropositive status by developing a healthy body image. Respondent 7 described this phenomenon:

> Body building ... is a way of masking it. Just because they
> look healthy doesn't mean they haven't got HIV ... but I
> think some people may take the attitude that I am less
> likely to be suspected of having HIV if I look healthy.

Respondent 17 was not deceived by the face validity of the new gay
muscular body symbol:

> You might see that they have got a great body ... but I
> don't allow myself to presume that they are not HIV.

In summary, many of the respondents relied on information
about their potential sexual partner's HIV serostatus by 'reading'
their body images, even though they seriously doubted its validity.
Perhaps this confusion arose from the lack of other reliable and
visible symbols, or because a muscular body image communicates
an almost universal message of health and well-being.

The symbolic meaning of age and experience

The age and experience of party patrons communicated to
many of the respondents the possible increased likelihood of risky
sexual behaviour. Many of the 'older' respondents (in their late
twenties or older), believed that younger gay men (whom they saw
as 'inexperienced') were more likely to have engaged in risky sexual
and drug-related behaviour. Respondent 8 endorsed these general-
izations:

> The younger group of people [are] very inexperienced.
> They're the risk group for the HIV problem. ... People like
> me who are up the other end of the scale ... are mature
> and got it together.

Conversely, some of the younger respondents (in their early
twenties) attributed the current HIV/AIDS crisis to the promiscuous
behaviour of older gay men. Respondent 5 described this phenomenon:

> It would be the older crowd who came out when
> anonymous sex and promiscuity was big.

Perhaps some of the younger respondents believed they were insulated from the HIV/AIDS virus because they restricted their sexual relationships to men from a similar age group, who like themselves had 'come out' or self-identified as gay men after the discovery of the HIV/AIDS virus. However, this interpretation ignored the possibility of HIV/AIDS infection through intra-age group transmission.

The young are subjectively immortal, according to Reanney (1991), often oblivious to the inevitability of death (Evans, 1988). Respondent 26 described these widespread misconceptions among younger gay party patrons:

> A lot of younger people do relate older men to AIDS ...
> [they] thought there is no way a young gay guy could have
> AIDS or HIV. ... They're taking risks because they didn't
> realize that they could catch it from having sex with guys
> their own age.

Respondent 31 was concerned about some younger gay men's fallacious interpretation of their risky sexual behaviour and advocated a pragmatic educational intervention model:

> Younger gay guys should start reading the *Star Observer*'s
> death notices. ... Just look at the date of birth and the date
> of death.

However, Patton (1991) attributed this risky sexual behaviour among younger gay men to their lack of experience in negotiating safer-sexual guidelines. Many of the respondents suggested that the type of drugs used by party patrons signified their level of maturity or experience. Respondents 30 and 26, respectively, considered this typology a reliable indicator of the age and experience of a party patron. Respondent 30 said

> The drugs give you a signal about ... what they've
> experienced in their lives.

Respondent 26 said:

> You can tell ... a more experienced person would take
> MDA compared to a lot of the younger people who take
> Acid at the parties.

The overuse of drugs by younger party patrons often indicated anxiety problems, lack of social adjustment or unresolved psychological angst relating to their identity, according to many of the respondents. As described by Respondent 12:

> You can predict that for someone to take seven Ecstasies they are desperate to lose control . . . or they don't feel comfortable with themselves. . . . They're usually young or inexperienced . . . and want desperately to be accepted.

Some party patrons over-used drugs to help them cope with a recent HIV-seropositive diagnosis, according to Respondent 7 whose suggestion was supported by his personal experience as a dance party drug dealer:

> Some younger gay men are still taking six Ecstasies at a time. . . . I found out they were just recently diagnosed HIV-positive.

Respondent 13 also suggested that some people over-used drugs to help them escape problems in their everyday reality:

> If someone takes a lot of drugs . . . sometimes they're escaping reality. I do that myself.

However, Respondent 31 was concerned that many younger gay men were increasing their risks of HIV infection by excessively using consciousness-changing substances:

> I can get as messed as the best of them, but too much all the time removes you too much from reality. . . . Lots of young guys are losing control . . . and that's when they might do something unsafe.

Respondent 14 also cautioned against the over-use of psychoactive substances and the increased likelihood of risky sexual behaviour:

> That's when you might [be] caught off guard . . . [and] have unsafe sex. . . . You're more likely to do something you wouldn't do otherwise . . . sexually, and might put yourself at risk. . . . [If] they meet someone who is into screwing

around without a condom then that means their chances of being HIV infected are increased enormously.

Respondent 7 advocated the use of cognitive 'pre-programming' as a prophylactic against this increased risk of HIV/AIDS infection:

> It's a matter of personal control. . . . When I take drugs . . . I keep a little corner in my mind very straight . . . It says to me 'it's all right, it's just the drugs, so calm down'.

Kelley (1972) demonstrates that people tend to attribute other people's behaviour to internal causes (including personality traits, motives, intentions and maturational stages) whereas they attribute their own behaviour to external determinants (their social and physical world). Perhaps some of the respondents used this attribution process to reduce their anxiety and responsibility for the continuing HIV/AIDS crisis among their subculture. These self-serving biases may have also reflected some of the respondents' needs to rationalize or reduce the inconsistency or incongruency between their knowledge of safer-sexual guidelines and their risk-laden behaviour. These responses may have been biased by the respondents' efforts to 'look good' in the eyes of others, including the researcher (Greenberg *et al.*, 1982).

The straighter-than-straight gay identity symbol

Many of the respondents suggested that there was a growing trend among the inner-city gay dance party patrons to look and act 'straighter-than-straight'. Respondent 18 described this phenomenon:

> There's a whole new sort of gay . . . who's moving into the party scene . . . really straight-acting.

McDowell (1992) suggested that this new gay identity emerged during the last decade when 'the masculine boy became the new icon. Tough and hard with firm pectorals and tight muscles . . . the very antithesis of the pansy and the poofter. He was not effeminate' (p. 102).

Sociopolitical dimensions

Respondent 25 described the inherent sociopolitical message in this new 'straighter-than-straight' gay symbol:

> No longer do gays want to be seen as being wimpy or being able to be knocked around or even killed.

The widespread desirability of these masculine attributes were mirrored in the classified personal advertisements section of the inner-city gay media (such as the *Sydney Star Observer* and *Capital Q*) which were biased in favour of 'straight looking and acting' gay men. Evans (1988) also notes a similar trend among 'American gay men [where] the ideal fantasy lover is big, hard-faced and muscle-bound ... and otherwise "straight appearing" (a phrase that often turns up in the personal ads section of gay newspapers)' (p. 179).

Political reactions to stigmatized identity

Respondent 25 described one of the embedded political meanings in this new gay identity symbol:

> They want to be better ... than the straight community. ... They want to rise above it ... straighter than straight.

Evans (1988) argued that the new gay identity was a powerful social and political statement that communicated the gay subculture's rebellion against their stigmatized marginal status within the dominant culture. He said this new body-building trend represented 'the extreme lengths to which many American gay men now feel they have to go in order not to be taken for "sissies" ' (pp. 178–9). This new gay image may have similarly represented a rebellious reaction against the previous stigmatizing attributes of the effeminate gay stereotype among the inner-city gay subculture. Respondent 18 described the powerful political message embedded in this new gay body symbol:

> It's gay power to protect us from the straight men and to be more dominant over the straight men.

Goffman (1974) suggested that a 'stigma ... is really a special kind of relationship between attribute and stereotype. ... [It] is almost everywhere in our society discrediting' (p. 14), similar to the traditional stigma ascribed to gay men in Western cultures.

Stereotyping

Some of the respondents were indignant about the predominance of this stereotyping as a new gay 'ideal type'. Respondent 10 described the inherent message in this identity symbol:

> The body culture ... they perceive that they're personifying the image that gay men are supposed to be like.

According to most of the respondents, this new gay symbol had usurped the previous discredited gay stereotype and was being propagated by many inner-city gay institutions, including newspapers, magazines, saunas, gyms and dance parties. Respondent 20 described the prescriptive norms embodied in this new gay-regimented image:

> I work in the sauna industry and they've taken out everything that was related to the stereotypical leather man and come in with the new gay look of the 90's ... the muscle bound super steroid-taking bodies. ... Gay men who are into body culture are body fascist.

Respondent 24 endorsed the persuasiveness and pervasiveness of this new gay identity:

> There's posters ... at the dance parties now [that] are indicating that LOOK is a more ... they call it body fascism in the States ... and it's being presented as an ideal thing.

This apparently powerful gay symbol warrants serious consideration for its incorporation into future intervention programmes. Foster and McGrath (1988) noted that this symbol was used by many Western gay subcultures. They suggested that today 'the fantasy figures of the gay pinup revolve around "straight-looking" types' (p. 28). Respondent 24 suggested that the healthy muscular youthful gay identity was anathema to many of the HIV-seropositive gay men:

> It's not fair at all ... [to] my age group [who] are going
> through the crisis full-on. ... The majority of us don't
> really have the time to go to a gym ... let alone have the
> money. ... And it's being held up as being the gay ideal
> while our bodies are fading away ... it's pretty shocking.

Perhaps, this multi-faceted muscular 'straighter-than-straight'
image was the symbolic representation of the inner-city gay subculture's recent development and enfranchisement; or perhaps it
was a reaction to their stigmatized social status, accumulated fears
and anxieties about the prevalance of the HIV/AIDS virus and death
in their subculture. Wotherspoon (1991) noted that oppressive
social sanctions continued to exist even after the political legitimation of the gay identity in New South Wales.

However, some of the respondents suggested that some party
patrons may have 'tricked' themselves and others by relying on
flawed or unreliable dance party symbols to communicate information about the HIV serostatus of a potential sexual partner.

Reactions to homonegativity

Most of the respondents suggested that they had been stigmatized or oppressed to varying degrees by the dominant culture's
homonegative sanctions of their gay identity. The heavily biased
distribution of HIV diagnoses and related issues among the Western
gay subcultures legitimized these increased homonegative sanctions,
as Davenport-Hines (1990) notes. According to many of the respondents the new gay masculine body symbol was the antithesis of the
stereotypic prescription defined by the dominant culture. Respondent 20 provocatively interpreted the new gay muscular body within
the context of the dance party:

> So you want to oppress us? Here we are, we aren't hiding,
> we look the way we want to look and that's ... the way the
> gay people do [it] at the dance parties.

Evans (1988) argued that the 'upshot of this conformity is that a new
gay stereotype is being created that is almost a satire on masculinity.
Among such gay men there is often an extreme hostility to feminine-
identified men. ... The prevailing notion seems to be, "I may be gay
but at least I'm not a queen".' (p. 179). Perhaps some gay men felt

betrayed by these effeminate men because they symbolized or mirrored the dominant culture's stigmatizing stereotypical prescriptions of the gay identity. According to Respondent 8 the new gay symbol lacked sufficient potency to transform this stigmatized status:

> There's now the real gay image of the muscle men and still they call us queers.

Goffman (1974) notes that 'we use specific [derogatory] terms ... in our daily discourse as a source of metaphor and imagery, typically without giving thought to the original meaning' (p. 15). These discrediting homonegative definitions may have been internalized by some of the gay dance party patrons, undermining their self-esteem, pride in their identity and will to survive the AIDS virus. Evans (1988) suggests that many gay men have 'internalized homophobic values ... [and] the majority of American gay men were acutely anxiety-ridden about their masculinity' (p. 179). Much of the respondents' data indicated that the new gay symbol was designed to deconstruct their stigmatized gay identity and redress many gay men's low self-esteem. It appeared to help them counteract the destructive effects of their discredited or 'spoiled identity' (Goffman, 1974). Respondent 12 described some of the underlying psychophysiological dimensions of this recent gay metamorphosis:

> People put a lot of time and effort into their body ... it's not a pure assumption that they've got good self-esteem ... it could be the reverse.

However, this identity transformation may have increased levels of anxiety, stress and inter-group alienation, rather than reduced them, according to Goffman (1974). Evans (1988) describes the new 'compulsive body-building' trend among gay men as 'internalized homophobic values ... and so intense is their self-deprecation that they have fallen in love with the image of their worst homophobic oppressors' (p. 179). Some gay dance party patrons may have believed they had escaped their stigmatized identity and risk of HIV infection by emulating their oppressors – an identification with the oppressor.

The risk of losing gay identity

As suggested by most of the respondents, some gay dance party patrons developed muscular bodies so they could 'pass' as straight men and reap 'the great rewards in being considered normal: almost all persons who are in a position to pass will do so on some occasion by intent' (Goffman, 1974, p. 95). Respondent 18 described the advantages of passing between the social boundaries:

> I'll go back to where I was when I was a straight person except now I'm just sexual and I'm accepted in both worlds.

Many of the respondents personally identified with the new 'straighter-than-straight' gay identity symbol, although most of them were concerned about its degenerative effects on the social legitimation and future self-determination of the gay subculture. Respondent 25 suggested that this *normalizing* symbol masked the gay identity through the process of assimilation:

> Straight acting is exactly what it is . . . it involves them closing themselves in a box.

This new gay stereotypic symbol was similar to Hans Christian Andersen's story of 'The Emperor's New Clothes' in which the Emperor only exchanged one form of oppression for another (in this case, a similarly scantily-clothed one to the dance party patron). Most of the respondents indicated that many gay dance party patrons denied their stigmatized gay identity by 'passing' (Goffman, 1974) as straight men. Respondent 29 denied his association with the stigmatized gay stereotypic symbol:

> I'm not like other gay men as you can see . . . I'm very straight.

Goffman (1974) also suggested 'the more allied the individual is with normals, the more he will see himself in non-stigmatic terms, although there are contexts in which the opposite seems true' (p. 131). Perhaps, some of these gay men believed their new image 'magically' transformed their stigmatized identity by making their gay identity 'invisible'. Respondent 25 suggested that this new 'straighter-than-straight' image was a form of homonegativity:

> They're not accepting their homosexuality. . . . People are saying for whatever reason 'well I want to be straight again'.

According to Respondent 21 there were some dance party patrons who oscillated between denial of, and association with, the gay identity:

> By saying they're straight they can live within the straight world . . . and pass it off as some sort of sexual experience . . . but never have to admit that they're gay . . . because if they're gay then people will align them with AIDS and align them with all the negative things.

Respondent 29 described the delusory characteristics of this Janus-faced identity symbol:

> A guy I know . . . very well built, goes to the gym . . . the outside might look fine [but] he's HIV. . . . He sleeps with anything, has unsafe sex and blames it on the drugs . . . knowing full well that he is HIV . . . and he won't go for an AIDS test.

Similarly, Respondent 31 was critical of these life-threatening deceptions:

> They don't tell you about it unless you ask . . . it's very irresponsible. . . . If there's an intent it's usually [a] consensual act in reference to becoming a sexual act between two people who have taken drugs.

For some HIV-seropositive dance party patrons, it may have been easier to externalize the virus by attributing it to the gay identity (which they did not identify with) rather than to internalize the reality of it as a part of their personal identity. Some gay dance party patrons, according to many of the respondents, did not disclose their HIV serostatus because they feared the stigma, including rejection by a sexual partner. They may have also controlled this information because of the fear of being a pariah to their own subculture.

Respondent 27 described the condemnatory effects of self-identifying as an HIV-seropositive person:

> I do tend to be pretty upfront about my positive status although for a long time I wasn't. .... It's very difficult for people who are HIV-positive to be up front about it ... because it's like coming out all over again. .... It's like saying you've got leprosy.

Respondent 30 described the double-bind situation of disclosing his HIV status to a potential sexual partner:

> The first time you're going to go to bed with someone you don't tell them ... It's so difficult to say I'm HIV. It kills it ... it kills it ... and very often that's going to be the end of it anyway.

Thus, his double-bind becomes a 'double-blind':

> I recently met someone and we went to bed a couple of times and ... the subject came up like after the first week and ... he asked me straight out 'What's your HIV status?' and I told him I was positive and that was the last time he touched me. He was totally uninformed ... and totally hysterical about the whole thing.

Goffman (1974) suggests that a person who lives a double life 'also suffers from "in-deeper-ism"; that is, pressure to elaborate a lie further to prevent a given disclosure' (p. 105). Some of the respondents also appeared to be confused or ambivalent about disclosing information to the researcher related to their safe-sexual behaviour. There was a consistent pattern of initial denial of risky sexual behaviour usually followed by a reverse discourse which they generally rationalized in accordance with flawed information. Respondent 22 described this phenomenon:

> I haven't had unsafe sex since I was diagnosed, not to my knowledge ... well okay I've done things that are unsafe in terms of not using condoms but I've been very careful that no body fluids are exchanged. There have been a few isolated incidences that I've felt bad about afterwards ... I guess I don't practise a hundred per cent safe sex but I'm

careful not to exchange body fluids ... and especially not
from me to anybody else because I'm aware that I'm HIV
and that would play on my conscience ... and I don't want
to aid and abet the virus in any way.

Goffman (1974) suggested that even 'where an individual has quite
abnormal ... beliefs, he is likely to have quite normal concerns and
employ quite normal strategies in attempting to conceal those
abnormalities from others' (p. 156). Respondent 30 criticized the
irresponsibility of some party patrons' belief systems that were
constructed by denial of their reality:

There are a lot of people who are HIV infected and they
don't know ... who won't even go and have a test because
they're so heavily into denial of their sexuality let alone the
disease.

As suggested by many of the respondents this 'double-double-
identity' symbol may have increased the risk of HIV infection among
the dance party patrons. The gay activists' slogan 'Silence = Death'
appears to encapsulate the essence of this 'double-double-identity'
denial. The denial appeared to be sustained by four magical beliefs:
(1) the 'straighter-than-straight' persona provides a passport
between the dominant culture and the gay subculture, (2) the
healthy muscular body masks an HIV-positive status, (3) a person
may 'trick' themselves and a potential partner by their healthy
muscular appearance, and (4) they may 'trick' the AIDS virus,
including its degenerative effects and possible transmission.

Magical prophylactic qualities of the new gay identity symbol

Respondent 28 was committed to the prophylactic properties
of this new body armour:

It's a reaction against AIDS because I believe the healthier I
am, if I ever get exposed to the virus the more chance I
have of not getting it ... that's one of the reasons other
people do it.

Most of the respondents' data indicated that the new 'straighter-than-straight' muscular gay identity symbol was not only a form of denial of the gay identity, but it was also adopted by some party patrons to 'trick' the deadly AIDS virus. Respondent 27 described this self-deception:

> I think that people believe that the more robust they are the more resistant they are going to be to the virus. . . . So there's certainly a lot more emphasis on health and looking healthy as well.

Respondent 2 summarized the self-deluding ideology behind this fallacious belief system:

> They're saying 'I haven't got AIDS, I won't get AIDS, I'm too strong a person . . . I'm too powerful a person to come under this banner'.

Respondent 25 also described some of the rationalizations underlying this self-deception:

> They might escape the repression and AIDS by looking and acting straight . . . If you just be straight you won't get AIDS . . . 'cause straight guys don't get AIDS.

Some of the respondents' data indicated that there was a large contingent of dance party patrons who had sex with other men but denied their gay identity. They also suggested that some of these men believed they were 'tricking' the virus by self-identifying as heterosexual males. Similarly, Altman (1990) notes that 'there are large numbers of men having sex with other men . . . who don't self-identify as part of a gay community' (p. 56). Some of the respondents seemed to believe that they had 'magically tricked' the AIDS virus through sexual association with 'straight' men. Respondent 34 described this phenomenon:

> This is a personal exposure. . . . I like to have casual encounters with people that are completely withdrawn from the gay scene . . . mostly straight boys if possible, that is my preference. . . . But the straight boys . . . acted as though it [the AIDS virus] didn't affect them even though they were having unsafe gay sexual encounters.

Perhaps, one of the reasons he preferred 'straight' men was that 'straight guys don't get AIDS' (as Respondent 25 suggested). However, as he implied, this 'magical-thinking' may have increased, rather than decreased, his risk of HIV infection. Frazer (1976) defined these magical thoughts and actions as 'sympathetic magic whereby like [actions, objects or thoughts] produces like, or that an effect resembles its cause; and second, that things which have once been in contact with each other continue to act on each other at a distance' (p. 14). All these forms of magical thinking appeared to be embedded in the symbolic characteristics of the 'straighter-than-straight' identity symbol within the context of the inner-city gay dance party milieu.

Anonymous sex in backrooms

According to many of the respondents some party patrons had *en masse* anonymous sex in the unlit backrooms of the dance party venues, whilst under the influence of psychoactive substances. Respondent 27 described the cognitive distorting effects these transformed realities had on some participants' personal identity:

> In those backroom situations at the dance parties ...
> you've got a group of people who are on drugs ... and
> there's no lights ... with a lot of people around you. ... It
> gets a bit freaky, you feel like you're losing your identity in
> this mass of moving flesh ... and you lose touch with
> reality.

This blurring of individual boundaries between 'selfness' and 'self-lessness' in this anonymous sexual setting may have also reduced some party patrons' concept of personal responsibility for safe-sexual guidelines. One of the main motivating factors for participating in these backroom sexual venues was this sense of 'selflessness' or anonymity, as described by Respondent 13:

> I have seen a group of guys in the toilets with all the lights
> out ... basically it's very anonymous, that tends to be very
> important ... that gives them satisfaction as well.

Perhaps Respondent 13 was speaking from first-hand experience because 'seeing' in these unlit areas would have required extraordinary visual perception. Some of the respondents suggested that these anonymous settings provided some of the older party patrons with access to younger sexual partners. Respondent 20 described the disinhibiting effects of these anonymous sexual interactions:

> I have a wonderful time . . . in the toilets and a lot of people put it down by calling us all those AIDS-ridden old queens down there doing what they can't give up. It was mostly very young people . . . I felt so liberated . . . there were a lot of people who hadn't done it before.

However, these depersonalized anonymous sexual venues may have contributed to reduced interpersonal responsibility between potential sexual partners (as mentioned already), and increased their likelihood of HIV infection. Zimbardo (1969) found that anonymity or depersonalization diffuses personal responsibility for the consequences of one's actions. Individuals in an anonymous setting often demonstrate less self-control, diminished responsibility and impulsive risky behaviour (Diener, 1980).

Finally, some of the dance party patrons may have believed they had 'tricked' the AIDS virus by being 'invisible' or anonymous in the unlit backroom.

Conclusion

Symbols may be the basis of man's survival, as Rapaport (1965) suggests, but some party patrons may have increased their risk of contracting a life-threatening disease by depending too heavily on seriously flawed symbols, including the 'straighter-than-straight' gay identity symbol to access the HIV/AIDS serostatus of a potential sexual partner, and whether or not to have unprotected anal intercourse.

Three different core categories emerged from the respondents' data to describe the meanings, attitudes and belief systems attributed to the chameleon characteristics of this 'straighter-than-straight' gay identity symbol. Some patrons lived a double-identity to escape the stigma of the gay identity; others used a similar strategy to deny the dual stigma of the gay identity and its association with the HIV/AIDS crisis; whilst others adopted a 'double-double-identity' to reduce the discrediting characteristics of the gay identity, escape the stigma of being an HIV-seropositive man and the reality of this diagnosis. That is, some HIV-seropositive gay men may have been deceiving themselves by the prophylactic and antidotal qualities of their 'double-double-identities'. After all, the AIDS virus is invisible to the *host* and the *audience*, as there is usually a long asymptomatic stage during which there are no apparent changes to the physical organism.

The data indicated that the respondents' memory functions, including recall and decoding of safer-sexual guidelines were impaired by a diverse range of external and internal symbols (including loud music, subdued lighting, unlit areas and use of consciousness-changing substances), within the context of the dance parties. This was consistent with the findings of Jenkins (1974) among a sample of amphetamine users who were exposed to similar cognitive-masking stimuli. These state- and context-dependent cognitive inhibitors emphasized the importance and development of non-verbal communication symbols, such as clothing, face, eyes and body image.

It is imperative to administer the safer-sexual educational intervention programmes whilst dance party patrons are in an altered state of cognition or consciousness to control for possible state-dependent learning deficits. According to Goddard (1992), research in this area 'is essential to assist planning future campaigns in preventative education ... [because] the overwhelming majority of new HIV diagnoses [and probably new seroconversions] are due to homosexual transmission' (p. 12). Dance party argot or symbols, such as the muscular body, should be incorporated or submerged in the safer-sexual intervention model to increase its efficacy. This bonding process should help to strengthen the association between the muscular body symbol (complete with penile erection), condom use, and the eroticism of this combination. Further, these safer-sexual stimuli would be powerfully reinforced by the universal association of the male body with male sexuality. The main objective of the educational programme would be to cue previously encoded safe-sexual information. These intervention programmes are important because one of the main ideological tenets of the dance party milieu is 'escaping from everyday reality': where the meaning of safer-sexual behaviour is learnt. Whilst these two dynamics would appear to be polarized, bonded together they may provide a powerful medium for the communication of safe-sexual intervention information within this social context.

Chapter nine

Conclusions and Suggestions for Future Research and Intervention Programmes

We hate the thing we fear, the thing we know may be true and may have a certain affinity with ourselves, for each man hates himself. ... To overcome hatred is to take a step towards self-knowledge, self-mastery, self-justification and consequently towards an end of suffering.

Cesare Pavese (as quoted in Davenport – Hines, 1990)

And ye shall know the truth, and the truth shall make you free.

St John 8:32

Limitations

BEFORE summarizing the findings of this qualitative and ethnographic research it is important to acknowledge the limitations of this non-random sample of sixty-three gay men and the pilot nature of this investigation. Although it is clear from the data that unsafe sexual behaviour does occur at the dance parties, no conclusion can be drawn about the prevalence or generalizability of this risky behaviour in the larger gay subculture or the recreational drug-using dance party population. Thus, the dance parties cannot be held responsible for possible risky sexual behaviour when it may be a minority of people using drugs. The data may also be restricted by some unknown or unanticipated biases in respondents' inclusions, although attempts were made to avoid biases by selecting evidence from a variety of sources. Douglas (1986) suggests that 'people whose perception is being studied are living in a world constructed from their own concepts' (p. 26) which they may or may not choose to disclose totally. Future research needs to be conducted among a more representative sample of recreational drug-using gay dance party patrons to evaluate the possible magnitude of this risk-laden behaviour, and the strength of the attitudes and belief systems that may sustain it.

Glaser and Strauss's Grounded Theory (1967) model proved to be the 'best-fit' for this pilot study as it had the flexibility and robustness to allow the researcher to experiment and generate a variety of innovative methods, concepts, categories, theory and analyses to help in the formulation of possible hypotheses for future research and subsequent intervention models. According to Moore (1992), this 'ethnographic method has the potential to answer many important questions within the alcohol and other drug field by providing access to those drug users who are "invisible" ' (p. 322). The data and analyses in this qualitative investigation also took into consideration Durkheim's (1954) suggestion that people's perception or world-view emerges directly out of their social experiences and usually mirrors the norms and values of their social groups.

The significance of the respondents' data should not be ignored, both because of their considerable number of actual sexual encounters, and the consistent and concurrent supportive evidence in the gay media and other sources. For example, the pre-Mardi Gras cartoon 'Living with Adam' (Figure 3) in *The Sydney Star Observer* (a bi-monthly gay newspaper) graphically supports the familiarity and significance of these findings (including the unlit backrooms, set and setting, drug use and sexual behaviour) among the Sydney gay subculture. After all, a cultural joke or comedy is generally not meaningful to its audience unless it is common knowledge.

Although there is an abundance of research and literature concerning the association between substance use and risky sexual practices in similar gay samples (Butt, 1989; Gold, 1989; Stall and Ostrow, 1989) there appears to be no previous research on the inner-city gay dance parties, party drugs and increased risk of HIV infection. This pilot study attempted to examine the sociopsychological and political dimensions that contributed to the evolution of the inner-city gay dance party institution and place it in its HIV/AIDS and drug-related context. Several core categories and their properties emerged from the data to describe these phenomena. They include, the dance party milieu, its evolution, set and setting, meanings and functions, and their relationship to patrons' belief systems, attitudes and possibility of increased risky sexual behaviour within this context.

Evolution of the dance party institution

The findings suggest that the rapid growth of the inner-Sydney gay dance party institution (including Mardi Gras, Sleaze Ball and other parties) mirrored the social and political evolution of its subculture. The first Mardi Gras Parade in 1978 announced the inception of the inner-Sydney gay subculture and its members' growing dissatisfaction with their lack of social and political enfranchisement. Although a well-established covert gay community with a wide range of social institutions existed prior to this significant social and political watershed (Wotherspoon, 1991) it took another three years after the inaugural Mardi Gras demonstration for the partial legitimation of the gay subcultural identity with the enactment of the anti-discrimination law (in 1982). This major political victory provided the catalyst for the development of an independent gay subculture. It was now permitted to lease a public venue (the Hordern Pavilion) from the local authorities to launch their first

Figure 9.1: reprinted by permission of Jeff Allan

Mardi Gras Party in 1982 to celebrate this semi-legitimation. The acquisition of this major public venue helped accelerate the development of the gay subculture and its 'coming of age' with the decriminalization of homosexuality in New South Wales in 1984. Many informed gay entrepreneurs capitalized on this previously closeted population (Wotherspoon, 1991) by organizing gay-oriented dance parties at the Hordern Pavilion on an almost weekly basis for crowds often in excess of 7000 patrons.

The dismantling of the large-scale private dance parties at the Hordern Pavilion

Ironically, the unprecedented popularity of these privately organized parties at the Hordern Pavilion contributed to the termination of their leasing arrangements in late 1990. The findings suggest that two major social factors contributed to this situation. First, there was a strong residential lobby for their prohibition on the basis of public inconvenience and noise pollution; and a large contingent of homonegative heterosexuals (from the outer Sydney suburbs) threatened to overwhelm the homogeneity of these gay social events. To avoid these negative social forces many of the gay party patrons opted for smaller gay-oriented underground dance parties usually held in inner-city warehouses or sports stadiums.

Functions of the dance party institution

The data reveal that this inner-city gay dance party phenomenon is an important multi-dimensional institution for a significant number of mainly younger gay men and their subculture. It provides some party patrons with a gateway or initiation into the gay subculture where they may experience positive social and sexual reinforcement for their gay identity without the customary condemnation of the dominant culture. These 'homoempathic' environments positively reinforce or validate their patrons' lifestyle, contrasting with their stigmatized everyday realities. The findings also indicate that the dance party institution serves a similar function to the traditional family or a religious institution for its members. This institutional socialization similarly provides its patrons with a subgroup identity, friendship network, belief system, reality and ritualized behaviour, including the use of consciousness-changing stimuli. The dance party institution helps many of the patrons cope with the stress embedded in their everyday reality, such as the fear of HIV/AIDS infection, the loss of a significant other or a recent HIV-seropositive diagnosis.

Reaction to HIV/AIDS crises

It is rare in contemporary Western cultures for large numbers of people, the size of the gay subculture, to face the possibility of premature death from an incurable disease. However, there are many similarities between the gay subculture's life-affirming responses (including the dance party institution) to the HIV/AIDS pandemic and reported behaviour among other populations facing life-threatening crises (Douglas, 1986; Helman, 1990; Zoja, 1989), particularly when established medical and religious paradigms fail to provide an effective cure for deadly diseases (Evans, 1988; Frankl, 1984; Helman, 1990; Nohl, 1971; Reanney, 1991; Zoja, 1989). These responses include similar survival media, symbols, rituals, music, theatre, art, dance, costume and the use of consciousness-changing substances to help participants escape everyday reality. It is difficult to conceptualize or communicate what psychological impact the HIV/AIDS pandemic has had on this traditionally stigmatized gay subculture since the first diagnosis in Australia in 1982. Many of these gay men face HIV/AIDS-related hardships (including their own or a significant other's premature death) often without support from their family of origin, or many social support systems within the dominant culture. According to the findings, this major social institution appears to be the main sociopsychological buffer or safety-valve for a considerable subgroup of gay men who have been immersed in one of the most existentially and scientifically distressing periods in recent history.

The risk-related properties of dance party symbols and belief systems

According to Douglas (1986), 'disastrous processes with casualties mounting by hundreds or thousands over the years, produce different profiles of risk characteristics' (p. 25) similar to risk-related properties that emerge from the core categories in this investigation. They include seriously flawed symbols, fallacious belief systems and desensitization to the safer-sexual guidelines within the context of the inner-city gay dance party milieu. Many of these properties are premised on 'magical thinking' relating to their prophylactic qualities against the AIDS virus. As the findings reveal, these flawed belief systems and symbols emerge out of a unique set of interrelated aetiological social and political factors. They include the gay subculture's struggle to survive the growing devaluation or stigmatization of their gay identity since the reality of the HIV/AIDS pandemic (Davenport-Hines, 1990). This concept of survival is implicitly communicated in the incredible growth and high public profile of the Mardi Gras Festival, the gay subculture, the dance party institution, its rituals and argot and the new gay identity symbol of the muscular 'straighter- than-straight' *acting* gay man. Douglas (1991) notes that the body has also been used as a medium of communication by other cultures confronting similar life-threatening crises. Paradoxically, this important 'straighter-than-straight' identity symbol has only surface validity when used to assess the HIV status of potential sexual partners, according to the respondents' data. The data also indicate that the face, particularly the area around the eyes, is a reliable non-verbal interpersonal communication symbol within the set and setting of the dance party milieu. This finding may have important implications for future safer-sexual educational models.

The paradoxical meaning of 'straight-acting' as an identity symbol

As Pronger (1992) notes, the style or argot of the gay sub-culture grows out of its 'experience of the paradox, the deep intuition of gender as a form, and of passing [sic], the conscious appropriation of forms for the sake of survival' (p. 228). The findings suggest that the gay subculture and its identity symbols reflect and absorb the paradoxical characteristics of their marginalized status. Ironically, the findings also reveal these symbols are also saturated with the concept of survival. The 'contradictory realities' of the gay subculture's social and political status are embedded in the meaning of the new muscular gay symbol. It is, paradoxically, the most powerful symbol of the dominant culture or their oppressors: the male body. One only has to be in the company of a gay friend or friends at a predominately heterosexual gathering to appreciate the potential social discomfort from these incongruities. The data also suggest that some gay men's self-esteem is sufficiently undermined by this lack of social acceptability that they are willing to mirror their oppressors' image to escape this unrelenting stigma. Simpson (1992) said 'By definition no self-identifying SA [Straight Acting] is truly happy with their sexuality, confident about who and what they are – otherwise they would not be so driven to define themselves in terms of what they're not – non-camp, not effeminate' (p. 50). Callaghan (1993) argues that 'gay men subconsciously hunger for ... heterosexual approval ... the popularity of ... "straight acting" ... represents the greatest homosexual cringe of all ... It implies that only heterosexual men are truly masculine, and that butch gay men are simply "acting" that way' (p. 49). The data demonstrate that some gay men are prepared to risk their lives, rather than risk losing their self-delusions as personified in this 'straighter-than-straight' image. Similarly, Pronger (1992) found that these chameleon characteristics are adopted by 'gay men, in order to survive, [whereby they] become keenly aware of how to behave in different circumstances. This is at the heart of passing and the fluidity of the gay world' (p. 219). The new gay identity symbol appears to have a 'miraculous' ideological underpinning similar to the Christian doctrine of salvation through the body of Christ, whereby you 'change your body and change your life! ... and these images have an irresistible appeal to some gay men, who have spent most of their lives treated as sexual outcasts, as second rate specimens of masculinity' (Callaghan, 1993, p. 50). This new masculine gay identity symbol and the effeminate 'limp-wristed' stereotype share similar disempowering characteristics, and are flip-sides of the same coin: the former emulates the *power* of their oppressors, whilst the latter is defined in terms of its opposite: *powerlessness*. These discrediting characteristics of the effeminate stereotype may be literally translated as being less than 'real' men.

Internalized homophobia and loss of social identity

The findings reveal these two gay identity symbols (effeminate and 'straighter-than-straight') may lead to self-hatred, internalized homophobia, self-destructive behaviour (including risky sexual and drug-related behaviour), similar to the subcultural genocide of the Aboriginal Australian (Lewis, 1992), and many other cultures facing life-threatening crises (Fanon, 1977; Helman, 1990; Sartre, 1977; Zoja, 1989). In support of this finding Evans (1988) states that 'many gay men have also internalized homophobic values. ... So intense is their self-deprecation that they have fallen in love with the image of their worst homophobic oppressors. ... Anxiety-ridden about their masculinity and driven by eroticized self-hatred' (p. 179).

Pronger (1992) argues that 'for a man to behave effeminately is an expression of [this] paradox ... such gestures are violations of masculinity, insults to the meaning of manhood. This is why they are met with such contempt by so many, including many gay men who long for the power of patriarchy' (p. 221). Similarly, heterosexual men 'find themselves in a double bind: they are sexually attracted to a class of humans whom they also believe are inferior': women (Evans, 1988, p. 179). As these findings suggest, the new straight-acting identity symbol creates, absorbs and reflects a multitude of paradoxes within the gay subcultures, because it 'is' what it is not: heterosexual.

Drugs used as a medium of control

Many of the party patrons intentionally used drugs to transform or control their internal moods or external environments, as previously reported (Beck *et al.*, 1989; Newcombe, 1992; Solowij *et al.*, 1992). These findings also indicate that this potentially life-threatening concept of control has its origin in some party patrons' ability to sculpt their bodies into a muscular masculine form and manipulate their mind and environment by the use of drugs. The party drugs, including the drug Ecstasy, are attributed similar 'magical-controlling' qualities to the new 'straighter-than-straight' gay identity symbol. The combination of these two 'magical' media reinforces some straight-acting patrons' beliefs in their prophylactic qualities against both the homonegative patriarchal system and the AIDS virus.

Drugs' magical medium of escape

The data also suggest that Ecstasy retains its popularity among party patrons because it helps them develop an alternative reality where they may feel good, have fun and escape their everyday responsibilities, as Solowij *et al.* (1992) also found. Its arrival around 1984–5 (Chesher, 1990; Solowij *et al.*, 1992) coincided with the gay subculture's growing awareness of their newly acquired political enfranchisement and the impact of the HIV/AIDS pandemic.

Paradoxically, the data indicate that these reality-transforming illusions may contribute to increased risky sexual and drug-related behaviour within the context of the dance party and recovery party venues.

Inherent risks of loss of control

Ironically, these fallacious beliefs often lead to *loss* of control and possible increased risk of HIV infection. Solowij *et al.* (1992) found that 'twenty-eight percent of the[ir] sample admitted to having experienced problems related to their use of Ecstasy ... [including] loss of reality [and] loss of control' (p. 1170). Specific drugs are often used or discarded in accordance with their controlling attributes. According to the findings, being out of control, 'out of it' or 'messy' is negatively sanctioned behaviour among the gay dance party patrons because of its association with risky behaviour. According to the data the highly valued attributes of the drug Ice were far outweighed by potentially dangerous biochemical effects, that may have resulted in unpredictable or unstable behaviour such as loss of discrimination or judgement, possible compulsive-obsessive sexual behaviour, episodic dependency on the drugs and increased risky sexual behaviour. These findings are supported by previous findings among Ice-using populations in the USA (DEA, 1989; Miller and Tomas, 1989).

The meteoric rise and fall in popularity of Ice among the party patrons was mainly due to its 'consciousness-controlling' capacity. Previous research also found that people often used recreational drugs to control their minds and bodies but ironically, consciously or unconsciously, abdicated responsibility for their subsequent behaviour by using often unreliable (sometimes toxic), illegal substances (Beck *et al.*, 1989; Newcombe, 1992; Solowij *et al.*, 1992). This concept of control should be one of the key symbols to emphasize in future safe sexual intervention programmes.

Magical paradoxical realities

The findings suggest that 'magical-thinking' is an important determinant of risky sexual and drug-related behaviour within the dance party milieu. Similarly, many Australian Aboriginals (also a stigmatized minority) use alcohol, another significant patriarchal symbol, as their 'sympathetic magic' medium for the transformation of their status to adult white male. For example, 'A Pintupi man from Central Australia was reported to say "Citizens we are now. We can drink liquor." A Yalata (South Australia) person was also reported as saying "when I drink I'm like a white fella" ' (Lewis, 1992, p. 161). Douglas (1986) describes these ideologies or beliefs as 'so-called laws of magic [whereby] the magician can change events either by mimetic [or sympathetic] action [or symbols] or by allowing contagious forces to work' (p. 23).

The Gay Activist's terms for this magical-transformation are 'deconstruction' and 're-appropriation' (Bad Object-Choices, 1991). As Simpson (1992) suggests, they take over the symbols of their oppressors or cultural images and make them their own. These ambiguous or incongruent meanings are embodied in, and determined by, the self-destructive characteristics of the 'straight-acting' gay identity symbol. Ironically, this phenomenon is also reflected in the epidemiology of HIV with its invisible deconstruction and re-appropriation or cellular invasion of the immune system or human body.

The magical meaning of the gay identity symbol

The contradictory realities of the virus also contribute to the increased likelihood of self-delusion or 'magical' belief systems (Simpson, 1992). Many HIV-seropositive gay men continue to sculpt a muscular healthy body image during the often lengthy asymptomatic phase, thus possibly 'tricking' themselves or a potential sexual partner into believing they are not infectious. This denial or delusion helps reduce the accumulated life-threatening incongruencies of living with a possibly terminal disease.

Previous research supports the presence of this unconscious response among similar populations facing life-threatening crises, such as chronic illness, terminal diseases, plagues (Helman, 1990) and natural disasters (Douglas, 1986, 1991). It provides the individual or group with a psychological buffer against the life-effacing effects of being daily confronted with the reality of premature death.

The new 'straighter-than-straight' gay identity symbol is also undermined by its 'magical' prophylactic qualities against the AIDS virus, because the data suggest that 'straight men don't get AIDS'. This powerful male social 'myth' is also imbued with concepts of longevity and youthfulness which provide little, or no, guidance, or assistance to the large number of gay men facing premature death. To the contrary this powerful symbol is charged with dangerously flawed meanings of immunity or immortality in the context of the HIV/AIDS pandemic, as the data indicate. These findings are supported by a wide range of literature (Evans, 1988; Douglas, 1986; Helman, 1990; Reanney, 1991).

The magical prophylactic qualities of age

The data indicate that most of the party patrons are gay adolescents or young adults, with the majority in their twenties to early thirties. Some of these party patrons believe their age magically shields them from HIV infection because they 'came out' after the AIDS virus was inherently embedded in the gay subcultural identity. Linn *et al.* (1989) found that this age-related risky behaviour was mainly due to their lack of experience in safer-sexual negotiations. Future safe-sexual intervention programmes need to educate younger party patrons in negotiation or communication skills to control for their inexperience.

A magical passport between the two realities

However, the data suggest that this dual identity symbol provides some men with an anonymous 'passport' into the inner-city gay dance party milieu (including the use of illegal substances and sexual activity with other men) without responsibility to, or identification with, the gay subculture, thereby increasing the likelihood of HIV transmission.

Simpson (1992), a gay media spokesperson, also describes the paradoxical meanings inherent in the new straight-acting identity symbol. He argues that 'It is not always just a reaction to stereotypes and stigma, but often represents a desire to "pass", to be taken for a heterosexual; the spirit of the closet' (p. 48). This desire to 'pass' may even be compounded by the additional stigma of HIV infection on top of homosexuality. Pronger (1992) again notes, that 'gay muscles ... are the lie that tells the truth ... ' (pp. 275–6). This metamorphic identity symbol is compromised by its lack of identity-integrity to the dominant culture, the gay subculture or the person himself: as he does not identify with any of these social categories.

Magical qualities of the anonymous sexual venues

According to the findings the *unlit* sexual venues or back-rooms at the dance parties also afford some men an anonymous cover or 'closet' to disappear into and invisibly participate in casual sexual interactions with other men without responsibility to the gay identity or subculture. However, Douglas (1986) points out that the 'more isolated [or anonymous] a person ... [is] the less his decisions are subject to public scrutiny, and the more he sets his own norms of reasonable risk' (p. 69). The findings reveal that this measure of 'reasonable risk' is often determined by the degree of identification these straight-acting men have with the gay identity and possible risk of HIV infection.

Some of these men are self-deluded by the 'magical' qualities of the unlit environment where they are able to avoid the stigma of the gay identity and the constant emphasis on safer sexual behaviour. The cruel irony of this 'magical thinking' is that they cannot hide from the invisible virus, HIV: it does not disappear when the lights are out, nor does it discriminate according to a person's sexual identity. As Altman (1991) has commented, 'there is nothing inherently homosexual about a virus ...' (p. 12). It 'is a lethal disease that attacks *people*, regardless of age, colour, sex, sexual orientation, or any other variable; the virus does not discriminate' (p. 84).

These anonymous unlit sexual venues may also provide mixing and possible increased transmission of HIV/AIDS between age groups, according to the data.

The incongruency between knowledge and risky behaviour

The data reveal a multitude of potentially dangerous incongruities between the respondents' knowledge of safe-sexual guidelines and their risky behaviour following their use of psychoactive substances at the dance parties or later at the recovery parties held at various gay venues (such as bars, nightclubs, saunas and private homes). Seigel *et al.* (1989) suggest that 'many homosexual men continue to engage in risky sexual behaviour, despite their high levels of awareness concerning which sexual practices carry the greatest risk of transmission' (p. 561). The respondents appeared to be deeply concerned about this incongruity and its potential dangers when discussing it later with the researcher. This memory deficit may be partly explained in terms of state-dependent learning theory whereby an intoxicated person may have difficulty in recalling the significance of information previously encoded when sober. Conversely, individuals who learnt whilst intoxicated report similar cognitive impairment when sober (Haaga, 1989; Lowe, 1988). However, there is no significant difference between the two groups' ability to recall information as long as they are in the same cognitive state as when the information was encoded (Eich *et al.*, 1975; Eich, 1977; Jenkins, 1974).

The similarities between these two learning situations are important factors to consider in future safer-sexual and drug-related educational intervention programmes among the dance party patrons. Supporting this, Douglas (1986) also argues 'in the case of human memory what is stored and retrievable depends on control of attention, and since attention depends on social signals and social pressures ... [the analyst needs to focus] on the individual's coding of social experiences' (pp. 30–31). Previous safe-sexual and drug-related educational programmes among drug users appear to overlook or ignore the possible serious public health implications of these confounding effects. The efficacy of future intervention programmes may be improved by educating the target population in both state-dependent conditions, within the context of the possible risk-related behaviours.

Confounding cognitive effects of external or context-dependent stimuli

As the findings suggest, the drugs and the congruent environment (including the loud music and the subdued fantasy-lighting) also distort or confound some party patrons' perception of sexual and drug-related risk. These state-, mood- or context-dependent learning impairments may be conditioned by: previous positive associations, intentions, beliefs (Stall *et al.*, 1986) or mind-set prior to use (Beck *et al.*, 1989; Stevens, 1988; Zoja, 1989). They may intentionally use drugs, attend the parties (or recovery parties) and participate in sexual activity to help them feel good and forget the pain and fear of their stigmatized identity and the omnipresent HIV/AIDS pandemic. These powerful belief systems appear to become ritualized or conditioned over time by the positive effects of the external and internal stimuli (including the context, atmosphere, lighting, music, sexual activity and drugs).

Low self-esteem and increased risky behaviour

Sullivan *et al.* (1986) report that deficient self-esteem is 'a source of pain, often imperceptible but not negligible, in a person's life. Relief from this pervasive pain is often sought, consciously or unconsciously, in the analgesic state induced by drug use' (p. 93). Two significant interrelated factors, self-esteem and control, consistently emerge from the data to describe the psychotherapeutic effects of the dance party institution. These dimensions also reflect the party patrons' need for social legitimation and the effects of a spoilt or stigmatized identity, according to Goffman (1974). As Pronger (1992) agrees 'it is true there are many "sad homosexuals"; a history of oppression is not easily eradicated' (p. 229). Callaghan has noted (1993) that the need for approval among some gay men is 'so great that they are willing to . . . fry their livers with steroids – and sacrifice a long, healthy life – in the interests of inflating their bodies for just one more dance party' (p. 50).

Giblin *et al.* (1988) also found that self-esteem and control were important determinants of a stable self-concept and a person's capacity to deal with a stressful reality, among a similar sample of adolescent drug users. The data disclose that the transformational media of the dance party milieu also boost the depleted self-esteem of many gay patrons by contrast to their disempowered everyday lifestyle.

Paradoxically, the findings also suggest that this need to 'feel okay' by using artificial forms of control (such as intoxicating substances) often distorted many of the respondents' perception of risk within the 'other-worldliness' of the dance party and post-party venues. However, previous research shows that individuals make closer approximations of risky behaviour when immersed in their everyday reality (Green, 1980; Green and Brown, 1981). They were more likely to overestimate the risk of rare events and underestimate common or familiar events (Harvey, 1979; Slovic *et al.*, 1979, 1981).

Lalonde (1974) also found that most people tend to evaluate the outcome of a risky situation more optimistically when they are involved. On their own these previous findings are cause for concern, but when they are associated with the use of psychoactive substances and possible risk of HIV infection, as in this preliminary study, they become potentially dangerous self-delusions or belief systems.

Low self-esteem and self-destructive behaviour

Garnefski *et al.* (1992) found 'low self-esteem and the use of drugs were particularly strongly related to suicidal thoughts and behaviour' (p. 189). Although there is a growing number of investigations into the association between low self-esteem, destructive behaviour and the use of psychoactive substances in relatively young drug-using subpopulations (Dembo et al., 1989; Fenley and Williams, 1991; Slap et al., 1991; Uribe and Ostrov, 1989), there appears to be little research in this area among gay populations. According to Evans (1988), many gay men have 'internalized homophobic values [and] . . . display intense self-hatred' (p. 179). This self-hatred or homophobia often has its origin in a lifetime of gay-aversive conditioning which is usually reinforced through the primary agents of culture, religion, family of origin and peers. They are also constantly exposed to homonegative messages via other socializing media, such as, communication networks, education, entertainment and employment. Several studies suggest an association between the number of stressful life-events and a history of self-destructive ideations and behaviours (Garnefski et al., 1992; Smith and Crawford, 1986). Douglas (1986) argues that when 'uncertainty is at a very high level and everyone is taking big risks, the cultural norms will encourage more risk-seeking' (p. 75), as the findings also suggest.

Gay-oriented contexts reduce ambiguities

The data also suggest that the closed social boundaries of less ambiguous gay social contexts often distort patrons' perception by engendering a false sense of security (Ringdal, 1991) or immunity from the AIDS virus particularly following their use of psychoactive substances within these eroticizing contexts. However, these disinhibiting or liberating media provide an important safety valve for the dissipation of some party patrons' accumulated stress, frustration, aggression and pain, and from being daily immersed in a homonegative and life-threatening HIV/AIDS reality. Sartre (1977) warns that if 'this suppressed fury fails to find an outlet, it turns in a vacuum and devastates the oppressed creatures themselves. In order to free themselves they [may] even massacre each other' (p. 16). Perhaps, a similar phenomenon accounts for some gay party patrons' risky drug-related and sexual behaviour: that is, this potentially deadly combination may correlate with an unconscious or conscious self-destructive ideation which has its causal pathway in their double-stigma of a discredited identity or lifestyle and their HIV-seropositive status (within the dominant culture and the gay subculture).

Post-party or recovery party venues and possible risk-related behaviour

As the data indicate, many party patrons attend these venues at the conclusion of a dance party for a variety of reasons. These gay recovery parties systematically filter the heterogeneous or heterosexual male composition out of the original dance party population refining it to a less ambiguous environment for their gay patrons. This funnelling process reinforces gay subcultural boundaries, cohesiveness, solidarity, congruency, pride or self-esteem and identity-affirmation. It also reduces the impact or trauma of being confronted with the sober reality of their everyday lives by providing smaller homoempathic venues where patrons may continue to use drugs and participate in backroom sexual activity. These post-party venues are often located in, or adjacent to, the inner-Sydney gay business district and everyday reality.

The data indicate that some of the party patrons use more drugs (particularly alcohol) to help them come down off their hyperstimulated condition or to 'trick' their consciousness into a sober state, although in reality they are still intoxicated, as Hall and Hando (1993) also found among young drug users in Sydney.

The findings suggest that the less ambiguous or more sexually specific the venue (including the backrooms at the dance parties and the saunas) the greater the risk of unsafe sexual behaviour.

Less ambiguous gay venues increase the likelihood of risky sexual behaviour

The findings suggest that several group dynamics and sanctioned behaviours, including diffusion of responsibility (Wallach *et al.*, 1974), anonymity, the presence of others (Diener, 1980; Zimbardo, 1969) or the use of psychoactive substances (Butt, 1989; Stall *et al.*, 1986) contribute to increased risky sexual behaviour within these less ambiguous homoeroticizing venues. These findings have important public health implications for future research in this area and in the design of sexual and drug-related intervention programmes.

Less ambiguous private post-party venues reduce the likelihood of risky behaviour

Paradoxically, the least risky sexual post-party settings are those held in private homes where the guests directly or indirectly know each other. The findings support the importance of developing open and honest rapport between potential sexual partners in familiar private settings. This process of social interaction enables the sexual partners to negotiate safer-sexual guidelines whilst engaged in 'eye-to-eye' contact. These findings have important public health implications for the future efficacy of safer-sexual educational messages.

Intervention suggestions

Future safer-sexual and drug-related intervention strategies should target the dance party population at several different levels. First, the patrons should be taught the technique of cognitively 'pre-programming' their memory by keeping a 'little corner in [their] mind very straight', following their use of psychoactive substances within the context of the dance party institution. Second, they need to learn how to negotiate safer-sexual guidelines with a potential sexual partner in an open and honest manner (similar to some of the samples' reported behaviours at private parties) rather than relying on flawed symbols, such as the 'straighter-than-straight' identity symbol. Third, the dance party and recovery party venues should openly reinforce safer-sexual behaviour by reminding their patrons about the importance of safe-sexual and drug-related behaviour via a wide range of context-related media. These safer-sexual messages (or conditioned stimuli) should also be widely promoted within the gay subculture and its institutions, to reinforce party patrons' conditioned responses (or safer-sexual behaviour) whilst in the context of the dance party milieu, or everyday reality to control for either state-dependent learning conditions, intoxicated or sober.

Efficacy increased by incorporation of dance party argot

The efficacy of any future dance party intervention model may depend on the incorporation of the dance party argot or symbols (including the magical thinking) into these safer-sexual educational programmes. This process would re-frame, bond and strengthen these potentially flawed communication symbols by redefining or reappropriating their meaning to a safer sexual message. Douglas (1986) argues that 'survival involves the human kind of communicating, and this involves establishing the conceptual categories of public discourse' (p. 39). The deconstruction and reappropriation of the flawed dance party symbols should 'magically' empower the safer-sexual message through the laws of sympathetic magic, as defined by Frazer (1976). This synthesis should also help reduce previous ambiguities in the arena of HIV/AIDS-related promotions, increase self-esteem by offering patrons an opportunity to take control of their sexual negotiations, and raise some party patrons' awareness of their often seriously unreliable mode of communicating interpersonal information while intoxicated (such as using the healthy muscular body facade or image to assess the HIV serostatus of a potential sexual partner).

Recommended form, structure and context of intervention messages

The deconstruction and reappropriation of the gay identity symbol should also help reduce reported resistance (or adversive conditioning) to condom use (Chapman and Hodgson, 1988) by eroticizing the safer-sexual stimuli (the muscular, healthy body image), or by creating a paired association with the safe-sexual message. According to Chapman and Hodgson, there is a 'need to conceptually re-position the condom ... [It is] in general disrepute, widely regarded as pleasure-inhibiting, uncomfortable, unnatural ... [and] in dire need of a new image' (p. 104). Pronger (1992) also found strong resistance among some gay men 'who don't like using condoms because they ... have not yet been able to eroticize them' (p. 233).

Interventions that incorporate these eroticizing elements and the use of 'semantic classical conditioning' should help modify some party patrons' risky sexual behaviour within the context of the dance party milieu. Any subsequent safe-sexual behaviour (or conditioned response) may be continuously reinforced by the party patrons' constant exposure to the 'straighter-than-straight' symbol (one of the paired-associate stimuli of the safe-sexual message) in their everyday lives. This should help to reveal the 'truth' or remove the veil of illusion surrounding these non-verbal communication symbols and the often ambiguous HIV/AIDS-related educational messages.

In summary, the widespread use of this important gay identity symbol within the gay subculture may continue to reinforce previously encoded safe sexual information and cue the party patrons' memories for this vital information. The 'new' eroticized symbol could also be given maximum exposure on posters and other modes of visual communication within the context of the gay subculture and its social institutions to further reinforce these associative effects with the safe-sexual message.

Safer-sexual messages communicated by a variety of media

The media used to communicate these safe-sexual messages need to be modified to take into account numerous external environmental factors, such as the unlit sexual venues at the dance parties and the recovery parties or other poorly lit venues. Luminous materials should be used in the composition of the posters so that they continue to transmit their important safer-sexual information regardless of the level of lighting within these settings.

The dance party audio-visual equipment also provides effective channels for the communication of these safe-sexual intervention messages. They could be regularly interspersed with the music, video clips and other dance party settings, to maximize their impact whilst the patrons are intoxicated on party drugs. These safer-sexual messages should be introduced in the early stage of the dance party evening, around 1 to 2 am when most of the party patrons are in attendance and 'peaking' on their drugs. This procedure may also help control for possible state- and context-dependent learning impairment. These conditioned stimuli could be reinforced by regular intervals of exposure peaking prior to patrons' departure to post-party venues within the context of the dance parties.

Locations of interventions

It is necessary to seek the co-operation of the owners, managers or staff of these gay social institutions before implementing any intervention programmes within their venues. The organizers in this study indicated their willingness to assist in the design and implementation of the future intervention programmes within the context of their dance party organizations. Such programmes could be administered to the target population within the dance party and recovery party contexts and other gay social institutions (such as the gay media, coffee lounges, restaurants, public toilets and private venues) to ensure maximum exposure of safer-sexual guidelines to as many party patrons as possible whilst they are in a sober or intoxicated state. This procedure should help control for possible state-dependent learning contamination and reinforce the significance of safe-sexual behaviour through the 'semantic classical-conditioning' model (Maltzman, 1977).

Drug-related harm-reduction recommendations

Newcombe (1992) argues that 'one of the most urgent harm reduction issues stems from the illegality of dance drugs which means there are no controls of their content or purity' (p. 16). An in-field drug counsellor should be available at the dance parties to offer patrons advice, assistance and, if necessary, referral to drug agencies outside this reality. A comprehensive pamphlet giving the latest information about recent seizures of illegal drugs and the drug-related risk of HIV/AIDS infection should be available to party patrons, and promoted in the gay media. It should include the statistical characteristics, chemical composition, toxicity and possible consequences of over-use or poly-use of current 'street-drugs'. This information should be based on reliable sources, such as dance party organizers, representatives of the gay recreational drug-using subculture, local drug agencies, research institutes and law enforcement authorities.

A multi-dimensional advisory committee composed of representatives from these various organizations should be established to pool their collective experience, knowledge, expertise and recommendations for future harm-reduction policies and intervention programmes within the context of the dance party institution. This co-operative approach should ensure that party patrons make an informed decision about using specific drugs rather than relying on often inaccurate anecdotal information and dangerous personal experimentation.

The prohibition of these drugs has not controlled their use (in Australia, or internationally) and the continued denial of this reality has directly or indirectly contributed to a growing number of drug-related problems among young recreational drug-using populations (Beck *et al.*, 1989; Chesher, 1990; Newcombe, 1992; Peroutka, 1990; Solowij *et al.*, 1992; Miller and Tomas, 1989). The gay-activists' expression 'Silence = Death' poignantly encapsulates the potential risk of party patrons' denial (including 'magical thinking') and the possible increased risk of HIV transmission or other risk-laden behaviour.

A harm-reduction intervention model will allow the gay patrons to take responsibility for their actions from an informed premise whilst enjoying the benefits of these multi-dimensional social institutions. These educative messages should help reduce the dangerous ambiguities embedded in some of the dance party symbols that currently heighten the risk of HIV transmission among the inner-city gay dance party patrons. This research highlights the importance of understanding the set and setting of the social and subcultural institutions which are developing in the gay subculture and the factors which influence their form. The use of party drugs, and the setting which has evolved in interaction with their use and with the HIV pandemic, are both a response to the threat of HIV infection and, paradoxically, a contributor to it.

Appendix

Qualitative and Descriptive Research Methodology

Theoretical model

GLASER and Strauss' Grounded Theory (1967) was considered the 'best-fit' for this investigation 'because of its emphasis on the generation of *theory* and the *data* in which that theory is *grounded*' (Strauss, 1987, p. 22). During the early stages of this pilot study it emerged as a versatile and workable model. It was also flexible enough to accommodate the diversity, complexity and sensitivity of the inner-city gay dance party institution, including some of the gay patrons' possible increased risk of HIV infection following their use of illegal psychoactive substances within these social contexts. Goddard (1992) also suggests that 'HIV/AIDS ... is complex medically, scientifically, socially and politically. Paradoxes abound and the simple answer is very seldom the right answer' (p. 14). The researcher considered it essential, given the potential importance of the area under investigation, to find a theoretical and methodological model that would provide some 'right questions' to ask or hypotheses to test and that these be generated by the *participants* rather than the *researcher*.

Research model

The research segments often overlapped, finding the researcher performing a variety of roles, including interviewing a block of subjects during the same week as attending a dance party (as a participant-observer) and concurrently recording in-field findings, transcribing subjects' taped interviews, contracting the data for analyses and writing up these descriptions and findings.

The participant-observation stages afforded the researcher the opportunity for serendipity, that is the emergence of significant unanticipated discoveries (in this previously unresearched area) by contrast to the constraints of the *a priori* assumptions of a questionnaire survey, as noted by Whyte (1984). This methodological approach was also in accordance with Neugarten's (1977) research recommendations to psychologists who 'would do well to make greater use of the person himself as the reporting and predicting agent, and by gathering systematic and repeated self-reports along with other types of data, to combine the phenomenological and the "objective" perspectives' (pp. 639–40).

In accordance with the Grounded Theory model the researcher progressively acquired a detailed grounding in the research topic by systematically categorizing the emerging properties and intensively analyzing, often word by word, the field notes and the transcribed interview data. The emerging properties were consistently compared for similarities or underlying uniformity and coded in accordance with their core category. Strauss (1987) suggested that these core categories be given a 'best fit' label as soon as possible to enable the researcher to think about their relationship with other categories of data. This process continued until: (1) no new core categories emerged from the respondents' data and (2) all the existing categories were coded, verified and saturated (Strauss, 1987). The term 'respondent' is used in preference to 'subject' in this book because the latter term tends to imply that an experimental manipulation has been carried out by researchers, whereas in this study the respondents themselves determined the data and direction of the investigation. The theory generated from these core categories accounted for some of the respondents' patterns of sexual attitudes and behaviour within the context of the dance party milieu following their use of psychoactive substances. The included data are meant to provide readers with sufficient information to understand the phenomenon under investigation within its sociopsychological and HIV/AIDS-related contexts.

Field work

The ethnography of interactions with illicit drug dealers and users is described in detail by Adler (1985) who describes her work with an upper-level drug-dealing and smuggling community in southern California. Such work is part of a significant history of investigative field research on drug users and dealers, with the emphasis on personal observation, interaction and experience being often the only way to acquire accurate knowledge about deviant behaviour. Adler (1985) makes the point that investigative techniques are especially necessary for studying groups such as drug dealers and users because the highly illegal nature of their occupation makes them secretive, deceitful, mistrustful and paranoid. She notes, in fact, that the lack of detailed scientific information about such groups is lacking precisely because of the difficulty social researchers have in penetrating into these subcultures (p. 11). While her goals and values precluded her becoming converted to complete membership in the trafficking activities, she was able to assume a peripheral membership role by being a member of their social world and participating in their daily activities on that basis. This model of involvement was followed in the present research. In Adler's research, the respondents' general level of suspicion and the highly illegal nature of dealing in illicit drugs made it essential to keep a covert role. However, in the gay dance party scene, the widespread use of 'party drugs', the large numbers of participants involved in a small geographical area, and the numbers of gay people involved in research-associated activities in both the National Centre for HIV Social Research at the University of New South Wales, and the next door HIV/AIDS ambulatory care clinic, made contacts comparatively easy. One of the research supervisors (MR) was a gay man nationally known to be involved in HIV/AIDS research, and since there is a long tradition of close friendships between gay men and 'straight' women that includes close social partnerships, the involve-ment of the investigator and field researcher (LL) in the dance parties was an unexceptional and fully acceptable one in the 'friend' role. Further, details of the study were reported in the gay press and advertisements for participants carried in the same media. The study was thus a relatively overt one and at no time were interviewees unaware of the nature and purpose of the study – indeed, the respondents were eager to be of assistance in the investigation. The development of trust that followed from these structural aspects of the research context, and additionally from the rapport built up with the investigator by those respondents who were interviewed, was also to a large extent based on the facilitation of the study by an 'unofficial gatekeeper' who introduced the investigator to his social group and a large number of friends. Whyte (1984) suggested that an unofficial gatekeeper is usually an established member of the research population who 'can either facilitate entry and encourage access to information or see to it that the researcher never penetrates beyond superficial acquaintance' (p. 37). Moore (1992) also empha-sized the importance of having the assistance of a 'cultural broker' (or unofficial gatekeeper) when investigating 'the sometimes secre-tive worlds of illicit drug use' (p. 314).

Glaser and Strauss' Grounded Theory (1967) model pro-vided the naive researcher with a compass for guidance through this previously unmapped territory. The participant-observation stages helped the researcher to formulate some of the important research questions and items to ask the respondent during the subsequent interview sessions. It also assisted the researcher in interpreting the significance of these observations within the framework of the norms and values of the dance party milieu, which may be important determinants of possible risky sexual and drug-related behaviours, as Whyte (1984) notes.

We also found that the different stages of the field work were important building blocks in: (1) the evolution of the research design, (2) the generation of theory, the research questions and initial items for the interview schedule, (3) the development of empathic interactions with the respondents during the interview sessions, (4) the comparative evaluation of their evolving data and (5) the final analyses of these data.

This longitudinal in-field research procedure also helped the researcher to monitor the social evolution of the gay dance party milieu over a three-year period. However, we were consistently aware of previous ethnographers' warnings about the possible loss of scientific objectivity the deeper a researcher penetrates or identifies with the social reality of their target population (Kidder & Judd, 1986; Moore, 1992). Two naturally occurring phenomena helped control some researcher-biases in this study: the gender of the researcher who carried out the interviews and observations precluded her from self-identifying as a gay male dance party patron, and the literature review, the transcriptions and analyses were carried out in another city eighty kilometres south of the inner-city gay dance party milieu.

Although the researcher could never become an undetectable 'insider' she was accepted with a high degree of respect and acquired an almost 'invisible' status, as 'an honorary gay dance party patron'. This transformation, or rite of passage, occurred after the researcher danced through the night (for approximately eight hours) with a group of party patrons (including the unofficial gatekeeper). Moore (1992) also reported similar in-field experiences where the researcher's status was transformed from outsider to insider.

Researcher's familiarization, education and preparation stages

In the initial stages the researcher spent a considerable amount of time familiarizing herself with the social context including the norms, values and behaviour (Glaser and Strauss' theory, 1967) of the inner-city dance party milieu, often in the company of the 'unofficial gay gatekeeper'. In this investigation the gatekeeper facilitated entrance into the target population and provided the researcher with social support, information and introductions to key informants (including drug dealers, media representatives, gay political leaders and several dance party organizers). The gatekeeper's introductions implicitly validated or legitimized the integrity of this researcher with most of the respondents, as Moore (1992) also found among a similar marginal population.

Potential target population

Approximately 17,000 dance party patrons attended the annual Gay Mardi Gras dance party celebration at the main Sydney Showground in 1992 (Gough, 1992). This location is situated within walking distance from the main inner-city gay residential areas (including the suburbs of Darlinghurst, Kings Cross, Paddington and Surry Hills). There were numerous other gay-oriented dance parties regularly catering for thousands of patrons at the Alexandria Basketball stadium (only minutes from the inner-Sydney suburbs) and other inner-city underground venues.

Sample characteristics

The respondents were sixty-three self-identified gay men who regularly attended the inner-city gay dance parties. The sample consisted of sixty party patrons who regularly attended the gay dance parties whilst intoxicated on psychoactive substances (including one community dance party organizer, a gay activist and two illegal drug dealers, or key informants) and three of the more successful private inner-city gay dance party organizers.

Age

The respondents' mean age was twenty-eight years, ranging from nineteen years to forty-three years with 56 per cent in their twenties.

Place of birth

Most (69 per cent) of the sample were Australian-born, 16 per cent were born in New Zealand, 8 per cent were born in the UK and 7 per cent nominated another country as their place of origin.

Education

Over half (56 per cent) of the sample had completed tertiary education, 13 per cent had attempted or commenced tertiary education, 18 per cent had completed secondary educational level (equivalent to the New South Wales Higher School Certificate or year twelve) and only 13 per cent had only attempted some secondary schooling (with one case missing).

Employment status

The majority of the sample were in full-time (53 per cent) or part-time (18 per cent) employment. Fifteen per cent were retired or on a pension and only 3 per cent were students. The respondents' occupations were scored in accordance with Daniel's (1983) Occupational Prestige Scale. This scale ranges from 1.0 to 7.0 with 1.0 representing the highest occupational status. The mean of the sample was 5.0, representing a middle range of occupational status that included 11 per cent of the sample scoring 4.6 (insurance agents, cooks and an assistant manager) and 12 per cent scoring 4.9 (this included a parole officer, patternmaker and a drafting assistant). There were seven missing cases, which reflected the nine respondents (15 per cent) who were either retired, unemployed or on pensions. A diverse range of occupations (with scale scores) were included in the sample, from a barrister (1.7), dentist (2.3) to two sex workers (or 'prostitute' on the Prestige Scale, 6.9), two drug dealers and four students.

Residential address

The majority (97 per cent) of respondents resided in the inner-Sydney post code (PC) zones, including Darlinghurst and Surry Hills (PC 2010, 42 per cent), Kings Cross (PC 2011, 11 per cent) and Paddington (PC 2021, 7 per cent). Their domicile arrangements were relatively stable with 58 per cent living in the same residence for more than six months, including 24 per cent of these living at the same address for more than eighteen months (data missing for two cases). However, 32 per cent of the sample had changed residence more than six times in five years with a range of one to fifteen moves during this period (data were not available for ten cases).

Religious identity and strength of affiliation

The majority of the sample (80 per cent) did not identify with any religious institution, although 37 per cent of these self-identified with a 'personal spiritual' belief system. This skewed distribution may reflect the respondents' disillusionment with the traditional homonegative attitudes of most mainstream Judeo-Christian belief systems and may also partly account for the strength of the reported ritualized behaviours within the context of the inner-city dance party institutions (see Chapter Six). Only 11 per cent of the sample were classified as either Roman Catholic (5 per cent) or Protestant (6 per cent) with only 10 per cent nominating themselves as 'other' (one case missing). A similar percentage (10 per cent) accounted for those who self-identified as Christian-oriented (see above); they also scored high ('7', 'strong religious affiliation') on the seven-point Likert-scale which asked the question 'How strong is your religious affiliation at the present time?' compared with 57 per cent of the sample who scored one ('weak [or no] religious affiliation') on the continuum.

Patterns of drug-related issues

More than half (60 per cent) of the sample were initiated into recreational drug use by their eighteenth year (which was also the mean age of the sample's onset of use), and by nineteen years 73 per cent had used recreational drugs within the context of the dance parties. The age range for this phenomenon was from eleven years to thirty-six years, with a modal age of eighteen years. Almost three-quarters of the sample (73 per cent) nominated Ecstasy (3, 4-methylenedioxymethamphetamine [MDMA]) as the drug they 'most usually use at the dance parties', 'Speed' (amphetamine) ranked second with 64 per cent, and Marijuana was almost as popular with 61 per cent use. Alcohol followed close behind with 58 per cent, LSD (lysergic acid diethylamide) was used by 39 per cent and Amyl Nitrite followed with 27 per cent. Cocaine with 19 per cent was almost as popular as methylenedioxyamphetamine (MDA) and Valium which were 17 per cent and 16 per cent respectively. Ice (d-methamphetamine hydrochloride), Quaaludes, Heroin and 'Special K' or Ketamine were only used by a few respondents.

Relationship status and sexual behaviour

One hundred per cent of the sample self-identified as sexually active gay men. Seventy per cent of these were single and the remaining 30 per cent were in a 'lover/partner' relationship with only 13 per cent co-habiting. Over a third of these relationships were open to other sexual relationships and 17 per cent were monogamous. There was missing data for just over a third of cases (twenty-two people).

When asked their number of sexual partners over the last twelve months, only 5 per cent of the sample had one sexual partner, 31 per cent had been with two to six partners, and the majority (64 per cent) had been with more than six different sexual partners (no missing data). Fifty-three per cent of the sample reported they had engaged in risky sexual behaviour following their use of psychoactive substances within the context of the party or afterwards at another venue (at some stage). Thirty-eight per cent had not had unsafe sex (with 9 per cent of cases missing data).

HIV status

Almost half (49 per cent) of those who voluntarily provided information about their current HIV/AIDS status were seronegative, 9 per cent did not know their current status and a third (n = 16) of the reported cases (n = 49, with 15 missing cases) were seropositive, which represented 25 per cent of the sample.

Sample source

The main sources of referral for the respondent participation were through friendship networks, the Albion Street (AIDS) Centre, the AIDS Council of New South Wales, the gay Darlinghurst bookshop in Oxford Street and articles in the free gay media (*The Sydney Star Observer*, and *Capital Q*).

Interview procedure

The in-field (participant-observation) experiences also helped in the ongoing education and training of the initially naive researcher, as Moore (1992) notes. This evolving process partly determined the structure and content of the interview segments. It played a multi-faceted function by providing the researcher with a general information base for the generation of some exploratory items (Glaser and Strauss's theory, 1967) particularly during the early stages. These items were subsequently incorporated into the interview schedule as non-threatening introductory items.

This procedure also helped by affording the interviewer a frame of reference for the development of open and honest rapport during these interview sessions (Moore, 1992). The interviewer utilized her counselling training to facilitate an empathic interviewing environment (Kidder and Judd, 1987).

Location

Four of the six interview segments were conducted at the University of New South Wales National Centre in HIV Social Research, conveniently located in the inner-Sydney suburb of Surry Hills, part of the inner-city gay locale and next to the Albion Street AIDS Centre. These six interview segments were administered over an eighteen-month period, at approximately six-monthly intervals. All interviews followed a similar format and procedure (including the various stages of analyses). Any deviations from procedure were noted and discussed where appropriate.

Sequence of interview segments

The first (one-and-a-half hour) taped interview was with Organizer 1, closely followed (about a week later) by a block of sixteen interviews (of between one and three hours' duration) over three consecutive days in the University of New South Wales National Centre in HIV Social Research. Organizers 2 and 3 were interviewed concurrently about a week later for three hours at their inner-Sydney residence.

The second block of ten interviews were carried out approximately six months later (at the Centre) around the same period as Organizers 2 and 3 were re-interviewed (at their residence) in regard to the emerging data and theory (Glaser and Strauss's theory, 1967) and the rapid evolution of the inner-city gay dance party institution. Organizers 2 and 3 were very co-operative throughout this investigation by providing the researcher with invaluable information (following several spontaneous telephone interviews) and open access to the target population.

The final bracket of thirty-four interviews were conducted at the University of New South Wales National Centre in HIV Social

Research over a three-week period about six months after the previous block of ten interviews (i.e. one year after the first block).

Appointment schedule

The daily appointment schedule usually included four to five interviews and only the first name and initial for surname were recorded. Many of the respondents were only available in the evening after office hours (9 a.m. to 5 p.m.).

Context and equipment

The interviewing area at the University of New South Wales National Centre in HIV Social Research was relatively soundproof, well-ventilated and private (approximately three metres by four metres). The taping equipment was located on a desk immediately in front of the respondents for optimum recording conditions.

The tapes were marked with the interviewees' first name only and allocated a number corresponding to their position on the interview schedule. The taping equipment was checked before each interview and placed in a non-conspicuous position until the respondents provided informed consent for its use during the interview sessions, when it was turned on.

Interview ethics

Two different ethical procedures were carried out by the researcher for the sixty respondents and the three organizers to comply with the conditions prescribed for the study by the relevant university ethics committee which had approved it. The first group were assured that: (1) their raw data would remain the confidential property of the researcher, (2) their identity would remain anonymous, and (3) they may withdraw from the interview at any point. They all subsequently signed informed consent forms and completed the included biographical and demographic sample characteristics questionnaire and interview.

The interviewer informed the three organizers that they may be identifiable because of (1) the small number of original and current dance party organizers (approximately ten in Sydney), and (2) the idiosyncratic nature of the data they supplied during these interviews. All three subsequently provided permission or informed consent to use their data under these conditions.

The interviewer endeavoured to protect the dignity of the respondents by affording them respectful recognition of the risks they took in disclosing information that was potentially compromising from either a social or legal point of view.

Interview sessions

Cannell and Kahn (1968) suggested that the first few minutes were critical determinants in the establishment of an amicable, honest and open interview session. The respondents were more likely to lie when they did not trust the researcher, according to Jourand (1969). Conversely, they were more honest and open with a professionally competent interviewer who was committed to: protecting their anonymous status, ensuring confidentiality, discussing the aims and objectives of the investigation, demonstrating respectful familiarity with the research topic, administering the items schedule in an interesting and fluid manner, self-disclosing where appropriate, dealing with any research questions or distressing issues as they arose, rephrasing the items when necessary without biasing the data, and sensitively re-focusing the interview without leading or restraining response.

The interviewer refrained from using gay dance party argot during interview sessions because it seemed professionally and contextually inappropriate and may have offended some of the respondents (Read, 1980; Whyte, 1984). The researcher also consistently checked with the respondents and the organizers, throughout the interview segments to determine if they were offended by the terminology of the items. These prescriptions were considered important given the sensitivity of the issues being tapped. Strauss (1987) argued that the integrity of the respondents' data was determined by the successful integration of these ethical and moral dimensions into the interview session.

The respondents were thanked for their valuable participation and paid A$20 (about £9) by a cash cheque at the conclusion of the interview. The organizers received no financial consideration for their participation in this investigation. Most of the respondents and organizers were interested in the findings of the research and furnished the researcher with their telephone numbers for future contact.

Generation of open-ended items and schedule

The interview schedule opened with a block of open-ended exploratory or general questions followed by more sensitive probes or items relating to the respondents' sexual beliefs, communication systems and subsequent behaviour after their use of illicit drugs at the dance parties. This funnelling process was used to (1) control for possible respondent discomfort and resistance and (2) establish a frame of reference to help cue previously encoded information about these attitudes and behaviours, as suggested by Warwick and Lininger (1975).

The more sensitive items were administered to the respondents approximately fifteen to twenty minutes into the interview session which was determined by the respondents' relaxed body language (including sitting back in their chair, unfolding their arms, resting their hands at the back of their head, taking off their jacket, gesticulations and inflections in speech). This behaviour signalled to the interviewer that the respondent was in a more receptive or open mood and willing to provide honest responses to items about their sexual and drug-related behaviour within the context of the dance parties.

The introductory items were generated from information in the gay media, the respondents' data and the in-field observations. New items were generated from the respondents' data at the conclusion of each interview segment and incorporated into the emerging interview schedule. They were concisely phrased to help control for possible ambiguities.

The flexibility of the interview schedule also enabled the respondent to describe most of their data in depth and allowed the interviewer to clarify further any ambiguities (Warwick and Lininger, 1975).

Researcher debriefing

The researcher had available professional debriefing during various stages of this investigation to help her cope with many distressing aspects of this research project. The interview sessions were often extremely stressful because some of the respondents sought therapeutic advice in respect of unresolved lifestyle crises (including drug use and related behaviour, the presence of HIV among their community, the unknown results of recent HIV/AIDS tests, a recent HIV-positive diagnosis of a significant other or himself and fear of contracting HIV or being diagnosed with AIDS). A psychological support system may also provide other solo interviewers with an important safety-net to help them off-set possible professional 'burn-out', as Bennett and Kelaher (1993) found among a group of HIV/AIDS health-care professionals.

Sixteen respondents (25 per cent of the sample) were HIV-positive, with some respondents confirming their previous HIV/AIDS pathology tests as positive at a later stage (usually by telephoning the researcher). Sadly, six respondents died from HIV/AIDS-related diseases during this research project.

Respondent debriefing

The interviewer concluded the interview session with an extensive debriefing programme which included: acknowledgement of the respondent's valuable contribution to this investigation; answering respondents' queries about the interview (Kidder and Judd, 1987); providing drug- and HIV/AIDS-related educational information derived from the research findings and the recent literature; agreeing to provide interested respondents with the research findings at the conclusion of the investigation, and by furnishing the respondents with a professional card (with home and office telephone numbers) to enable them to contact her if they needed to resolve any issues arising from these interview sessions.

All of the respondents appeared to leave the interview sessions with their self-esteem intact and the reputation of behavioural science enhanced rather than diminished. As indicated by Kelman (1967) 'we have a responsibility toward the subject as another human being whose dignity we must preserve' (p. 7). Some of the respondents subsequently contacted the researcher to discuss various aspects of their interview and many remained in contact with the researcher throughout the research project. These respondents often provided the researcher with an invaluable internal control by monitoring the validity of the emerging analyses, as Moore (1992) recommends.

Analysis of the emerging data

The respondents' taped face-to-face interviews were transcribed verbatim onto a computer using Microsoft Word 4.0. These tapes were generally typed in blocks of four to five at the conclusion of the daily interview schedule. They were roughly shuffled, chosen haphazardly, renumbered and transcribed to further control for respondent anonymity and confidentiality.

A professional typist assisted in the transcription of thirty-three of the taped interviews. The interviewer cross-verified these transcriptions with the respondents' and the organizers' original taped data and corrections were made where necessary.

The analysis of the data

These data were: (1) systematically collated for consistency of response or properties, (2) collapsed into the emerging core categories and (3) funnelled into their corresponding categories on the interview schedule and the results sections of this book. This funnelling format was designed to control for possible respondent and reader biases by presenting the least provocative items or issues first, rather than beginning with the more sensational sexual and drug-related items.

The introductory core categories provided the reader and the researcher with: (1) a social and political context to ground the emerging theory in, (2) descriptive analyses of these categories and their properties and (3) a broader and deeper frame of reference for understanding the respondents' data. It took the researcher many months before she was 'more or less certain of them and very many more before those core categories . . . [were] saturated, and linked in a multiplicity of ways with other categories', as Strauss (1987, p. 23) suggests.

Several of these properties, such as sexual venues at the parties, ritualized behaviour, and the use of consciousness-changing media to help patrons escape homonegative and HIV/AIDS-related issues, consistently emerged throughout the six pilot investigations. They have been included in the analyses to illustrate and support their consistency and relevance to the 60 respondents' and the 3 organizers' perceptions, attitudes and belief systems in relation to the social construction and sexual behaviours within the context of the inner-city gay dance party institution.

The language used by the researcher in this book to describe the inner-city gay subculture, including the dance party milieu and HIV/AIDS-related issues was also selected from a variety of gay-sensitive sources. These sources included: media, literature, videos, key informants, respondents and a leaflet of *Buzzwords* (to avoid) produced by ACT UP (AIDS Coalition to Unleash Power).

Tools of analysis

The researchers cast a wide net to encompass a range of disciplines and other sources (including anthropology, sociology, psychology, history, communications and popular gay novels, videos and media) for the analyses of the respondents' diverse and complex data. These sources included extensive database searches; literature reviews of the various disciplines; personal contact (by telephone or mail) with professional experts (in Australia and internationally) in most of these areas; and ongoing discussions with some of the respondents (including many of the key informants).

The reported evidence need not necessarily be accurate beyond a doubt nor was this investigation concerned with minute accuracy: its primary functions were to help formulate theory and generate hypotheses for future investigations.

Conclusion

Glaser and Strauss' Grounded Theory (1967) model afforded the researchers an effective pilot study strategy to generate theory and formulate hypotheses for a future quantitative investigation in this previously unresearched area.

In summary, this theoretical format reflected the emergence or evolution of the research project, including the researchers' experiences (in the field and interview sessions), accumulative knowledge and skills, combined with theoretical assumptions and hypotheses (Strauss, 1987).

References

Abbott, A. and Concar, D. (1992) A trip into the unknown, *New Scientist*, 135(1836) pp. 30–34.

Abcarian, R. and Klotz, M. (1982) *Literature: The Human Experience* (New York, Holt, Rinehart and Winston).

Adler, P. A. (1985) *Wheeling and Dealing* (New York, Columbia University Press).

AIDS and Youth: High Risk Youth Workshop (1989) *National AIDS Bulletin*, 3(7) pp. 24–7.

Allport, G. (1937) *Personality: A Psychological Interpretation* (New York, Holt, Rinehart and Winston).

Altman, D. (1982) *The Homosexualization of America* (Boston, Beacon Press).

Altman, D. (1991) Safe sex and the pornographic vernacular, in: Bad Object-Choices (eds), *How do I Look?: Queer Film and Video* (Washington, Bay Press).

American Psychiatric Association (1988) *Diagnostic and Statistical Manual of Mental Disorders*, 3rd edn (Washington, American Psychiatric Association).

Achilles, N. (1967) The development of the homosexual bar as an institution, in: J. H. Gagnon and U. Simon (eds) *Sexual Deviance*, pp. 228–244 (New York, Harper & Row).

Asch, S. E. (1951) Effects of group pressure on the modification and distortion of judgement, in: H. Guetzkow (ed.) *Groups, Leadership and Men* (Pittsburgh, Carnegie Press).

Augustine, Saint (1973 ed.) *Confessions*. Translation and Introduction by R. S. Pine-Coffin (London, Penguin).

Bad Object-Choices (eds) (1991) *How do I Look?: Queer Film and Video* (Washington, Bay Press).

Bagnall, G., Plant, M. and Warwick, W. (1990) Alcohol, drugs and AIDS-related risks: results from a prospective study. *AIDS Care*, 2, pp. 309–317.

Barash, D. (1981) *Sociobiology: The Whisperings Within* (New York, Harper & Row).

Baron, R. A. and Byrne, D. (1987) *Social Psychology: Understanding Human Interaction* (Needham Heights, MA, Allyn & Bacon).

Bateson, G. (1972) *Steps to an Ecology of Mind* (San Francisco, Chandler).

Batke, S. L. (1988) Treatment of intravenous drug users with AIDS: the role of methadone maintenance, *Journal of Psychoactive Drugs* 20(2), pp. 213–216.

Battjes, R. J., Leukefeld, C. G., Pickens, R. W. and Haverkos, H. W. (1988) The acquired immunodeficiency syndrome and intravenous drug abuse, *The Bulletin of Narcotics*, 11 (1), pp. 21–34.

Beck, J., Harlow, D., McDonald, D., Morgan, P., Rosenbaum, M. and Watson, L. (1989) Exploring Ecstasy: a description of MDMA users, *Institute of Scientific Analysis Final Report to the National Institute of Drug Abuse*, pp. 1–252.

Beck, J. (1990) The public health implications of MDMA use, in: S. J. Peroutka (ed.) *Ecstasy* (Boston, Kluwer Academic Publishers).

Bell, A. P. and Weinberg, M. S. (1978) *Homosexualities: A Study of Diversity Among Men and Women* (New York, Simon and Schuster).

Bennett, G., Chapman, S. and Bray, F. (1989) A potential source for the transmission of the human immunodeficiency virus into the heterosexual population: bisexual men who frequent 'beats', *Medical Journal of Australia*, 6, pp. 314–318.

Bennett, L. and Kelaher, M. (1993) Longitudinal determinants of patient care-related stress in HIV/AIDS health professionals. Presentation, *IXth International Conference on AIDS*, Berlin, 6th–11th June. Abstract No. 21-4062.

Berger, P. L. (1977) *Face Up To Modernity* (Harmondsworth, Penguin Education).

Berger, P. L. and Luckmann, T. (1975) *The Social Construction of Reality* (Harmondsworth, Penguin).

Berkelman, R. L., Heyward, W. L., Stehr-Green, J. K. and Curran, J. W. (1989) Epidemiology of Human Immunodeficiency Virus Infection and Acquired Immunodeficiency Syndrome, *American Journal of Medicine*, 86, pp. 761–770.

Bertalanffy, L. von (1965) On the definition of the symbol, in: Joseph R.

Royce (ed.) *Psychology and the Symbol: An Interdisciplinary Symposium* (New York, Random House).

Birdwhistell, R. L. (1970) *Kinesics and Context: Essays on Body Motion Communication* (Philadelphia, University of Pennsylvania Press).

Blacker, P., Wodak, A., Tindell, B. and Cooper, D. (1986) Exposure of the intravenous drug users to AIDS retrovirus, Sydney, 1985. *Australian New Zealand Medical Journal*, 16, pp. 686–690.

Bogoras, W. (1979) Shamanistic performance in the inner room, in: W. A. Lessa and E. Z. Vogt (eds) *Reader in Comparative Religion: An Anthropological Approach*, 4th edn (New York, Harper & Row).

Borges, J. L. (1976) Tion, Uqbar, Orbis, Tertius, *Ficciones* (London: Harrap).

Bradley, C. W. (1978) Self-serving biases in the attribution process: a re-examination of the fact or fiction question, *Journal of Personality and Social Psychology*, 35, pp. 56–71.

Brandt, A. M. (1985) *No Magic Bullet: A Social History of Venereal Diseases in the United States Since 1880* (New York, Oxford University Press).

Brehm, J. W. (1966) *A Theory of Psychological Reactance* (New York, Academic Press).

Brennan, T. and Auslander, N. (1979) Adolescent loneliness: an exploratory study of social and psychological predispositions and theory, *Journal of National Institute of Mental Health*, 1, pp. 12–21.

Brettle, R. P., Bisset, K., Burns, S., Davidson, J., Davidson, S. J., Gray, J. M., Inglis, J. M., Lees, J. S. and Mok, J. (1987) Human immunodeficiency virus and drug use: the Edinburgh experience, *British Medical Journal*, 295, pp. 421–4.

Brettle, R. A. and Nelles, B. (1988) Special problems of injecting drug-misusers, *British Medical Bulletin*, 44(1), 149–60.

Brown, S. A., Goildman, J. M., Inn, A. and Anderson, L. (1980) Expectancies of reinforcement from alcohol: their domains and relation to drinking patterns, *Journal of Consulting and Clinical Psychology*, 48, pp. 419–426.

Bruner, J. (1962) The conditions of creativity, in: H. E. Gruber, G. Terrell and M. Wertheimer (eds) *Contemporary Approaches to Creative Thinking*, pp. 12–13 (New York, Atherton Press).

Buffum, J. (1988) Substance abuse and high-risk sexual behaviour: drugs and sex – the dark side, *Journal of Psychoactive Drugs*,

20(2), 165–8.

Burnstein, E. (1983) Persuasion as argument processing, in: M. Bradstatte, J. Davis and G. Stoker-Kreichgauer (eds), *Group Decision Processes* (London, Academic Press).

Butt, L. (1989) Alcohol and disinhibition: 'One more drink and I'll be under the hose', *Connexions* 9(5), pp. 2–8.

Cabaj, R. P. (1989) AIDS and chemical dependency: special issues and treatment barriers for gay and bisexual men, *Journal of Psychoactive Drugs* 21(4), 387–393.

Callaghan, G. (1993) Pumping ironies: gay body image in the '90s, *Campaign: Australia*, 56, pp. 47–50.

Camus, A. (1947) *La Peste* (France); Eng. transl. (1967) *The Plague* (Harmondsworth, Penguin).

Cannell, C. F. and Kahn, R. L. (1968) Interviewing, in: G. Lindzey and E. Aronson (eds) *Handbook of Social Psychology*, 2nd edn (Reading, MA., Addison-Wesley).

Carlson, N. R. (1984) *Psychology: The Science of Behaviour* (Needham Heights, MA, Allyn & Bacon).

Carnes, M. (1985) *Out of the Shadows: Understanding Sexual Addiction* (Minneapolis, CompCare).

Carroll, T. E. and Loy, J. G. (1989) The drug offensive – a review of its approach and progress from April 1986 to September 1988, *Australian Drug and Alcohol Review*, 7, pp. 487–98.

Cartwright, D. and Zander, A. (1968) Pressures to uniformity in groups, in: Cartwright, D. and Zander, A. (eds) *Group Dynamics: Research and Theory*, 3rd edn (New York, Elsevier North-Holland).

Cassell, J. (1976) The contribution of the social environment to host resistance, *American Journal of Epidemiology*, 104, pp. 107–123.

Catania, J., McDermont, L. and Wood, J. (1984) Assessment of locus of control: situational specificity in the sexual context, *Journal of Sex Research*, 20, pp. 310–324.

Centres for disease control (1989) Morbidity and mortality weekly reports. Acquired Immunodeficiency Syndrome associated with intravenous drug use – United States, 1988, *Journal of the American Medical Association*, 261(16), pp. 2314–2316.

Chaisson, R. E., Bacchetti, P., Osmond, D., Brodie, B., Sande, M. A. and Moss, A. R. (1989) Cocaine use and HIV infection in intravenous drug users in San Francisco, *Journal of the American*

Medical Association, 261(4), pp. 561–565.

Chaisson, R., Moss, A. and Oniski, R. (1987) Human immunodeficiency virus infection in heterosexual intravenous drug users in San Francisco, *American Journal of Public Health*, 77, pp. 169–172.

Chapman, S. and Hodgson, J. (1988) Showers in raincoats: attitudinal barriers to condom use in high-risk heterosexuals, *Community Health Studies*, 12, pp. 97–105.

Chesher, G. (1990) Some views on Ecstasy, *Modern Medicine of Australia*, April, pp. 81–85.

Cho, A. K. (1990) Ice: a new dosage from an old drug, *Science*, 34, pp. 631–634.

Cohen, S. (1971) *Images of Deviance* (Harmondsworth, Penguin).

Cohn, N. (1970) *The Pursuit of the Millennium* (New York, Oxford University Press).

Collison, R. and Collison, M. (1980) *Dictionary of Foreign Quotations* (London, Macmillan Press).

Cowan, G., Drinkard, J. and MacGavin, L. (1984) The effects of target, age, and gender on use of power strategies, *Journal of Personality and Social Psychology*, 47, pp. 1391–1398.

Cozby, P. C. (1985) *Methods in Behavioural Research*, 3rd edn (London, Mayfield).

Crimp, D. and Rolston, A. (1990) *AIDS Demographics* (Seattle, Bay Press).

Crowne, D. P. and Liverant, S. (1963) Conformity under varying conditions of personal commitment, *Journal of Abnormal and Social Psychology*, 66, pp. 547–555.

Crowne, D. P. and Marlowe, D. (1964) *The approval motive: studies in evaluative dependence* (New York, Wiley).

Culler, J. (1988) *Framing the Sign: Criticism and its Institutions* (Oxford, Basil Blackwell).

Cvetkovich, G. and Grote, B. (1983) Adolescent development and teenage fertility, in: D. Bryne and W. Fisher (eds) *Adolescents, Sex and Contraception* (Hillsdale, NJ, Erlbaum).

Daniel, A. (1983) *Power, Privilege and Prestige: Occupations in Australia* (Melbourne, Longman Cheshire).

Dank, B. M. (1971) Coming out in the gay world, *Psychiatry*, 34, pp. 189–197.

Dass, Ram (1976) *The Only Dance There Is* (New York, Aronson).

Davenport-Hines, R. (1990) *Sex, Death and Punishment: Attitudes to Sex and Sexuality in Britain since the Renaissance* (London, Collins).

Day, N. A., Houston-Hamilton, A., Deslondes, J. and Nelson, M. (1988) Potential for HIV dissemination by a cohort of black intravenous drug users, *Journal of Psychoactive Drugs*, 20(2), pp. 179–183.

DEA (Drug Enforcement Administration) Strategic Intelligence Section Domestic Unit, Washington, DC (1989) A special report on 'Ice' (D-Methamphetamine Hydrochloride), *Epidemiologic Trends in Drug Abuse, Proceedings*. Community Epidemiology Work Group Public Health Service, December, pp. 69–83.

Defoe, D. (1966 ed.) *A Journal of the Plague Year* (Harmondsworth, Penguin) (First published 1722).

Delaney, M., Goldblum, P. and Brewer, J. (1989) Substance use and abuse. A gay men's health manual for the age of AIDS, *National AIDS Bulletin*, 6, pp. 29–34.

Dembo, R., Williams, L., La Voie, L., Berry, E., Getreu, L., Wish, E., Schmeidler, J. and Washburn, M. (1989) Physical abuse, sexual victimization, and illicit drug use: replication of a structural analysis among a new sample of high-risk youths, *Violence and Victims* 4(2), pp. 121–137.

Deren, M. (1975) *The Voodoo Gods* (St. Albans, Thames & Hudson).

DesJarlais, D. C., Friedman, S. R. and Hopkins, W. (1985) Risk reduction for the acquired immunodeficiency syndrome among intravenous drug users, *Annals of Internal Medicine*, 103(5), pp. 755–759.

Diener, E. (1980) Deindividuation: the absence of self-awareness and self-regulation in group members, in: P. Paulus (ed.) *The Psychology of Group Influence* (Hillsdale, NJ, Erlbaum).

Donoghoe, M. C., Stimpson, G. V., Dolan, K. and Alldritt, L. (1989) Changes in HIV risk behaviours in clients of syringe-exchange schemes in England and Scotland, *AIDS* 3(5), pp. 267–272.

Donoghoe, M. C., Stimpson, G. V. and Dolan, K. A. (1989) Sexual behaviour of injecting drug users and associated risks of HIV infection for non-injecting sexual partners, *AIDS Care*, 1(1), pp. 51–57.

Dorn, N. and South, N. (1990) Communications, education, drugs and HIV, in: J. Strang and G. Stimson (eds), *AIDS and Drug Misuse* (New York, Routledge).

Douglas, M. (1986) *Risk: Acceptability According to the Social Sciences* (London, Routledge & Kegan Paul).

Douglas, M. (1991) *Purity and Danger: An Analysis of the Concepts of Pollution and Taboo* (New York, Routledge).

Duffin, R. (1992) Mardi Gras & HIV: a personal reflection, *The Guide: Sydney Gay & Lesbian Mardi Gras* (Rushcutters Bay, New South Wales: Sydney Gay and Lesbian Mardi Gras Ltd., Workshop C).

Durkheim, E. (1954) The theory of decision-making, *Psychological Bulletin*, 51, pp. 380–417.

Eatts, T. (1989) The truth about: designer drugs, *New Woman*, September, pp. 89–91.

Eich, J. E. (1977) State-dependent retrieval of information in human episodic memory, in: I. M. Birnbaum and E. S. Parker (eds), *Alcohol and Human Memory* (Hillsdale, NJ, Erlbaum).

Eich, J. E., Weingartner, H., Stillman, R. C. and Gillin, J. C. (1975) State-dependent accessibility of retrieval cues in the retention of categorized list, *Journal of Verbal Behaviour*, 14, pp. 408–417.

Ekman, P. and Friesen, W. V. (1975) *Unmasking the Face* (Englewood Cliffs, NJ, Prentice-Hall).

Ekstrand, M. and Coates, T. (1990) Maintenance of safer sexual behaviours and predictors of risky sex: the San Francisco men's health study, *American Journal of Public Health*, 80(8), pp. 973–977.

Eliade, M. (1957) *The Sacred and Profane* (New York, Harcourt, Brace & World).

Eliade, M. (1974a) *Patterns in Comparative Religion* (New York, NAL Penguin).

Eliade, M. (1974b) *From Primitives to Zen* (New York, Harper & Row).

Eliade, M. (1956) *Forgerons et Alchimistes* (Paris: Flammarion); reprinted in: *The Forge and the Crucible: The Origins and Structures of Alchemy*, 2nd edn (London: The University of Chicago Press).

Ellis, A. (1970) *Rational-emotive therapy, in: L. Hersher (ed.) Four Psychotherapies* (New York, Appleton-Century Crofts).

Ellis, A. and Harper, R. A. (1975) *A New Guide to Rational Living* (Englewood Cliffs, NJ, Prentice-Hall).

Evans, A. (1988) *The God of Ecstasy: Sex Roles and the Madness of Dionysus* (New York, St Martin's Press).

Faltz, B. G. (1988) Counseling substance-abuse clients infected with human immunodeficiency virus, *Journal of Psychoactive Drugs* 20(2), pp. 217–221.

Fanon, F. (1977) *The Wretched of the Earth* (Harmondsworth, Penguin).

Feather, N. T. (1985) Attitudes, values and attributions: Explanations of unemployment, *Journal of Personality and Social Psychology*, 48, pp. 876–889.

Feather, N. T. and Tiggerman, M. (1984) A balanced measure of attributional style, *Australian Journal of Psychology*, 36, pp. 267–283.

Feldman, H. W., Espada, F., Penn, S. and Byrd, S. (1991) Street status and the sex-for-crack scene in San Francisco, in: *Crack Pipe as Pimp: An Eight-City Ethnographic Study of the Sex-for-Crack Phenomenon*, Task Order Number 1, final report submitted to the National Institute on Drug Abuse, pp. 1–22.

Fenley, J. M. and Williams, J. E. (1991) A comparison of perceived self among drug addicts and nonaddicts, *The International Journal of the Addictions*, 26(9), 973–979.

Festinger, L. and Carlsmith, J. M. (1959) Cognitive consequences of force compliance, *Journal of Abnormal and Social Psychology*, 58, pp. 91–101.

Fiefield, L. H., Latham, J. D. and Phillips, C. (1977) *Alcoholism in the Gay Community: The Price of Alienation, Isolation and Oppression* (Los Angeles, Gay Community Services Centre).

Finnegan, D. G. and McNally, E. B. (1987) Alcoholism, recovery, and health: lesbians and gay men, presented at *National Council on Alcoholism Forum*, Seattle, 3–4 May.

Fischer, C. S. (1975) Toward a subcultural theory of urbanism, *American Journal of Sociology*, 80(6), pp. 1319–1341.

Flexser, A. J. and Tulving, E. (1978) Retrieval independence in recognition and recall, *Psychological Review*, 85, pp. 153–171.

Foucault, M. (1976) *La Wolonte de Saviour* (Paris, Gallimard); Eng. transl. (1990) *The History of Sexuality: An Introduction*, 1 (London, Penguin).

Forsyth, D. R. (1983) *An introduction to group dynamics* (Monterey, CA, Brooks-Cole).

Foster, A. and McGrath, R. (1988) *Behold the Man: the Male Nude in Photography: Stills* (Edinburgh, Stills Gallery).

Frankl, V. E. (1984) *Man's Search for Meaning* (Boston: Washington Square Press).

Frazer, J. G. (1976) *The Golden Bough: A Study in Magic and Religion* (London, Macmillan).

Freud, S. (1953) An outline of psychoanalysis (J. Strachey, transl.), in: *The Standard Edition*, 23 (London, Hogarth).

Freud, S. (1957) Instincts and their vicissitudes (J. Strachey, transl.), in: *The Standard Edition*, 14 (London, Hogarth).

Freud, S. (1983 ed.) *New Introductory Lectures on Psycho-analysis* (New York, Norton) (First published 1953-74).

Fromm, E. (1976) *To Have or to Be?* (New York, Harper and Row).

Fustel de Coulanges, N. D. (1956) *The Ancient City: A Study on the Religion, Laws, and Institutions of Greece and Rome* (Garden City, Doubleday Anchor).

Gagnon, J. H. and Simon, W. (1974) *Sexual Conduct: The Social Sources of Human Sexuality* (London, Hutchinson).

Gailbraith, L. (1991) We will survive! 13 Challenging Years, *The Guide: Sydney Gay + Lesbian Mardi Gras 1991* (Rushcutters Bay, New South Wales: Sydney Gay Lesbian Mardi Gras Ltd).

Garber, M. (1992) *Vested Interests: Cross-dressing & Cultural Anxiety* (New York, Routledge, Chapman and Hall).

Gardner, H. (1973) *The Arts and Human Development: A Psychological Study of the Artistic Process* (New York, John Wiley).

Garnefski, N., Diekstra, R. F. W. and de Heus, P. (1992) A population-based survey of the characteristics of high-school students, with and without a history of suicidal behavior, *Acta Psychiatr Scand*, 86, pp. 189–196.

Gavin, D., Ross, H. and Skinner, H. (1989) Diagnostic validity of the drug screening test in the assessment of DSM 111 drug disorders, *British Journal of Addiction*, 84, pp. 301–307.

Gay, G., Newmeyer, J., Perry, M., Johnson, G. and Kurland, M. (1989) 'Love and haight', the sensuous hippie revisited: drug/sex practices in San Francisco, 1980–81, *Journal of Psychoactive Drugs*, 14(1/2), 111–123.

Giblin, P. T., Poland, M. L. and Ager, J. W. (1988) Clinical applications of self-esteem and locus of control to adolescent health (review), *Journal of Adolescent Health Care*, 9(10), pp. 1–14.

Ginzburg, H. M., French, J., Jackson, J., Hartsock, P. I., MacDonald, M. G. and Weiss, S. H. (1986) Health education and knowledge assessment HTLV-111 diseases among intravenous drug users, *Health Education Quarterly* 13(4), pp. 373–382.

Ginzburg, H. M., MacDonald, M. G. and Glass, J. W. (1987) AIDS, HTLV-111 Diseases, minorities and intravenous drug abuse, *Advances in Alcohol & Substance Abuse*, 6(3), pp.7–21.

Ginzburg, H. M. (1984) Intravenous drug users and the acquired immune deficiency syndrome, *Public Health Reports*, 99(2), pp. 206–212.

Ginzburg, H. M., Weiss, S. H., Macdonald, M. G. and Hubbard, R. L. (1985) HTLV-III exposure among drug users, *Cancer Research* (Suppl.), 45, pp. 4605s–4608s.

Glover, J. (1988) *The Philosophy of Psychology of Personal Identity*, 1 (London: Penguin).

Goddard, M. (1992) *The AIDS Crisis: Getting the Story Situations of Mental Patients and Other Inmates* (New York, Doubleday).

Goffman, E. (1963) *Asylums: Essays on the Social Situation of Mental Patients and other Inmates* (Harmondsworth, Penguin).

Goffman, E. (1974) *Stigma: Notes on the Management of Spoiled Identity* (Englewood Cliffs, NJ, Prentice-Hall).

Goffman, E. (1980) *The Presentation of Self in Everyday Life* (Harmondsworth, Penguin).

Gold, R. (1989) Places, times, reasons. Report of research carried out for the Victorian AIDS council. *National AIDS Bulletin*, 3(5), pp. 22–26.

Gold, R. S. and Skinner, M. J. (1992) Situational factors and thought processes associated with unprotected intercourse in young gay men, *AIDS*, 1, pp. 241–246.

Gold, R., Skinner, M. J. and Ross, M. W. (1994) Unprotected intercourse in HIV-infected and non-HIV-infected Gay Men, *Journal of Sex Research*, 31, pp. 59–77.

Goldsmith, M. (1988) Sex tied to drugs = STD spread, *Journal of the American Medical Association*, 260(14), p. 2009.

Goodwin, J. P. (1989) *More Man 'than you'll ever be!': Gay Folklore and Acculturation in Middle America* (Bloomington, IN, Indiana University Press).

Gough, A. (1992) Let's have a party!, *The Guide: Sydney Gay & Lesbian Mardi Gras* (Rushcutters Bay, Australia, Sydney Gay and Lesbian Mardi Gras Ltd., Workship C).

Grant, M. (Transl.) (1979) *Cicero: Selected Political Speeches* (Harmondsworth, Penguin).

Graves, T. D. and Graves, N. B. (1974) Adapted strategies in urban migration, *Annual Review of Anthropology*, 3, pp. 117-152.

Green, C. H. and Brown, R. A. (1981) The accuracy of beliefs about risk, *Atom*, 295, pp. 129–131.

Green, C. H. (1980) Risk: beliefs and attitudes, in: D. Cantor (ed.) *Fires and Human Behaviour* (New York, Wiley).

Greenberg, J., Pyaczynaki, T. and Solomon, S. (1982) The self-serving attributional bias: beyond self-presentation, *Journal of Experimental Social Psychology*, 18, pp. 56–67.

Guinan, M. E., Thomas, P. A., Pinksy, P. F., Goodrich, J. T., Selik, R. M., Jaffe, H. W., Haverkos, H. W., Noble, G. and Curran, J. W. (1984) Heterosexual and homosexual patients with the acquired immunodeficiency syndrome: a comparison of surveillance, interview, and laboratory data, *Annals of Internal Medicine*, 100, pp. 213–218.

Haaga, D. (1989) Mood state-dependent retention using identical or non-identical mood inductions at learning and recall, *British Journal of Clinical Psychology*, 28(1), 75–83.

Hacker, F. J. (1965) Psychology and psychopathology of symbolism, in Joseph R. Royce (ed.) *Psychology and the Symbol: An Interdisciplinary Symposium* (New York, Random House).

Hamilton, E. (1969) *Mythology: Timeless Tales of Gods and Heroes* (Boston, The New American Library).

Hammersmith, S. K. and Weinberg, M. S. (1973) Homosexual: changing patterns of awareness, *Drinking and Drug Practices Surveyor*, 18, pp. 3–7.

Hando, J. and Hall, W. (1992) Amphetamine use among young adults in Sydney, Australia, *State Health Publication* (NSW Drug and Alcohol Directorate: Research Grant Report Series).

Hanna, J. L. (1987) *To Dance is Human: A Theory of Nonverbal Communication* (Chicago, University of Chicago Press).

Hanna, J. L. (1988) *Dance, Sex, and Gender: Signs of Identity, Dominance, Defiance, and Desire* (Chicago, University of Chicago Press).

Harris, N., Gordon, D., Bley, L. and Sweeney, P. (1991) Why is HIV concentrated among IV amphetamine users in the Pacific North-West of the United States?, Abstract from the VII International Conference on AIDS in Rome.

Hart, G. J., Sonnex, C., Petherick, A., Johnson, A. M., Feinmann, C. and Adler, M. W. (1989) Risk behaviours for HIV risk infection among injecting drug users attending a drug dependency clinic, *British Medical Journal*, 298, pp. 1081–1083.

Harvey, M. (1979) *Project Summary: Improving the Social Management of Technological Hazards* (Eugene Ore, Clark University Center for Technology and Decision Research).

Hawkes, T. (1977) *Structuralism and Semiotics* (London, Methuen).

Hays, R. B., Kegeles, S. M. and Coates, T. (1990) High HIV risk-taking among young gay men, *AIDS*, 4, pp. 901–907.

Hearst, N. and Hulley, S. B. (1988) Preventing the heterosexual spread of AIDS: are we giving our patients the best advice?, *Journal of the American Medical Association*, 259(16), pp. 2428–2432.

Heger, H. (1986) *The Men with the Pink Triangle* (Boston, Alyson).

Helman, C. G. (1990) *Culture, Health and Illness*, 2nd edn (Tiptree: Butterworth-Heinemann).

Henry, J. A. (1992) Ecstasy and the dance of death, *British Medical Journal*, 305, pp. 6–7.

Herdt, G. H. (ed.) (1982) *Rituals of Manhood: Male Inititiations in Papua New Guinea* (Berkeley and Los Angeles, CA, University of California Press).

Herek, G. M. (1984) Beyond 'Homophobia': a social psychological perspective on attitudes toward lesbians and gay men *Journal of Homosexuality*, 10(1/2), pp. 19–21.

Herek, G. M. and Glunt, E. K. (1988) An epidemic of Stigma: public reactions to AIDS, *American Psychologist*, 43(11), pp. 886–891.

Hertz, R. (1960) *Death and the Right Hand* (London, Cohen and West).

Hewstone, M. and Jaspars, J. (1982) Explanations for racial discrimination: the effects of group decision on intergroup attributions, *European Journal of Social Psychology*, 12, pp. 1–16.

Hingson, R. W., Strunin, L., Berlin, B. M. and Heeren, T. (1990) Beliefs about AIDS, use of alcohol and drugs, and unprotected sex among Massachusetts adolescents, *American Journal of Public Health*, 80(3), pp. 295–298.

Hirabayashi, J., Willard, W. and Kemnitzer, L. (1972) Pan-Indianism in the urban setting, in: T. Weaver and D. White (eds) *The Anthropology of Urban Environments*, Society for Applied Anthropology Monograph Series, 11, pp. 77–88.

Hollander, E. P. (1978) *Leadership Dynamics: A Practical Guide to Effective Relationships* (New York, Free Press).

Horwitz, T. (1986) High and low on Ecstasy, *Sydney Morning Herald, Good Weekend*, August, pp. 15–17.

Houston, J. P. (1986) *Fundamentals of Learning and Memory*, 3rd edn (Orlando, FL, Harcourt, Brace Jovanovich).

Howard, J. H. (1976) The plains gourd dance as a revitalization movement, *American Ethnologist*, 3(2), pp. 243–260.

Hubbard, R. L., Marsden, M. E., Cavanaugh, E., Rachal, J. V. and Ginzburg, H. M. (1988) Role of drug-abuse treatment in limiting the spread of AIDS, *Review of Infectious Diseases*, 10(2), pp. 377–384.

Hull, J. G. and Bond, C. F. (1986) Social and behavioral consequences of alcohol consumption and expectancy: a meta-analysis, *Psychological Bulletin*, 99, pp. 347–360.

Humphreys, L. (1970) *Tearoom Trade* (London, Duckworth).

Humphreys RAL (1979) Exodus and identity: the emerging gay culture, in: Levine, M. (ed.) *Gay Men: The Sociology of Male Homosexuality* (New York, Harper & Row).

Huxley, A. (1954) *The Doors of Perception* (London, Harper & Row); rev. edn, 1974.

Huxley, A. (1932) *Brave New World* (London, Harper & Row); rev. edn, 1986.

Inge, W.R. (1971) The Penguin Dictionary of Modern Quotations: Compiled by J.M. and M.J. Cohen (Harmondsworth, Penguin).

Jaspers, K. (1959) *Truth and Symbol* (New Haven, CT, College of University Press).

Jenkins, J. J. (1974) Remember that old theory of memory? Well forget it!, *American Psychologist*, 29, pp. 785–795.

Jones, E. E. and Davis, K. E. (1965) From acts to disposition: the attribution process in person perception, in: L. Berkowitz (ed.) *Advances in Experimental Social Psychology*, 2 (New York, Academic Press).

Jones, E. E. and Nisbett, R. E. (1971) *The Actor and the Observer: Divergent Perceptions of the Cause of Behaviours* (Morristown, NJ, General Learning Press).

Jourand, S. M. (1969) The effects of experimenters' self-disclosure on subjects' behavior, in: C. Spielberger (ed.) *Current Topics in Community and Clinical Psychology* (New York, Academic Press).

Käll, K. I. (1992) Effects of amphetamine on sexual behavior of mail IV drug users in Stockholm-A pilot study, *AIDS Education and Prevention*, 4(1), pp. 6–17.

Käll, K. L. and Olin, R. G. (1990) HIV status and changes in risk behaviour among intravenous drug users in Stockholm 1987–1988, *AIDS*, 4, pp. 153–157.

Kamath, M. V. (1978) *Philosophy of Death and Dying* (Honesdale, PA, Himalayan International Institute of Yoga Science and Philosophy).

Kaplan, C. D., Grund, J.-P., Dzoljic, M. R. and Barendregt, C. (1992) Ecstasy in Europe: reflections on the epidemiology of MDMA. Unpublished paper, Addiction Research Institute and Department of Pharmacology, Medical and Health Sciences Faculty, Erasmus University, Rotterdam.

Kaplan, H. B., Johnson, R. J. and Bailey, C. A. (1988) Explaining adolescent drug use: an elaboration strategy for structural equations modelling, *Psychiatry*, 51, pp. 142–163.

Keeping the Gay & Lesbian in Mardi Gras (1992) *The Guide: Sydney Gay and Lesbian Mardi Gras* (Rushcutters Bay, NSW, Sydney Gay and Lesbian Mardi Gras Ltd., Workshop C).

Kelley, H. H. (1972) Attribution in social interaction, in: E. E. Jones *et al.* (eds) *Attribution, Perceiving the Causes of Behavior* (Morristown, NJ, General Learning Press).

Kelley, K. (1986) *Females, Males, and Sexuality* (New York, State University of New York Press).

Kelley, K., Cheung, F. M., Rodriguez-Corrillo, P., Singh, R., Wan, C. K., Becker, M. C. and Eberly, C. (1986) Chronic self-destructiveness: conceptualization and locus of control in cross-cultural perspective, *Journal of Social Psychology*, 126(5), pp. 572–579.

Kelman, H. C. (1967) Human use of human subjects: The problem of deception in social psychological experiments, *Psychological Bulletin*, 67, pp. 1–11.

Kidder, L. H. and Judd, C. M. (1986) *Research Methods in Social Relations*, 5th edn (New York, Dryden Press).

Klee, H. (1991a) The sexual behaviour of injecting women: heroin and amphetamine users compare, *Ist International Conference: The Biopsychosocial Aspects of HIV Infection*, Amsterdam, 22-5 September 1991, pp. 1–6.

Klee, H. (in press) Sexual risk among amphetamine misusers: prospects for change, *Social Aspects of AIDS Conference*, London, March 1991, pp. 1–21.

Kohlberg, L. (1969) Stage and sequence: the cognitive-developmental approach to socialization, in: D. A. Goslin (ed.), *Handbook of Socialization Theory and Research* (Chicago, Rand McNally).

Korf, D., Blanken, P. and Nabben, T. (1992) *Een nieuwe wonderpil? Verspreiding effecten en risico's van ecstasygebruik in Amsterdam* (Amsterdam: Jellinekreeks).

Kramer, T. H., Canellieri, F. R., Ottomanelli, G., Mosely, J. A., Fine, J. and Bihari, B. (1989) A behavioural measure of AIDS information-seeking by drug and alcohol in-patients, *Journal of Substance Use Treatment*, 6, pp. 83–85.

Krishner, G. (1973) *The Secret of Yoga* (London, Turnstone Books).

Kübler-Ross, E. (1975) *Death: The Final Stage of Growth* (Englewood Cliffs, NJ, Prentice-Hall).

Laing, R. D. (1978) *Self and Others* (Harmondsworth, Penguin Books).

Lalonde, M. (1974) *A New Perspective on the Health of Canadians: A Working Document* (Ottawa Ministry of National Health and Welfare, Government of Canada).

Lange, W. R. and Fralich, J. (1989) Nitrite inhalents: promising and discouraging news, *British Journal of Addiction*, 84, pp. 121–123.

Lansing, D. (1992) Drugs and alcohol: just a good time or long-term damage? *Capital Q: News for the Queer Capital*, 24 April, p. 8.

Lazarus, R. S. and Folkman, S. (1984) *Stress, Appraisal, and Coping* (New York, Springer).

Leach, E. (1976) *Culture and Communication* (Cambridge, Cambridge University Press).

Leach, E. R. (1978) *Levi-Strauss*, Revised edn (London, Collins).

Leary, T. (1968) *High Priest* (Cleveland, World Publishing).

Leigh, B. C. (1990) The relationship of substances used during sex to high-risk sexual behaviour, *Journal of Sex Research*, 27(2), pp. 199–213.

Levi-Strauss, C. (1967) *Structural Anthropology* (Garden City, Anchor).

Lewis, M. J. (1992) *A Rum State: Alcohol and State Policy in Australia* (Canberra, Australian Government Publishing Service).

Liester, M. B., Grob, C. S., Bravo, G. L. and Walsh, R. N. (1992) Phenomenology and Sequelae of 3,4-Methylenedioxymethamphetamine use, *Journal of Nervous and Mental Disease*, 180(6), pp. 345–352.

Lincoln, B. (1991) *Death, War, and Sacrifice: Studies in Ideology and Practice* (Chicago, University of Chicago Press).

Linn, L. S., Spiegel, J. S., Mathews, W. C., Leake, B., Lien, R. and Brooks, S. (1989) Recent sexual behaviours among homosexual men seeking primary medical care, *Archives of Internal Medicine*, 149, pp. 2685–2690.

Loudon, J. B. (1966) Private stress and public ritual, *Journal of Psychosomatic Research*, 10, pp. 101–108.

Lovejoy, N. C. and Moran, T. A. (1988) Selected AIDS beliefs, behaviours and informational needs of homosexual/bisexual men with AIDS or ARC, *International Journal of Nurses Studies*, 25(3), pp. 207–216.

Lowe, G. (1988) State-dependent retrieval effects with social drugs, *British Journal of Addiction*, 83(1), pp. 99–103.

McCusker, J., Westenhouse, J., Stoddard, A. M., Zapka, J. G., Zorn, M. W. and Mayer, K. H. (1990) Use of drugs and alcohol by homosexually active men in relation to sexual practices, *Journal of Acquired Immune Deficiency Syndromes*, 3, pp. 729–736.

McDowell, C. (1992) *Dressed to Kill: Sex Power & Clothes* (London, Hutchinson).

Mackay, C. (1991 ed.) *Extraordinary Popular Delusions: and the Madness of Crowds* (New York, The Noonday Press) (First published 1841).

McKirnan, D. J. and Peterson, P. L. (1988) Stress, expectancies and vulnerability to substance of use; a test of a model among homosexual men, *Journal of Abnormal Psychology*, 97(4), pp. 461–466.

McKirnan, D. J. and Peterson, P. L. (1989) Alcohol and drug use among homosexual men and women: epidemiology and population characteristics, *Addictive Behaviors*, 14, pp. 545–553.

Magli, P. (1990) The face and the soul, in: M. Feher, R. Naddaff and N. Tazi (eds), *Fragments for a History of the Human Body*, 2 (New York, Zone).

Malatesta, V., Pollack, R., Wilbanks, W. and Adams, H. (1979) Alcohol effects on the orgasmic-ejaculatory response in human males, *Journal of Sex Research*, 15(2), pp. 101–107.

Malinowski, B. (1927) *Sex and Repression in Savage Society* (London, Routledge & Kegan Paul).

Maltzman, I. (1977) Orienting in classical conditioning and generalization of the galvanic skin response to words: an overview, *Journal of Experimental Psychology*, 106, pp. 111–119.

Mansfield, S. and Owen, G. (1993) The use of Ecstasy and other recreational drugs in gay men and its association with unsafe sexual behaviour, presented at *IXth International Conference on AIDS*, Berlin 6–11 June, Abstract No. D06-3580.

Marin, G. (1989) AIDS prevention among Hispanics: needs, risk behaviours and cultural values, *Public Health Reports*, 104(5), pp. 411–415.

Marmor, M., DesJarlais, D. C., Friedman, S. R., Lyden, M. and El-Sadr, W. (1984) The epidemic of acquired immunodeficiency syndrome (AIDS) and suggestions for its control in drug abusers, *Journal of Substance Abuse Treatment*, 1, pp. 237–247.

Marmor, M., Desjarlais, D. C., Cohen, H., Friedman, S. R., Beatrice, S., Dubin, N., El-Sadr, W., Mildan, D., Yancovitz, S., Mathur, U. and Holzman, R. (1987) Risk factors for infection with human immunodeficiency virus among intravenous drug users in New York City, *AIDS* 1(1), pp. 39–44.

Martin, J. L. (1987) The impact of AIDS on gay male sexual behaviour patterns in New York City, *American Journal of Public Health*, 77, pp. 578–581.

Martin, J. L. (1990) Drug use and unprotected anal intercourse among gay men, *Health Psychology*, 9(4), pp. 450–465.

Martos, J. (1981) *Doors to the Sacred: A Historical Introduction to Sacraments in the Christian Church* (London, SCM Press).

Marx, K. (1930 ed.) *Capital,* translated from the 4th German edn by Eden and Cedar Paul. Introduction by Prof. G. D. H. Cole (London, Everyman's Library) (First published 1867-94).

Maslow, A. (1970) *Motivation and Personality* (New York, Harper & Row).

Maughan, W. S. (1977 edn) *The Summing Up* (New York, Arno Press) (First published 1938).

Maupin, A. (1992) *Maybe the Moon* (London, Bantam).

Merton, T. (1957) *The Silent Life* (London, Burns & Oates).

Miller, W. R. (1989) The preview of 1990 international conference, *Connexions*, 9(5), pp. 9–10.

Miller, D. T. and Ross, M. (1975) Self-serving biases in the attribution of causality: fact or fiction? *Psychological Bulletin*, 82, pp. 213–225.

Miller, M. A. and Tomas, J. M. (1989) Past and current methamphetamine epidemics, *Epidemiologic Trends in Drug Abuse, Proceedings* (Community Epidemiology Work Group, Public Health Service), December, pp. 69–83.

Mirin, S., Weiss, R. and Michael, J. (1988) Psychopathology in substance abusers: diagnosis and treatment, *American Journal of Drug and Alcohol Abuse*, 14(2), pp. 139–157.

Mitchell, J. C. (1956) *The Kalela Dance* (Manchester, Manchester University Press).

Monaghan, D. (1989) MDMA in the wards and 'ecstasy' in the press, *Connexions* 9(1), pp. 19–21.

Mondanaro, J. (1987) Strategies for AIDS prevention: motivating health behaviour in drug-dependent women, *Journal of Psychoactive Drugs*, 19(2), pp. 143–149.

Mooney, J. (1965) *The Ghost-Dance Religion and the Sioux Outbreak of 1890*, A. F. C. Wallace (ed.) (Chicago: University of Chicago Press) (First published 1896).

Moore, D. (1992) Review: penetrating social worlds: conducting ethnographic research into alcohol and other drug use within Australia, *Drug and Alcohol Review*, 11, pp. 313–323.

Moore, D. (1993) Social controls, harm minimisation and interactive outreach: the public health implications of an ethnography of drug use, *Australian Journal of Public Health*, 17(1), pp. 58–67.

Moscovici, S. (1980) Toward a theory of conversion behaviour, in: L. Berkowitz (ed.) *Advances in Experimental Social Psychology*, 13 (New York, Academic Press).

Murphy, D. L. (1988) Heterosexual contacts of intravenous drug abusers: implications for the next spread of the AIDS epidemic, in: R. Stall (ed.) *AIDS and Substance Abuse*, pp. 89–97.

Neugarten, B. L. (1977) *Social policy, social ethics, and the aging society* (Chicago, Committee on Human Development, University of Chicago Publishers).

Newcombe, R. (1988) Ecstasy: new drug, familiar panic!, *The Mersey Drugs Journal*, 2(4), pp. 12–13.

Newcombe, R. (1990) *Drug Use and Drug Policy in Merseyside*. Paper given at the *First Conference of European Cities*, Centre of Illegal Trade in Drugs, Frankfurt.

Newcombe, R. (1991) Raving and dance drugs: house music clubs and parties in north-west England. Unpublished report, Liverpool.

Newcombe, R. (1992) A researcher reports from the rave: an inside look at the risks of dance drugs and how to respond, *Druglink*, 7(1), pp. 14–16.

Newell, G. R., Mansell, P. W., Wilson, M. B., Lynch, H. K., Spitz, M. R. and Hersh, E. M. (1985) Risk factory analysis among men referred for possible acquired immune deficiency syndrome, *Preventative Medicine*, 14, pp. 81–91.

Newmeyer, J. A. (1988) The intravenous drug user and the secondary spread of AIDS, *Journal of Psychoactive Drugs*, 20(2), pp. 169–172.

Nietzsche, F. (1896) The grave song, in: A. Tille, trans, *Thus Spake Zarathustra: A Book for All and None* (London, H. Henry and Co.).

Nilsson, M. P. (1957) *The Dionysiac Mysteries of the Hellenistic and Roman Age* (Boston, Little, Brown).

Nohl, J. (1971) *The Black Death: A Chronicle of the Plague compiled from Contemporary Sources* (London, Unwin).

North, G. (1992) A letter from gerry north, in: *The Night of Your Life: Sydney Gay and Lesbian Mardi Gras* (Woolloomooloo, Sydney, Media Services Pty).

O'Sullivan, K. (1992) Sex crimes: a turbulent history of police/gay relations, *The Guide: Sydney Gay & Lesbian Mardi Gras* (Rushcutters Bay, Australia, Sydney Gay and Lesbian Mardi Gras Ltd., Workshop C).

Ogilvy, J. (1979) *Many Dimensional Man: Decentralizing Self, Society, and the Sacred* (New York, Harper & Row).

Ostrow, D. (1986) Barriers to the recognition of links between drug and alcohol abuse and AIDS, in: *Acquired Immune Deficiency Syndrome and Chemical Dependency* (Washington, DC, USGPO), pp. 15–20.

Overton, D. A. (1972) State-dependent learning produced by alcohol and its relevance to alcoholism, in: B. Kissen and H. Begleiter (eds) *The Biology of Alcoholism: Physiology and Behaviour*, 11 (New York, Plenum).

Parkes, C. M. (1975) *Bereavement* (Harmondsworth, Penguin).

Parsons, T. (1949) *The Structure of Social Action* (Glencoe, IL, Free Press).

Patton, C. (1991) Safe sex and the pornographic vernacular, in: Bad Object-Choices (eds), *How Do I Look?: Queer Film and Video* (Washington, Bay Press).

Paul, J. P., Bloomfield, K. A. and Stall, R. (1991) Gay and alcoholic; epidemiological and clinical issues, unpublished paper, National Institute of Mental Health/National Institute of Drug Abuse, pp. 1–27.

Paul, J. P., Stall, R. and Davis, F. (1993) Sexual risk for HIV transmission among gay/bisexual men in substance-abuse treatment, *AIDS Education and Prevention*, 5(1), pp. 11–24.

Peele, S. (1987) A moral vision of addiction: how people's values determine whether they become and remain addicts, *Journal of Drug Issues*, 17, pp. 187–215.

Penny, R., Marks, R., Berger, P., Marriott, D. and Bryant, D. (1983) Acquired immunodeficiency syndrome, *Medical Journal of Australia*, 1, pp. 554–557.

Perls, F. (1969) *Gestalt Therapy Verbatim* (California, Real People Press).

Peroutka, S. J. (1990) Ecstasy: the clinical, pharmacological and neuro-toxicological effects of the Drug MDMA, in: S. J. Peroutka (ed.) *Ecstasy* (Boston, Kluwer Academic).

Phares, E. J. (1978) Locus of Control, in: H. London and J. E. Exber (eds) *Dimensions of Personality* (New York, Wiley).

Phillips, C. (1991) From the president, *The Guide: Sydney Gay & Lesbian Mardi Gras* (Rushcutters Bay, Australia, Sydney Gay and Lesbian Mardi Gras Ltd., Workshop C).

Plant, M. A. (1990) Alcohol, sex and AIDS, *Alcohol Alcoholism*, 25, pp. 293–301.

Power, R. (1990) Drug-using trends and HIV risk behaviour, in: J. Strang and G. Stimson (eds) *AIDS and Drug Misuse* (New York, Routledge).

Prentice-Dunn, S. and Rogers, R. W. (1983) Deindividuation in aggression, in: R. Green and E. Donnerstein (eds) *Aggression: Theoretical and Empirical Reviews* (New York, Academic Press).

Pronger, B. (1992) *The Arena of Masculinity: Sports, Homosexuality, and the meaning of Sex* (London, GMP).

Quadland, M. C. (1985) Compulsive sexual behaviour: definition of a problem and an approach to treatment, *Journal of Sex & a Marital Therapy*, 11(2), pp. 121–132.

Quadland, M. C. and Shattls, W. D. (1987) AIDS, sexuality, and sexual control, *Journal of Homosexualtiy*, 14(1/2), pp. 277–298.

Raphael, B. (1986) *When Disaster Strikes: How Individuals and Communities Cope with Catastrophies* (New York, Basic Books).

Rapoport, A. (1965) Discussant 11, in: J. R. Royce (ed.) *Psychology and the Symbol: An Interdisciplinary Symposium* (New York, Random House).

Ratner, E. (1988) A model for the treatment of lesbian and gay alcohol abusers, *Alcoholism Treatment Quarterly*, 5(1/2), pp. 25–46.

Raymond, C. A. (1988a) Addressing homosexuals' mental health problems, *Journal of the American Medical Association*, 259(1), p. 19.

Raymond, C. A. (1988b) Study of IV drug users and AIDS finds differing infection rate, risk behaviours, *Journal of the American Medical Association*, 260(21), p. 3105.

Read, K. E. (1980) *Other Voices: The Style of a Male Homosexual Tavern* (USA, Chandler & Sharp).

Reanney, D. (1991) *The Death of Forever: A New Future for Human Consciousness* (Melbourne, Longman House).

Redhead, S. (1990) *The End of the Century Party: Youth and Pop Toward 2000* (Manchester, Manchester University Press).

Reilly, C. and Homel, P. (1987) 1986 survey of recreational drug use and attitudes of 15 to 18 year olds in Sydney, *Directorate of Drug Offensive* (NSW Dept of Health In-House Series).

Rest, J. R. (1974) The hierarchical nature of moral judgement: the study of patterns of comprehension and preference with moral stages, *Journal of Personality*, 41(1), pp. 92–93.

Rhodewalt, F. and Davidson, J. (1983) Reactance and the coronary-prone behaviour pattern: the role of self-attribution in response to reduced behavioural freedom, *Journal of Personality and Social Psychology*, 44, pp. 220-228.

Ringdal, N. J. (1991) *Bekjennelser fra en mann av gay-generasjonen: Lystens Dod* (Oslo, Aschenhoug).

Robinson, G. N., Thornton, N. J., Rout, J. and Mackenzie, N. (1987) AIDS-risk behaviours and AIDS knowledge in intravenous drug users, *New Zealand Medical Journal* 100(121), pp. 209–211.

Room, R. and Collins, G. (1983) Introduction: Alcohol and disinhibition: nature and meaning of the link, *NIAAA Research Monograph*, 12, pp. v–viii.

Ross, M. W. (1993) Men who have sex with men, *AIDS Care*, 5, pp. 514–516.

Ross, M. W. and Rosser, B. R. (1989) Education and AIDS risks: a review, *Health Education Research: Theory & Practice*, 4(3), pp. 273–284.

Ross, M., Wodak, A., Gold, J. and Miller, M. (1992) Differences across sexual orientations on HIV risk behaviours in injecting drug users, *AIDS Care*, 4, pp. 139–148.

Rotter, J. B. and Hochreich, D. J. (1975) *Personality* (Glenview IL, Scott Foreman).

Royce, J. R. (1965) Psychology at the crossroads between the sciences and the humanities, in: R. Royce (ed.) *Psychology and the Symbol: An Interdisciplinary Symposium* (New York, Random House).

Safe, M. and Sager, M. (1990) Ice, the new vice, *The Australian Magazine*, 26–7 May, pp. 8–12.

Sartre, J.-P. (1961) Introduction F. Fanon, *Les Damdes de la Terre* (Français Maspero); trans C. Farrington (1977) as *The Wretched of the Earth* (Harmondsworth, Penguin).

Schuster, C. R. (1988) Intravenous drug use and AIDS prevention, *Public Health Reports* 103(3), pp. 261–266.

Schutz, A. and Luckman, T. (1974) *The Structures of the Life-World* (London, Heinemann Educational).

Seigel, K., Mesagno, F. P., Chen, J. and Christ, G. (1989) Factors distinguishing homosexual males practicing risky and safe sex, *Social Science Medicine*, 28(6), pp. 561–569.

Selwyn, P. A., Feiner, C., Cox, C. P., Lipshutz, C. and Cohen, R. L. (1987) Knowledge about AIDS and high-risk behaviour among intravenous drug users in New York City, *AIDS* 1(4), pp. 247–254.

Sherif, M., Harvey, O. J., White, B. J., Hood, H. E. and Sherif, C. W. (1961) *Intergroup Conflict and Cooperation: The Robbers Cave Experiment* (Norman: Institute of Group Relations).

Sherry, C. (1988) AIDS Prevention: Facts from the Countries..., *Hygie* 7(3), pp. 38–41.

Shine, D., Moll, B., Emerson, E., Spigland, I., Harris, C., Small, C. B., Friedland, G., Weiss, S. and Bodner, A. J. (1987) Serologic, immunologic, and clinical features of parenteral drug users from contrasting populations, *American Journal of Drug and Alcohol Abuse*, 13(4), pp. 401–410.

Siegel, B. J. (1970) Defensive structuring and environmental stress, *American Journal of Sociology*, 76(1), pp. 11–32.

Siegel, L. (1986) AIDS: relationship to alcohol and other drugs, *Journal of Substance Abuse Treatment*, 3, pp. 271–274.

Simpson, M. (1992) No Effems, please, I'm straight-acting, *Campaign: Australia*, 210, pp. 47–57.

Single, E., Kandel, D. and Faust, R. (1974) Patterns of multiple drug use in High School, *Journal of Health and Social Behavior*, 15(4), pp. 344–57.

Sittitrai, W., Brown, T. and Sterns, J. (1990) Opportunities for overcoming the continuing restraints to behaviour change and HIV risk reduction, *AIDS*, 4(1), pp. 269–276.

Sivacek, J. and Crano, W. D. (1982) Vested interest as a moderator of attitude-behaviour consistency, *Journal of Personality and Social Psychology*, 43, pp. 210–221.

Slap, G. B., Chaudhuri, S. and Vorters, D. F. (1991) Risk factors for injury during adolescence, *Journal of Adolescent Health*, 12, pp. 263–268.

Sless, D. (1986) *In Search of Semiotics* (London, Croom Helm).

Slovic, P., Fischhoff, B. and Lichtenstein, S. (1979) Rating the Risks, *Environment*, 21(3), pp. 14–20.

Slovic, P., Fischhoff, B. and Lichtenstein, S. (1981) Perceived risk: psychological factors and social implications, *Proceedings of the Royal Society* (London), pp. 17–34.

Smith, S. M. (1979) Remembering in and out of context, *Journal of Experimental Psychology: Human Learning and Memory*, 5, pp. 460–471.

Smith, T. (1988) Counselling gay men about substance abuse and AIDS, *EAP Digest*, 8(4), pp. 41–44.

Smith, K. and Crawford, S. (1986) Suicidal behavior among 'normal' high school students, *Suicide Life Threat Behavior*, 16, pp. 313–325.

Smith, S. M., Glenberg, A. M. and Bjork, R. A. (1978) Environmental context and human memory, *Memory and Cognition*, 6, pp. 342–353.

Soloman, D. and Andrews, G. (eds), (1973) *Drugs and Sexuality* (St Albans, Panther).

Solowij, N., Hall, W. and Lee, N. (1992) Recreational MDMA use in Sydney: A profile of ecstasy users and their experiences with drug *British Journal of Addiction*, 87, pp. 1161–1172.

Sorrels, J. and Kelley, J. (1984a) Conformity by omission, *Personality and Social Psychology Bulletin*, 10, pp. 302–305.

Sorrels, J. P. and Kelley, J. (1984b) Illusory correlation in the perception of group attitudes, *Journal of Personality and Social Psychology*, 48, pp. 863–875.

Spencer, L. (1988) Prevention of AIDS among IV drug abusers, *Substance Abuse*, 9(1), pp. 29–40.

Stall, R., McKusick, L., Wiley, J., Coates, T. J. and Ostrow, D. G. (1986) Alcohol and drug use during sexual activity and compliance with safe sex guidelines for AIDS: the AIDS behavioural research project, *Health Education Quarterly*, 13(4), pp. 359–371.

Stall, R., Barrett, D., Bye, L., Catania, J., Frutchey, C., Henne, J., Lemp, G. and Paul, J. (1991) A comparison of younger and older gay men's HIV risk-taking behaviors, *Communication Technologies 1989 Cross-Sectional Survey*.

Stall, R. and Wiley, J. (1988) A comparison of alcohol and drug use patterns of homosexual and heterosexual men; the San Francisco men's health study, *Drug and Alcohol Dependence*, 22, pp. 63–73.

Stall, R. and Ostrow, D. G. (1989) Intravenous drug use, the combination of drugs and sexual activity and HIV infection among gay and bisexual men; the San Francisco men's study, *Journal of Drug Issues*, 19(1), pp. 57–73.

Stanovich, K. E. and West, R. F. (1983) The generalizability of context effects on word recognition: a reconsideration of the roles of parfoveal priming and sentence context, *Memory and Cognition*, 11, pp. 49–58.

Steiner, R. (1977) *Christianity and Occult Mysteries of Antiquity* (New York, Rudolf Steiner Publications).

Stephen, W. G. (1985) Intergroup relations, in: G. Lindzey and E. Aronson (eds), *Handbook of Social Psychology*, 3rd edn (New York, Random House).

Stevens, J. (1988) *Storming Heaven: LSD and the American Dream* (London, Paladin).

Stevenson, B. (ed.) (1967) *The Home Book of Quotations Classical and Modern*, 10th edn (New York, Dodd Mead and Co.).

Stoner, J. A. F. (1961) A comparison of individual and group decisions involving risk. Unpublished Master's thesis (Cambridge, MA, MIT). Cited in: R. A. Baron and D. Byrne (eds), *Social Psychology: Understanding Human Interaction* (Needham Heights, MA, Allyn & Bacon).

Strauss, A. L. (1987) *Qualitative Analysis for Social Scientists* (New York, Cambridge University Press).

Sullivan, A. P., Guglielmo, R. and Lilly, L. (1986) Evaluating, prevention and intervention procedures, *Journal of Drug Education*, 16(1), pp. 91–98.

Swanson, J. M. and Kinsbourne, M. (1979) State-dependent learning and retrieval: methodological cautions against theoretical considerations, in: J.F. Kihlstrom and F.J. Evans (eds), *Functional Disorders of Memory* (Hillsdale, N.J, Erlbaum).

Szasz, T. (1961) *The Myth of Mental Illness* (New York, Hoeber-Harper).

Tajfel, H. and Turner, J. (1979) An intergrative [sic] theory of intergroup conflict, in: W. G. Austin and S. Worchel (eds), *The Social Psychology of Intergroup Relations* (Monterey, CA, Sage).

Taylor, D. P. and Leonard, K. (1983) Alcohol and human physical aggression, in: R. Green and E. Donnerstein (eds), *Aggression: Theoretical and Empirical Reviews* (New York, Academic Press).

Tedder, R. S. (1988) HIV testing: problems and perceptions, *British Medical Bulletin*, 44(1), pp. 161–169.

Temple, M. T. and Leigh, B. C. (1992) Alcohol consumption and unsafe sexual behaviour in discrete events, *Journal of Sex Research*, 29(2), pp. 207–219.

Thera, N. (1983) *The Heart of Buddhist Meditation* (London, Rider).

Thomas, D. (1982) Do not go gentle into that good night, in R. Abcarian and M. Klotz (eds), *Literature: The Human Experience* (3rd edn) (New York, St Martin's Press) (First published 1946).

Tiger, L. (1971) *Men in Groups: A Controversial Look at All-male Societies* (London, Panther).

Tillich, P. (1952) *The Courage to Be* (New Haven, CT, Yale University Press).

Trebach, A. S. (1989) Tough choices: the practical politics of drug policy reform, *American Behavioural Scientist*, 32(3), pp. 249–258.

Trocki, K. F. and Leigh, B. C. (1991) Alcohol consumption and unsafe sex: a comparison of heterosexuals and homosexual men, *Journal of Acquired Immune Deficiency Syndromes*, 4, pp. 981–986.

Tuchman, B. W. (1978) *A Distant Mirror: The Calamitous 14th Century* (Harmondsworth, Penguin).

Uribe, V. M. and Ostrov, E. (1989) Correlations of substance abuse and self-image among socially diverse groups of adolescents and clinical implications, *Journal of Clinical Psychiatry*, 11(1), pp. 25–34.

US Department of Health and Human Services Report (1991–92), *NCADIP Publications Catalog*. Public Health Service Alcohol, Drug Abuse, and Mental Health Administration.

Vaillant, G. E. (1983) *The Natural History of Alcoholism: Causes, Patterns, and Paths to Recovery* (Cambridge, MA, Harvard University Press).

Van Gennep, A. (1960) *The Rites of Passage* (London, Routledge and Kegan Paul).

Waingarten, T. (1989) Dance party fever: feature, *Nine to Five*, September, pp. 6–7.

Wallach, M. A., Kogan, N. and Bem, D. J. (1974) Diffusion of responsibility and level of risk-taking in groups, *Journal of Abnormal and Social Psychology*, 65, pp. 75–86.

Warwick, D. P. and Lininger, C. A. (1975) *The Sample Survey: Theory and Practice* (New York, McGraw-Hill).

Weber, M. (1947) *The Theory of Social and Economic Organization*, A.R. Henderson and T. Parsons (eds and trans) (London, Hodge).

Weber, M. (1963) *The Sociology of Religion* (Boston, Beacon Press).

Weber, M. (1964) *Basic Concepts in Sociology* (New York, The Citadel Press).

Weddington, W. W. and Brown, B. S. (1989) Counselling regarding human immunodeficiency virus-antibody testing: an interactional method of knowledge and risk assessment, *Journal of Substance Use Treatment*, 6, pp. 77–82.

Weinberg, M. and Williams, C. (1974) *Male Homosexuals: Their Problems and Adaptations* (New York, Oxford University Press).

Weiss, S. H. (1989) Links between cocaine and retroviral infection, *Journal of the American Medical Association*, 261(4), pp. 607–609.

Wellman, P. I. (1958) *Death on the Prairie: The Terrible Struggle for the Western Plains* (London, Corgi).

Westermeyer, J., Seppala, M., Gassow, S. and Carson, G. (1989) AIDS-related illness and AIDS risk in homo/bisexual substance abusers: case reports and clinical issues, *American Journal Drug Alcohol Abuse*, 15(4), pp. 443–461.

White, K. (1989) Cofactors: do they influence HIV infection and progression? *AIDS Patient Care*, 3(3), pp. 24–27.

Whyte, W. F. (1984) *Learning from the Field: A Guide from Experience* (Beverly Hills, Sage).

Wilkinson, D. A., Leigh, G. M., Cordingley, J., Martin, G. W. and Lei, H. (1987) Dimensions of multiple drug use and typology of drug users, *British Journal of Addiction*, 82, pp. 259–273.

Wills, T. A. and Shiffman, S. (eds) (1985) *Coping and Substance Abuse* (Orlando, Academic Press).

Wilson, G. T. and Lawson, D. M. (1976) Expectancies, alcohol, and sexual behavior, *Journal of Abnormal Psychology*, 85(6), pp. 587–594.

Wodak, A. (1989) Heroin legalisation: to be or not to be?, *New Doctor*, 5, pp. 4–7.

Wohlfeiler, D. (1989) Supplement summary of presentations on drug use and AIDS. Adaptation of safer-sex workshops for gay and bisexual men, *V International Conference on AIDS*, Montreal, Canada, p. 847.

Wolk, J., Wodak, A., Morlet, A., Guinan, J. and Gold, J. (1990) HIV-related risk-taking behaviour, knowledge and serostatus of intravenous drug users in Sydney, *Medical Journal*, 152, pp. 453–458.

Wotherspoon, G. (1991) *City of the Plains: History of Gay Sub-culture* (Sydney, Hale and Iremonger).

Yobs Out! Mardi Gras members only ticket sales (1991) *Sydney Star Observer*, 169, p. 1.

Zaehner, R. C. (1978) *Mysticism: Sacred and Profane* (New York, Oxford University Press).

Zapka, J., McCusker, J. and Stoddard, A. (1988) Psychosocial factors and behaviour: Measurement and determinants, *Abstracts of the IV International Conference on AIDS*, Stockholm, Sweden, 12–16 June, p. 282.

Ziebold, T. O. and Mongeon, J. E. (eds) (1982) *Gay and Sober: Directions for Counseling and Therapy* (New York, Harrington Park Press).

Zillman, D. (1984) *Connections between sex and aggression* (Hillsdale, NJ, Erlbaum).

Zimbardo, P. G. (1969) The human choice: Individuation, reason and order versus deindividuation-impulse, and chaos, in: W. Arnold and D. Levine (eds), *Nebraska Symposium on Motivation*, 17 (Lincoln, NE, University of Nebraska Press).

Zinberg, N. E. (1984) *Drug, Set and Setting: The basis for Controlled Intoxicant Use* (New York, Yale University Press).

Zoja, L. (1989) *Drugs, Addiction and Initiation: The Modern Search for Ritual* (Boston, Sigo).

Index